Institutional Change in the Payments System and Monetary Policy

I0885547

Monetary policy has been at the centre of economic research from the early stages of economic thought, but payment system research has attracted increased academic attention only in the past decade.

Institutional Change in the Payments System and Monetary Policy initiates research on the interdependence of institutional change in the payments system and monetary policy, examining the different channels via which payment systems affect monetary policy. This volume explores important themes such as:

- conceptualisation and methods of analysis of institutional change in the payments system,
- determinants of institutional change in the payments system – political-economy versus technology
- empirics of institutional change in the retail and in the wholesale payments systems – policy initiatives and new technologies in the payments system
- implications of institutional change in the payments system for monetary policy and the instruments available to central banks to cope with it

The result is an accessible overview of conceptual and methodological approaches to institutional change in payment systems and a comprehensive and yet thorough assessment of its implications for monetary policy.

Stefan W. Schmitz is an Economist with the Austrian National Bank.
Geoffrey Wood is Professor of Economics at London's City University.

Routledge International Studies in Money and Banking

1 **Private Banking in Europe**
Lynn Bicker

2 **Bank Deregulation and Monetary Order**
George Selgin

3 **Money in Islam**
A study in Islamic political economy
Masudul Alam Choudhury

4 **The Future of European Financial Centres**
Kirsten Bindemann

5 **Payment Systems in Global Perspective**
Maxwell J Fry, Isaak Kilato, Sandra Roger, Krzysztof Senderowicz, David Sheppard, Francisco Soils and John Trundle

6 **What is Money?**
John Smithin

7 **Finance**
A Characteristics Approach
Edited by David Blake

8 **Organisational Change and Retail Finance**
An Ethnographic Perspective
Richard Harper, Dave Randall and Mark Rouncefield

9 **The History of the Bundesbank**
Lessons for the European Central Bank
Jakob de Haan

10 **The Euro**
A Challenge and Opportunity for Financial Markets
Published on behalf of *Société Universitaire Européenne de Recherches Financières (SUERF)*
Edited by Michael Artis, Axel Weber and Elizabeth Hennessy

11 **Central Banking in Eastern Europe**
Edited by Nigel Healey and Barry Harrison

12 **Money, Credit and Prices Stability**
Paul Dalziel

13 **Monetary Policy, Capital Flows and Exchange Rates**
Essays in Memory of Maxwell Fry
Edited by William Allen and David Dickinson

14 **Adapting to Financial Globalisation**
Published on behalf of *Société Universitaire Européenne de Recherches Financières (SUERF)*
Edited by Morten Balling, Eduard H. Hochreiter and Elizabeth Hennessy

15 **Monetary Macroeconomics**
A New Approach
Alvaro Cencini

16 **Monetary Stability in Europe**
Stefan Collignon

17 **Technology and Finance**
Challenges for financial markets, business strategies and policy makers
Published on behalf of *Société Universitaire Européenne de Recherches Financières (SUERF)*
Edited by Morten Balling, Frank Lierman, and Andrew Mullineux

18 **Monetary Unions**
Theory, History, Public Choice
Edited by Forrest H Capie and Geoffrey E Wood

19 **HRM and Occupational Health and Safety**
Carol Boyd

20 **Central Banking Systems Compared**
The ECB, The Pre-Euro Bundesbank and the Federal Reserve System
Emmanuel Apel

21 **A History of Monetary Unions**
John Chown

22 **Dollarization**
Lessons from Europe and the Americas
Edited by Louis-Philippe Rochon & Mario Seccareccia

23 **Islamic Economics and Finance: A Glossary, 2nd Edition**
Muhammad Akram Khan

24 **Financial Market Risk**
Measurement and Analysis
Cornelfis A. Los

25 **Financial Geography**
A Banker's View
Risto Laulajainen

26 **Money Doctors**
The Experience of International Financial Advising 1850–2000
Edited by Marc Flandreau

27 **Exchange Rate Dynamics**
A New Open Economy Macroeconomics Perspective
Edited by Jean-Oliver Hairault and Thepthida Sopraseuth

28 **Fixing Financial Crises in the 21st Century**
Edited by Andrew G. Haldane

29 **Monetary Policy and Unemployment**
The U.S., Euro-area and Japan
Edited by Willi Semmler

30 **Exchange Rates, Capital Flows and Policy**
Edited by Peter Sinclair, Rebecca Driver and Christoph Thoenissen

31 **Great Architects of International Finance**
The Bretton Woods Era
Anthony M. Endres

32 **The Means to Prosperity**
Fiscal Policy Reconsidered
Edited by Per Gunnar Berglund and Matias Vernengo

33 **Competition and Profitability in European Financial Services**
Strategic, Systemic and Policy Issues
Edited by Morten Balling, Frank Lierman and Andy Mullineux

34 **Tax Systems and Tax Reforms in South and East Asia**
Edited by Luigi Bernardi, Angela Fraschini and Parthasarathi Shome

35 **Institutional Change in the Payments System and Monetary Policy**
Edited by Stefan W. Schmitz and Geoffrey Wood

Institutional Change in the Payments System and Monetary Policy

Edited by
Stefan W. Schmitz and Geoffrey Wood

Routledge
Taylor & Francis Group
LONDON AND NEW YORK

First published 2006
by Routledge
2 Park Square, Milton Park,
Abingdon, Oxon OX14 4RN

Simultaneously published in the USA and Canada
by Routledge
711 Third Ave, New York, NY 10017

Routledge is an imprint of the Taylor & Francis Group, an informa business

First issued in paperback 2012

Typeset in Times by Keyword Group Ltd

British Library Cataloguing in Publication Data
A catalogue record for this book is available from the British Library

Library of Congress Cataloging in Publication Data
A catalogue record for this book has been requested

ISBN13: 978-0-415-38402-5 (hbk)
ISBN13: 978-0-203-09995-7 (ebk)
ISBN13: 978-0-415-64860-8 (pbk)

Contents

List of figures

List of tables

Notes on contributors

Angelo S. Baglioni, Università Cattolica del Sacro Cuore di Milano – General Istituto di Economia e Finanza, Largo Gemelli n.l, 20123 Milano, Italy. He is Associated Professor of Political Economy at the Catholic University of Milan, where he teaches courses on monetary economics and finance. His research interests include theory of financial intermediation, financial regulation, payment systems and monetary policy (e.g. II mercato monetario e la Banca Centrale. Liquidità bancaria, politica monetaria, sistemi di pagamento, II Mulino, Bologna, 2004.)

Ulrich Bindseil, European Central Bank, Postfach 16 03 19, D-60066 Frankfurt am Main, Germany. He is Deputy head of the ECB's Risk Management Division since 2004. Before, he was the head of the liquidity management unit in the ECB's Operations Analysis Division, and an Economist at the Deutsche Bundesbank. He has published on the organisation of markets, on decision making of EU institutions, and on monetary policy implementation.

Sujit 'Bob' Chakravorti, Federal Reserve Bank of Chicago, 230 South LaSalle Street, Chicago, Illinois 60604-1413, USA. Senior economist in the research department at the Federal Reserve Bank of Chicago. Chakravorti's research focuses on the economics of payments and the evolving structure of global financial markets. He has also been a visiting scholar at the European University Institute and the International Monetary Fund.

Forrest H. Capie, Cass Business School, 106 Bunhill Row, EC1Y 8TZ London; Professor of Economic History at CASS Business School, City University, London; currently seconded to Bank of England writing their history. He has taught at LSE, the universities of Warwick and Leeds and held various visiting appointments, including Aix-Marseille. He was editor of the Economic History Review from 1993 to 1999, and has published widely on monetary and financial history.

Cornelia Holthausen, European Central Bank, Postfach 16 03 19, D-60066 Frankfurt am Main, Germany. She is an economist at the ECB. Her main research interests are the economics of payment systems, such as competition, efficiency and pricing in large-value payment systems.

Stefan W. Schmitz, Oesterreichische Nationalbank, Otto Wagner Platz 3, A-1090 Wien, Austria. He initiated the research project 'Institutional Change and the Payments System and Monetary Policy' while at the Austrian Academy of Sciences (1998–2003). Since 2003 he is an economist at Oesterreichische Nationalbank. His research interests include payment systems, political economy of financial governance, and history of economic thought (e.g. Carl Menger and the Evolution of Payment Systems: From Barter to Electronic Money, 2002, ed. with M. Latzer).

Dimitrios P. Tsomocos, Bank of England, FMG LSE, and SBS Oxford, Threadneedle Street, HO-3 London EC2R 8AH, UK. University Lecturer in Finance and Fellow, Said Business School and St. Edmund Hall of the University of Oxford, Academic Consultant, Bank of England and Senior Research Associate, Financial Markets Group, LSE.

Lawrence H. White, University of Missouri, FA Hayek Professor of Economic History, Department of Economics SSB 408, 8001 Natural Bridge Road, St. Louis, MO 63121. Friedrich A. Hayek Professor of Economic History at the University of Missouri – St. Louis. His works on money and banking include Free Banking in Britain and The Theory of Monetary Institutions.

Geoffrey E. Wood, Cass Business School, 106 Bunhill Row, EC1Y 8TZ London. Professor of Economics at Cass Business School in London, and a Visiting Professor at the Centre for Commercial Law Studies at Queen Mary and Westfield College, London. His interests include financial regulation, monetary and financial history, and monetary policy.

Flemming Würtz, European Central Bank, Postfach 16 03 19, D-60066 Frankfurt am Main, Germany. He currently holds the position of Principal Economist within the liquidity management section of the European Central Bank, mainly focusing on issues relating to the ECB's liquidity management policy, its operational framework, and the formation of short term interest rates.

Institutional change in the payments system and monetary policy – an introduction

Stefan W. Schmitz and Geoffrey E. Wood[1]

The book presents the results of a research project on the interdependence between institutional change in the payments system and monetary policy. Monetary policy has been at the centre of economic research from the early stages of economic thought, but payment system research has attracted increased academic attention only in the past decade or so.[2] This book contributes to these so far largely separated fields by initiating research on the interdependence of institutional change in the payments system and monetary policy. (A neglected but instructive contribution to this field of study is the work of John Wheatley, who emphasised the interrelation between payment systems and monetary policy at the beginning of the nineteenth century.[3])

We are exploring the inevitable tension between the central bank's desire to control the monetary system – in order to ensure the effective implementation of monetary policy, the maintenance of financial stability, the smooth operation of the payment system and the collection of seigniorage – which in general is thought to require commercial banks to hold some reserve of central bank (CB) money, and their desire to economise on such reserves. The interaction of these forces drives institutional change in the payment system. What implications does institutional change in the payment system have for monetary policy? To answer this question, this book addresses two main subjects, the first of which is subdivided into two topics, and the second into three. These divisions are as follows:

1 Institutional change in the payments system

   a What is the appropriate conceptual framework to analyse institutional change in the payments system?
   b What are the relevant forces shaping institutional change in wholesale as well as retail and small value interbank payments systems?

2 Implications for monetary policy

   a What are the implications of alternative institutional structures of payment systems for the conduct and implementation of monetary policy?
   b What instruments are available for central banks to cope with institutional change in payment systems?
   c Are there alternative models of monetary policy implementation in a world without CB money?

A team of researchers from academia and central banks combined to analyse these topics from complementary perspectives – empirical economics (i.e., economic history), economic theory and institutional economics – and in different institutional environments of monetary policy (i.e. the Euro-area, the UK and the USA).

Institutional change of the payments system can affect monetary policy through various channels. Their institutional structure has an impact on the functioning of the money market. That market's reliable and predictable functioning is a prerequisite for effective liquidity management and monetary policy implementation. Intraday liquidity provision (which has little monetary policy implication) can spill over into the overnight market (possibly with monetary policy implications). Payments systems can affect the stability and predictability of the demand for CB money, which usually serves as the medium of final settlement in the interbank market.

In order to assess the extent to which institutional change in the payment system affects monetary policy, a number of theoretical and empirical questions are addressed.

- *Method*: What are the appropriate methods to investigate institutional change in the payments system?
- *Main drivers of institutional change in payment systems*: What are the relevant forces shaping institutional change in wholesale as well as retail and small value interbank payment systems (e.g. payment system policy; new technology enabling the emergence of new markets, new products, and new governance mechanisms; liberalisation, integration and consolidation of financial and product markets)?
- *Institutional change in payment systems*: What are the main institutional characteristics of payment systems? The institutional structures of payment systems show a great variety in different economic environments, for historic reasons[4] as much as for differences in the adoption of recent innovations. What are the major signs of institutional change in payment systems? A number of banks and non-banks, for example, mobile telecom operators, have entered the market for the provision of payment services in recent years with alternative means of payment. How are their operations linked with the central bank and how does that affect monetary policy?
- *Institutional change in the payment system and monetary policy*: How does institutional change in the payment system affect the stability and predictability of the demand for CB money? How does it impact on the quantity supplied and demand as well as the quality of the medium of final settlement? If effects are identified, can central banks adapt the instruments of implementation of monetary policy to cope with institutional change?
- *CB payment system policy*: Various central banks have moved to real time gross settlement (RTGS) and hybrid interbank payment systems in recent years, against previous trends towards deferred net settlement (DNS) systems. What are the implications of the alternative systems and their institutional features (i.e., availability of intraday credit in RTGS) for the conduct and

implementation of monetary policy? Which instruments are at the discretion of central banks to react to institutional change in the payments system?

- *The extreme case – a moneyless world*: Recent innovations in wholesale as well as retail and small value interbank payment systems are widely expected to reduce the demand for money and increase the interest sensitivity of the demand for money. Is the collapse of the demand for money to zero simply the limit of such an evolution and should it, therefore, be modelled accordingly? Or would a 'moneyless economy' reflect a different and incommensurable structure of the underlying economy? What are the appropriate methods to study such a fundamental institutional change? Is there a role for 'monetary policy' in a world without CB money?

The following pages attempt to lay the common foundations for the analyses presented in the main body of the book.

Method of analysis

The definition of the 'payments system' refers to the economy-wide web of payment systems and instruments in an economy. It consists of a number of individual payment systems, which are broadly categorised into two groups: wholesale as well as retail and small value interbank payment systems. A payment system is defined as '… incorporating a particular set of payment instruments, technical standards for the transmission of payment messages and agreed means of settling claims among system members, including use of a nominated settlement institution' (CPSS 2003: 9).

The analyses presented in this book utilise different but complementary approaches to investigate the impact of institutional change in the payment system on monetary policy: economic history (Lawrence H. White as well as Ulrich Bindseil and Flemming Würtz), general equilibrium analysis in Shubik's tradition of modelling monetary economies (Forrest H. Capie, Dimitrios P. Tsomocos, Geoffrey E. Wood), microeconomics of networks (Sujit Chakravorti), institutional economics (Stefan W. Schmitz), search models of money (Cornelia Holthausen) and empirical microeconomics and institutional economics (Angelo Baglioni).

The book advocates diversity in the methods of analysis. The different approaches are employed to complement each other, as they allow the highlighting of different conceptualisations, main drivers as well as potential directions and impacts of institutional change.

Main drivers of institutional change in the payments system

The following section relates institutional change in the payments system to its main interdependent drivers, which are broadly categorised in two groups: policy initiatives[5] (e.g. Core Principles; SEPA, EU New Legal Framework; Revision of Federal Reserve Policy on Payments System Risk (PSR policy), Amendments to

Money Transmitter Laws in many US states) and changing demand by banks (e.g. minimising opportunity costs of holding reserves) as well as final customers (i.e. increasing demand for cross-border payment services due to globalisation). New technologies are rarely drivers in their own right; more often they have an impact on institutional change by enabling the development of new products, new markets, and new governance structures.[6] This section provides a brief summary of the most important policy initiatives.

Johnson (1998) describes CB activities aimed at reducing settlement risk in the payments system by ensuring payment finality without explicit CB intervention. Measures taken include the containment of intraday exposure in deferred net settlement systems, collateralisation, loss-sharing agreements, the reduction of float, the implementation of RTGS (Real Time Gross Settlement) operated by central banks (e.g. the ECB's TARGET system, the Fed's Fedwire and the Bank of England's CHAPS) and the establishment of Lamfalussy standards for private DNS (Difference Net Settlement) systems in 1990.

As an extension of the Lamfalussy Standards for DNS systems, the Bank for International Settlements (BIS) initiated the Core Principles (CPSS 2001a) for systemically important payment systems[7] in 2001. The most important of the ten principles encourage payment systems to have a risk management procedure that clearly allocates responsibilities to the operator and participants, in order to be able to complete settlement in the case of failure of the largest net debtor in DNS systems, to settle in CB money, to permit fair and open access and disclose the relevant criteria and to have effective governance mechanisms in place. In addition, the BIS assigns certain responsibilities to central banks in relation to the Core Principles. Central banks' own payment systems should comply with the Core Principles, they should disclose their payment system objectives and policies, and they should oversee the compliance with the Core Principles in systematically important payment systems. The Core Principles were adopted by the ECB Council in 2001 and incorporated into the oversight standards for retail payment systems in 2003.[8] They were also incorporated into Federal Reserve Policy on PSR in 2004.[9]

Retail payment systems in the European Union are expected to undergo substantial institutional change in the next decade or so, due to increasing demand for cross-border payments and ensuing policy initiatives. Despite the introduction of the common currency in 1999 and 2002, the intersections of national retail payment infrastructures in the Internal Market remained inefficient and high price differential between national markets, as well as much higher costs for cross-border payments than for domestic ones, persisted. In response, the European Council initiated the Single Euro Payment Area (SEPA) Initiative in 2001 to promote the creation of a euro area-wide integrated retail payment infrastructure by the end of 2010. Effective as of 1 July 2002, it requires charges for cross-border electronic payments in euro within the Internal Market up to €12,500 (€ 50,000 after 2005) to be the same as for domestic payments in euro (Regulation (EC) No. 2560/2001). It contains a similar requirement (effective as of 1 July 2003) for cross-border credit transfers in euro within the Internal Market. The regulation promotes standardisation and straight through processing (STP) by the use of the

International Bank Account Number (IBAN) and the Bank Identifier Code (BIC) to decrease the costs of cross-border credit transfers. The European Payments Council (EPC) was set up by the banking industry to guide and implement the SEPA project. The milestones of the SEPA initiative were laid out in a White Paper in 2002. The operation of the first pan-European Automated Clearing House was envisaged for 2003. The EPC introduced a pan-European credit transfer instrument (Credeuro) in 2003 and plans to after a pan-European direct debit instrument (PEDD) in 2007. Recommendations for consistent tariffs for card schemes should be implemented in 2006. Full migration of customers to the SEPA is intended by 2010. The ECB plays a catalyst role, but has signalled to impose regulatory measures if the progress towards a SEPA were backtracked by banks. The European Banking Association (EBA) operates the first Pan European Automated Clearing House (PEACH), called STEP 2, as infrastructure for retail payments covered by the regulation.

The legal framework governing payment services in the EU is based on EU legislation and on national law. In order to remove legal barriers to an integrated European payments infrastructure and as part of the Commission's Financial Services Action Plan (FSAP), the European Commission proposed a New Legal Framework (NLF) for payments in the Internal Market. Its purpose is to review and consolidate community legislation as well as to harmonise legislation across the EU.[10] Its objective is to lower barriers to enable the entry of new payment service providers, to reduce compliance costs and legal uncertainties of dealing with 25 different legal environments, and to increase the quality and efficiency of payments in the Single Market. The basic principles of the NLF are that payment service providers should face prudential requirements proportionate to the risks involved and that a level playing field for all market participants, as well as appropriate consumer protection (i.e., information requirements, revocability of payment orders, and liability for non-execution, defective execution or unauthorised transactions), should prevail across the EU. The Payments Committee shall promote the consistent implementation of EU legislation. It consists of representatives of national authorities in the area of payment system oversight. The NLF covers all payments within the Single Market, which are initiated by payment instruments that present alternatives to cash, coins and cheques such as credit transfer, direct debit, card as well as electronic payments. The ECB is intensively involved in the legislative and political process concerning the NLF (as it also was in the case of the eMoney Directive 2000/46/EC).

Implementation of the SEPA initiative and of the New Legal Framework is likely to remain a driver of institutional change in European payment systems beyond 2010, due to the expected consolidation and integration of national payment infrastructures in Europe.

In the US, the fragmentation of the legal framework regarding payment services is substantial, too. Apart from Federal regulations such as the Electronic Fund Transfer Act (1978), the Monetary Control Act (1980), Federal Reserve Regulation E and the Federal Reserve Policy on PSR, state abandoned property laws and money transmitter laws apply to some payment services and instruments.

The Uniform Money Services Act was proposed in 2000 by the National Conference of Commissioners on Uniform State Laws. Its objective was to provide the states with a means to harmonise the regulatory framework across different types of money service businesses and to decrease compliance costs. It allows the states to amend and modify the act or not to adopt it at all. Understanding and complying with a large number of legal requirements remains a substantial burden for payment service providers in the US.

The main legal framework governing payment systems falls in the competence of legislatures. Nevertheless, central banks exert a high level of influence in drafting rules at the international level (e.g. Core Principles) and in shaping legislation by consulting governments and legislature (e.g. NLF, eMoney Directive 2000/46/EC). Furthermore, legal frameworks in the EU and US transfer substantial regulatory discretion concerning the regulation and oversight of payment systems to central banks (e.g. minimum reserve requirements, reporting requirements, ECB Minimum Standards, Regulation E).

Institutional change in the payments system

The central institutional characteristics of payment systems concern the medium of final settlement[11] in the payments system and its relation to the generally accepted medium of exchange in the economy, as well as to characteristics of clearing and settlement institutions. The generally accepted medium of exchange is the most liquid good in the economy, the good with the highest marketability and, thus, involves the lowest spread. Its incidental function is the unit of account function, because it is the good that embodies the unit of account. It also serves as the means of final settlement, because it is the only medium that is not a direct or indirect claim on future resources and that ensures settlement finality in the interbank payment system (in an economic sense rather than a legal sense). It is also a means of payment. However, not all means of payment (i.e. cheques, debit and credit cards, electronic money) are generally accepted media of exchange. Notwithstanding some exceptions (e.g. e-gold) means of payment are usually denominated and redeemable in the generally accepted medium of exchange.[12]

The characteristics of the clearing and settlement institutions (including the central bank as the usual institution of final settlement) include conditions of access to their accounts, conditions of access to credit facilities, and the nature of the clearing and settlement process (i.e. RTGS with or without intraday credit, DNS systems, hybrid systems). In addition, the surrounding institutional environment, in which the payment system operates, is of importance: the state of development of the interbank money market and the sophistication of participants' treasury management. Also, some features of monetary policy implementation have repercussions on the institutional characteristics of the payment system. The reserve maintenance system is of particular relevance in this respect (i.e. the averaging of minimum reserve requirements, the averaging period, its relation to the interval of central banks' refinancing operations and the potential employment of minimum reserves for settlement purposes).

These characteristics can be interrelated in important ways. The relationship between the generally accepted medium of exchange and the medium of final settlement, as well as the relationship between clearing and settlement institutions and the issuer of the generally accepted medium of exchange, can influence credit and liquidity risk of the payment system. If the medium of final settlement is not the generally accepted medium of exchange, potential demand for exchanging the medium of final settlement into the generally accepted medium of exchange imposes a liquidity risk on the participants of the payment system, as the generally accepted medium of exchange is by definition the most liquid asset in the relevant market. If the clearing and settlement institution is not the issuer of the generally accepted medium of exchange, its opportunity costs of holding sufficient reserves are positive and it can – in principle – go bankrupt, thus imposing a credit and liquidity risk on participants. However, there is no historical evidence of clearing and settlement institution bankruptcies we are aware of.

For monetary policy implementation the involvement of the central bank in issuing the generally accepted medium of exchange, and its role in the payment system, are critical. If the central bank acts as the clearing and settlement institution, the role of access to accounts[13] and credit at the clearing and settlement institution can give rise to risks for monetary policy implementation, due to potential spill-over of intraday credit to the overnight money market. If the clearing and settlement institution also performs oversight functions with respect to the participating institutions, potential economies of scope arise due to informational advantages. In historical examples of private clearing and settlement institutions, the institution also acted as oversight institution and often as quasi-regulator and supervisor of the participating institutions.[14] If the clearing and settlement institution is also the issuer of the generally accepted medium of exchange, the lender of last resort function can be fulfilled at lower marginal costs. It is sometimes claimed that conflicts of interest may arise with monetary policy objectives of the issuer of the generally accepted medium of exchange, but this is not an inevitable problem.[15]

Institutional characteristics influence the operational characteristics of the payments market, such as its efficiency (as measured for example by the turnover ratio – how often do intraday reserves turn over in the payment system; size of the float – the value of funds processed at any time and thus neither at the discretion of the payer nor the payee; execution time – the time it takes to execute a payment order), stability and reliability (stress resistance), the concentration of payment flows, the nature and intensity of competition among payment systems, structure and level of costs of access to the payment system and to intraday credit, and the degree of tiering in the payment system. The following subsections describe what we regard as the most important aspects of current institutional change in wholesale as well as retail and small value interbank payment systems:

Wholesale payment systems

According to the Committee on Payment and Settlement Systems (CPSS 2003), liberalisation, globalisation and consolidation have enormously increased the volumes handled in national wholesale (large value) payment systems and have thus increased awareness of potential threats to systemic stability. The hypothesis that the design of large value payment systems as DNS systems cause substantial externalities that justify public intervention, is disputed by Selgin (2005). He argues that these arguments reflect a fundamental misunderstanding of the functioning of large value payment systems and that recent reforms have other motives (e.g. seigniorage). (As the CPSS consists of CB delegates, it is less eager to stress the maintenance of seigniorage income as a driver of reform.) Nevertheless, the design of payment systems underwent considerable change. The spread of RTGS was intended to increase the safety of the large value interbank payment systems. These systems enabled the development of Delivery versus Payment (DVP – in security settlement), Payment versus Payment (PVP – in foreign exchange settlement), which also includes Continuous Linked Settlement (CLS) as a special form. Bilateral intraday payment obligations were harder to manage in DNS systems, as they remained largely invisible for most participants until end-of-day clearing. Bilateral intraday obligations result from the lag between sending payment messages and end-of-day settlement. Final settlement depends on the completion of all payment orders entered during the day. Thus, settlement cannot be considered final for a participant, even if the participant has no bilateral claim against the illiquid party.

Fry (1999) reports that unprotected DNS systems dominated in the large-value payment market internationally until the 1980s and that the associated risks were largely ignored. The Lamfalussy Report (BIS 1990) suggested 'Core Principles' for cross-border DNS systems for the containment of risks, in particular that the system should be able to settle even in the case of failure of the largest net debtor. Nevertheless, participants in DNS systems had to comply with minimum levels of creditworthiness, which in turn had to be monitored by other participants or the system operator, which restricted the number of direct participants. The number of participants in RTGS vastly exceeds the number of direct participants DNS systems usually had. In 2001, the CPSS (2001a) adopted the Core Principles for systemically important payment systems, which encourage clearing and settlement institutions to settle in CB money. All large-value payment systems in the Euro area settle in CB money.[16] The wholesale money market is the only financial market in the EU which is effectively integrated.[17] The establishment of the European large-value payment system TARGET (Trans-European Automated Real-Time Gross Settlement Express Transfer) in 1999 laid the foundations for this integration and, thereby, for the ECB to implement monetary policy effectively across the Euro area. TARGET is a decentralised system linking 15 individual large-value payment systems with the ECB Payment Mechanism (EPM). The technical infrastructure, the services offered and the pricing structures, largely differ among individual CB components within TARGET. The integration and consolidation of the European financial system and EU enlargement led to increasing demand for (largely) harmonised payment services, a more cost-efficient infrastructure and a single pricing structure. TARGET 2 aims at providing these by the implementation of a Single Shared Platform (SSP) for all CB components of the ECB's large-value payment system until 2007.[18] The provision of intraday credit as well as access to CB accounts remains the domain of the individual central bank.

McAndrews and Trundle (2001) argue that the remaining risks and the associated costs, even in protected DNS systems, led to the adoption of RTGS in all EU and G10 countries in the 1990s. The higher costs of liquidity in RTGS also gave rise to hybrids. They distinguish two main types – Continuous Net Settlement (CNS) and queue-augmented RTGS. The former evolved from DNS systems. Participants hold some liquidity with the system operator and enter payment orders throughout the day. These orders are queued, that is, not executed until an algorithm identifies those orders that can be netted without implying net positions of one of the participants that exceed its available liquidity balance. The algorithm operates frequently throughout the day and settlement occurs each time a group of payments complies with the relevant netting requirements. Technically the system remains a DNS system, but net settlement occurs so frequently that many payments are effectively settled in real time. The settlement risks associated with the interdependency of settlement in DNS systems is reduced by reducing the length of the settlement period.

Queue-augmented RTGS are an important form of RTGS. Payment orders are queued, if available liquidity is insufficient, and an algorithm searches for offsetting orders on a bilateral or even multilateral basis. Once a pair or group of orders fulfils the relevant criteria, they are settled on a gross basis. Legally and technically the system is a gross settlement system. The gain in liquidity saving in both CNS and in queue-augmented RTGS comes at the price of (potential) settlement deferral until a pair or group of payments complies with the relevant criteria. Usually netting occurs frequently during the day, so the deferrals are very short.

Centralised queuing mechanisms for CNS and queue-augmented RTGS all require sophisticated, reliable and cost-efficient ICT infrastructure. This underlines the role of technological advances in enabling institutional change in the payment system. McAndrews and Trundle (2001) argue that the related investment and operational costs may outweigh the ensuing benefits in terms of liquidity savings. This implies that sophisticated centralised queuing mechanisms are less attractive for payment systems with inexpensive intraday credit and highly concentrated payment flows among a small number of participants, who can more easily coordinate their payment orders. Fry (1999) highlights that DNS systems with a small number of large participants might entail a moral hazard problem, which should be taken into account in the analysis of the costs of DNS systems. For participants face an incentive to underinvest in mutual monitoring of counterparty risk, as they rely on the lender of last resort function of the central bank to bail out large participants, who are considered, perhaps erroneously, 'too big to fail'. The adoption of CNS and RTGS eliminates this moral hazard problem, as counterparty risk is reduced.

In RTGS, individual participants can reduce their working balances by delaying payments during the day. By entering payment orders after they have received sufficient funds, they can settle them from incoming payments and save liquidity costs. This incentive structure leads to payment delays and to potential risks that not all payments can be completed during the day. Market participants can solve the problem by cooperation mechanisms. McAndrews and Trundle (2001) distinguish ex ante mechanisms (e.g. participants set limits of net payments to individual counterparties; internal queues that release payments in response to incoming payments) and ex post mechanisms (e.g. rules of behaviour with ex post compliance monitoring, e.g., FBE (Federation Bancaire de l'union Europeene) Guidelines on Liquidity Management). In addition, system operators can contribute to the solution of the coordination problem by centralised queuing mechanisms, as the probability of netting and offsetting matches increases with the number of payment orders entered at specific batches.

In RTGS, intraday credit is usually provided explicitly by the clearing institution (often the central bank), so that the clearing institution rather than other participants bears the associated risks. The centralisation of credit risk exposure and the better availability of information improve credit risk management in payment systems. On the other hand, the demand for settlement reserves or CB intraday credit increases, so that the payment systems become more reliant on CB money (either in the form of intraday credit or in the form of settlement reserves with the central bank). McAndrews and Trundle (2001) argue that the evolution of hybrid systems constitutes a trade-off between central banks' desire for stability and market demands for efficiency.

CPSS (2003) reports empirical findings of the extent of tiering in selected large-value payment systems.[19] Out of the 29 payment systems analysed, 17 reported high degrees of tiering (i.e. less than 25 per cent of domestically located banks were direct participants), 6 reported mixed degrees of tiering (i.e. 25 per cent–75 per cent of domestically located banks are direct participants), and 6 reported low degrees of tiering (i.e. more than 75 per cent of all domestically located banks participate directly).[20] Only 22 payment systems provided figures concerning the degree of concentration in the value of payments handled. In seven of them the five largest participants accounted for more than 75 per cent of the value of all payments.[21] Data for 2002 show that banks' reserves at the central bank differ widely between the Euro area (5.7 per cent of narrow money), the UK (0.3 per cent of narrow money), and the US (1.7 per cent of narrow money), which is largely due to different MRR (Minimum Reserve Requirements) and tiering. The latter becomes evident from the share of banks' deposits at other banks of narrow money, which ranges from only 2.9 per cent in the US and 21.6 per cent in the Euro area to 51.3 per cent in the UK.[22] In some large-value payment systems the share of direct participants is 100 per cent (Fedwire US), while in CHAPS Sterling (UK) it is only 0.05 per cent. In ECB's TARGET the ratio is 45 per cent.

The Payments Risk Committee (PRC 2003) investigated options to cope with the internationalisation of payment services and to reduce the costs of liquidity at the international level. It recommended the development of new intraday liquidity services involving intraday real-time repos, cross-border collateral pool facilities, and intraday collateral and currency swaps. It also asked central banks to accept securities, which are traded on foreign markets and denominated in foreign currencies, as collateral in intraday liquidity enhancing operations. Central banks could increase the efficiency of international large-value payments by liberalising remote access to their domestic RTGS, central banks' accounts, and intraday credit for foreign participants and the establishment of multicurrency facilities. The decision is likely to be based on trading off the perceived benefits with respect to decreasing settlement risks and enhanced static efficiency due to central banks' involvement against the perceived costs stemming from increased risks for monetary policy implementation (e.g. potential problems in controlling the supply of aggregate overnight reserves due to the provision of intraday credit foreign participants) and from public involvement (e.g. barriers to market entry and innovation as well as reduced dynamic efficiency in the market for international payment services).

Retail and small value interbank payment systems

The efficiency and reliability of retail and small-value interbank payment systems (SVPS) affect consumer confidence in the financial system as well as in the central banks and currency in particular. Therefore central banks are regularly involved in payment system operation and/or oversight. However, their influence varies. Some have an operational capacity; others have merely an oversight function, and may act as catalysts for market developments.[23]

CPSS (2002) summarised recent trends in SVPS in the G-10 countries and in Australia:

- A shift from cash and paper-based instruments (i.e. paper cheques) to non-cash electronic payment methods (card-based – credit and debit cards – as well as account-based – direct debit and credit transfers);
- An increase of straight through processing (STP) due to enhanced interoperability of payment procedures based on common data protocols;
- The evolution of product innovation in the context of new payment methods (eMoney, mPayments) and in the area of access products (ATMs offer additional services, such as reloading prepaid mobile phone cards; internet banking). New products are usually captured by some sort of regulation in the EU (i.e. e-Money Directive or Banking Directives) and to some extent in the US, where large differences prevail across states.
- New entrants (e.g. market mobile phone companies, telecommunication operators, net-based scratch card companies) are often particularly innovative, and are more active in the area of new payment instruments (e.g. eMoney, Electronic Bill Presentment and Payment – EBPP), despite the fact that banks remain the main players in the payment system. New market entrants are usually subject to some form of regulation in the EU (i.e. eMoney Directive, Banking Directives and – in the future – New Legal Framework) and to some extent in the US, where large differences prevail across states.

BCG (Boston Consulting Group, 2003) expects the share of non-cash payments in Europe to increase from 42 per cent in 2003 to 57 per cent in 2010. In the US the share is expected to remain stable at 85 per cent. That corresponds to an annual growth rate of 6 per cent in Europe and 5.5 per cent in the US. The composition of non-cash payments shifts towards electronic payments. The Federal Reserve System (2004a) estimates the annual growth rate of the number of non-cash payments to have accelerated from 3.1 per cent (1979–2000) to 3.8 per cent (2000–2003). In 2003, the number of electronic non-cash payments (55 per cent of non-cash payments) exceeded that of checks (45 per cent of non-cash payments) for the first time. The processing of paper cheques decreased between 2000 and 2003 due to increased electronification of cheque payments at the point of sale and due to substitution of cheques by electronic payment instruments.

The Red Book and the Blue Book provide data on the evolution of cashless payment instruments in the Euro area, the UK and the US from 1998 to 2002. The number of cheque transactions decreased in all three areas, whereas the number of transactions by all other cashless instruments (credit/debit cards, credit transfers and direct debit, eMoney) increased. The total number of transactions by electronic cashless instruments exceeded that of cheques substantially in all three economies in 2002. The diffusion of debit/credit cards per inhabitant increased strongly during the period, as did the use of eMoney in the Euro area. The use of credit transfers and direct debits grew substantially in the US and only slightly in the Euro area and the UK, where diffusion was much higher already. The relative importance of cashless instruments by volume indicates that the US mostly relies on cheques and credit/debit cards, whereas the Euro area largely uses account based instruments (credit transfers and direct debits). The data on relative importance based on value show that direct transfers play the most important role in all three economies in high-value retail payments. The number of ATMs per 1 million inhabitants was much higher in the US than in the Euro area and the UK in 2002. The number of ATM transactions in the UK and the US is about twice as high as in the Euro area. Data on eMoney cards and terminals in the Euro area demonstrate continued growth from low levels. In 2002, about 22 million eMoney cards were issued in the Euro area with an average loading of €37. In general, the distribution of cards with various functions (credit, debit, cash, eMoney, cheque guarantee) differs widely among the three economies. The analysis of data concerning the retail payment systems in the Euro area, the UK and the US shows pronounced institutional variation.

Humphrey *et al.* (1996) argue that the pricing of payment services has a strong impact on the direction of institutional change in payment systems by shaping changes in demand. This point is frequently stressed with regard to the (creeping) diffusion of alternative payment instruments (i.e. eMoney). Additional factors influencing the economy at large do often have an impact on the payment system as well (e.g., the introduction of the Euro).

Account-based (e.g. direct debits and credit transfers) and card-based payment processes differ in important ways: whereas account-based transactions are executed at the expense of the account-holder (either on a per-transaction basis or in terms of total operating expenses of the account), card-based products involve a per-transaction fee payable by the merchant.[24] Account-based transactions are often cleared and settled via a National Automated Clearing House (NACH).

The organisational structure of retail and small-value interbank settlement and clearing differs substantially in G-10 countries, according to CPSS (2000), despite similar available technology. In some countries the functions of rule setting for and operation of the clearing process are combined, in others they are separated. Market structure differs widely, too. In some countries a single clearing arrangement operates for paper-based and for electronic payments, in others two separate mechanisms are in place, but there are also countries with more than 100 clearing arrangements. In many countries only private entities (often bank associations, groups of financial institutions) provide clearing services, while in others CB services coexist with private suppliers. After multilateral clearing, settlement usually takes place at the end of the day through accounts held at the central bank. The latter more often than not operates the settlement system.

In all European countries (except Austria, Finland and Russia) and in the US, NACHs operate in small-value payment systems as DNS systems. NACHs are run in the background as an infrastructure not visible to the customer. In Europe, central banks are actively involved in operating NACHs, many of which are owned and operated by central banks or by a company partly owned by a central bank. In the US, the Fed operates its own FedACH system, while the number of private competitors is declining. Card-based transactions are often cleared and settled via private, branded, networks. The visibility of these is a central, strategic issue for the operating company. Clearing and settlement often take place on the books of a private clearing and settlement institution. The share of paper cheques has fallen considerably as electronification, straight through processing (STP) and interoperability of non-cash payments has increased.[25] As a result, the Bank for International Settlements (CPSS 2002) reports increases in security, decreases in operational risk and reduced settlement lags.

Pan European Clearing Houses (PEACHs) were established as an industry response to the increased pressure on prices for cross-border transactions resulting from the SEPA initiative. Cross-border payments remain more expensive than domestic ones, due to a lower number of transactions, more complex technological requirements and stricter access criteria. Currently, a large share of cross-border payments is processed via correspondent banking relationships. These are costly to administer and complicate risk as well as treasury management. In order to cope with these disadvantages, European banks have developed alliances (such as the European Banking Association – EBA) and joint ventures. Cross-border mergers and acquisitions have increased the cheaper variant, in-house cross-border payment services. In addition, money remittance offices provide cross-border money transfer services and spread geographically. Card-based transactions feature prominently in cross-border payments in tourism and distant selling (i.e. eCommerce).

Advances in information and telecommunication technology, the role of economies of scale and scope in payment systems and political pressure, may lead to a consolidation and concentration of the European small-value payment systems market. Consolidation and concentration impact on efficiency and stability of the payment system in various ways. The BIS conjectures that competition enhances the innovative capacity and efficiency of market participants.[26] On the other hand, a fragmented market might leave potential economies of scale and scope partly unexploited, increase operational risk due to different procedural and technological standards and amplify legal risks due to differences in legal arrangements or regulatory provisions concerning different market participants. Cooperation among market participants is necessary to some extent, as common technological standards and interoperability increase the efficiency of the payment systems. 'Co-opetition' (competitors cooperate in selected areas – e.g. development of common standards – but compete in input and output markets) poses challenges for competition policy; these problems are not unique to the payments market.

In the US, the Federal Reserve System was founded in 1913 with the specific objective to prevent breakdowns of the payments system by establishing a national cheque clearing system. The motive for legislation was a breakdown of the payments system, which was considered to have contributed to the financial panic of 1907. Lacker, Walker and Weinberg (1999) challenge the view that the Fed's prominent role in cheque clearing was due to apparent inefficiencies in the prevailing system in the early twentieth century. In 1917, Congress authorised the Fed to prohibit commercial banks to charge the Fed cheque presentment fees, after the 'voluntary reciprocal plan' initiated in 1915 failed to attract a critical mass of member banks to participate in the Fed's cheque clearing business. Only after the Fed was granted the sole right of mail present at par (a legal privilege), it gained a competitive advantage and gained market share. According to Lacker, Walker and Weinberg (1999), the underlying motive was to attract members to the Federal Reserve System.

The dominant position in the small value payment systems market that the Fed had acquired since its foundation, led to the Monetary Control Act of 1980, which intended to promote private competition in the small value payment systems market by restricting the Fed's pricing policy to create a level playing field between the Fed and potential private competitors. In order to promote the efficiency of cheque clearing, the Fed was transferred further regulatory powers over cheques it did not process itself in the Expedited Funds Available Act in 1987. The Debt Collection Improvement Act of 1996 spurred the growth of ACH usage. It required the federal government to handle most of its payments electronically by 1999. Concerns about the service availability for smaller depository institutions and community banks led to the conclusion of the Rivlin Committee in 1998 that the Fed should continue to operate its FedACH service and should foster competition among commercial ACH providers, as well as stipulate market growth by enhanced services.[27] Thus, the Fed's prominent role in the US checking collection and ACH markets depend largely on politico-economic factors rather than on technological innovation.

Both innovation and new market participants pose questions concerning the adequacy of the current legal and regulatory framework including central banks' settlement and access policies. The payments system traditionally rests largely on commercial banks. Despite institutional change in the payments system leading to the blurring of boundaries of traditional financial sectors, banks still dominate the wholesale payment system. A number of product innovations in retail payment systems increased the role of non-banks in small value transactions. Although the active participation of non-banks in handling payments has a long history in the US and Europe (e.g. postal giro), the increasing diffusion of current innovations such as smart cards and online debit cards raises a number of interesting questions; some are addressed in studies by the Federal Reserve Bank of Kansas City[28] and the Bank of England[29] respectively. They presented evidence that non-banks engaged in a large number of payment activities, but that they are hardly involved in settlement activities. As the latter are conducted mainly through the banking system, the potential dangers for systemic risk and the impact on the efficacy of monetary policy due to participation of non-banks in the payments system is thought to be limited. In the EU, the ECB has successfully used its influence on the legislative process regarding the eMoney Directive 2000/46/EC and insisted on the incorporation of the redeemability requirement, which reinforced the link between electronic money schemes and the euro as the generally accepted medium of exchange, the medium of final settlement and the uniform unit of account. Similarly, the ECB is actively involved in the legislative process leading to the New Legal Framework (NFL), which will also cover payment service providers, which are not traditional banks.

Cross-border economic activity increases as a result of European integration and so does demand for cross-border small value interbank payments. This will affect the structure of the European market. Major participants in the cross-border market (PEACHs) might also attract domestic payments, albeit at the beginning of the integration process they do not offer competitive prices and quality for domestic payments. Large NACHs that expand into the cross-border market, on the other hand, might evolve into PEACHs. The emergence of an integrated cross-border payments market is likely to increase consolidation pressure on national markets. However, the market is still nationally fragmented and tendencies to delay integration are motivated by past investments in domestic payment system infrastructure, which are not yet fully depreciated. Consequently, switching from domestic to integrated small value interbank payment systems involves high investment under considerable uncertainty concerning future market structure. As a result of the high fixed costs of direct participation, due to the more stringent technological requirements in PEACHs than in NACHs, banks with low cross-border volume might find it more efficient to participate indirectly via a larger domestic hub. That institution can be the respective central bank or a domestic commercial bank. Most small value interbank payment systems in the EU are tiered to some extent; some are tiered to a large extent with the indirect participants by far outnumbering the direct ones. All systemically important payment systems in the EU settle in CB money.[30] But settlement in CB money occurs for the direct participants' clearing balances only. Although these include payment orders of indirect participants, the latter usually receive only commercial bank money after settlement.

Institutional change affects the choice between direct and indirect participation in interbank small value payment systems. The spreading collateral requirements and increasing technological sophistication increase costs of direct participation. Advances in ICT and increasing transaction volumes decrease the costs of operating and accessing payment systems at the margin for both direct and indirect participants. The impact on relative costs of direct and indirect participation remains ambiguous and the evidence so far is inconclusive.[31] In the cases of large nostro banks and 'quasi systems', small payment system participants settle on their books, which might give rise to stability concerns in tiered systems. The Ferguson Report (Group of Ten 2001) defined 'quasi systems' as financial institutions, which are not officially clearing and settlement institutions, that clear and settle large values relative to a well-defined notion of entire payment flows across their own books. Tiering is common in payment systems and often the result of central banks' policy concerning access to CB accounts.[32] Especially in correspondent banking systems a small number of banks might emerge as nostro banks. Many smaller banks hold accounts at these and settle across their books. Therefore, the extension of payment system oversight to these institutions might be called for.

Process (i.e. electronification, straight-through processing) and product innovations (e.g. m-payments offered by mobile phone companies) offered also by non-banks, as well as emergence of institutional innovations (e.g. increased tiering and new markets such as the integrated European payments market – PEACHs, Continuous Linked Settlement – CLS) are expected to lead to increases in efficiency and to decreases of CB money needed to support a given value of payments in a relevant market.

In the long-term evolution of payment systems, one of the most important instances of institutional change was the foundation of central banks (from the foundation of the Sveriges Riksbank in 1668 and of the Federal Reserve System in 1913 to the foundation of the European Monetary Institute in 1994 and the ECB in 1998), which are to be explained entirely by politico-economic considerations rather than by technological innovations. Similarly, the establishment of common currencies from the circulation of federal reserves notes in 1914 to the circulation of euro notes in 2001 was based on widespread technologies, but represented considerable institutional innovations based on politico-economic reasoning.

The analysis of recent developments indicates that central banks and commercial banks as well as final customers have diverging preferences with respect to the optimal risk/cost trade-off in payment systems. Institutional change in the payment system is driven by the politico-economic interaction of central banks' and commercial banks' (and end users') interests as well as their respective power resources rather than by technological innovations.[33] New technologies are not drivers in their own right; they have an impact on institutional change as tools in the development of new products, new markets, and new governance structures by changing the incentive and costs structure underlying particular institutional arrangements in payment systems.

We conceptualise technology as a production technology that transforms inputs (i.e. labour, capital) into outputs (i.e. payment services such as clearing and settlement). Rather than reducing the term technology to hard- and software (i.e. computers, telecommunication infrastructure), this conceptualisation also encompasses organisational structures, rules and procedures in the production of payment services.[34] While general purpose technologies, such as information and telecommunication technologies, can be assumed to be exogenous to the politico-economic tensions that drive institutional change in the payments systems, this does not hold true for more specific payment technologies. The latter are endogenous to the process of institutional change, as they are influenced by research and development efforts of payment system participants. Payment technologies depend on complementary innovations to become productive. First, these can be necessary at the firm level: the adoption of new payment technologies necessitates adaptations at the level of the individual payment institution in areas such as organisational structures, internal governance mechanisms and risk management models as well as skills. The adoption of new payment technologies at the firm level is often driven by the desire of commercial banks and their customers to minimise their costs of holding CB reserves. Second, complementary innovations can also be necessary at the level of the payments system and involve political decisions: these are institutional innovations such as the governance structure of the payments system (i.e. regulation and oversight of new payment institutions and technologies), the general legal framework (e.g. privacy protection and liability issues in payment systems). But they also involve complementary initiatives of private institutions such as monitoring credit histories of users of payment instruments (credit registers). Both specific payment technologies as well as their complementary institutions are (to a large extent) endogenous to the politico-economic tension that drives institutional change in the payments system. Thus, the statement 'Technology drives the adoption of payment instrument X' represents a naïve concept of payment technology. It wrongly regards payments technology as exogenous to the payments industry. It underestimates the need for complementary institutions to make new payment technologies productive and the complexity of the adoption of new payment technologies at the firm level.

Humphrey, Sato, Tsurumi and Vesala (1996) describe the long-term evolution of the payments systems in Europe, Japan, and the US. The authors explain the dominance of credit transfers in Europe by banking concentration, nationwide networks, and cooperation among banks. The relatively early emergence of credit transfers – despite the relatively late extension of banking services to the general public beyond merchants and the wealthy – can be ascribed to the development of postal giro services across Europe. This forced other credit institutions to offer similar payment services to compete for deposits. In the case of Japan, the authors consider the lower crime rate as the major reason for the larger reliance on cash at the point of sale compared to the US. The evolution of the Japanese payments system was largely driven by policy initiatives (i.e. the government initiative to develop a modern banking system after 1868; the National Centralised Domestic Exchange Settlement System (NCDE) operated by the Bank of Japan (BOJ) in 1943 as small value payment systems; the BOJ-NET in 1988 as large value payment system) and demand (i.e. a coordinated banking sector initiative that led to the ZENGIN system in 1973 to replace NCDE). In the US, banking services were offered relatively early to the general public. But due to regulatory constraints (i.e. branching restrictions), the resulting low concentration, and later the involvement of the Fed in and subsidisation of cheque clearing, the cheque system was more cost-effective than the one based on credit transfer.[35] The long-run evolution of payments systems in Europe, Japan and the US supports the predominance of institutional and politico-economic factors in shaping payment systems over technological innovations.

The institutional and organisational structures of the economy-wide payments system differ across time and across economies. But they all have in common that CB money serves as the generally accepted medium of exchange and the unit of account and all economically relevant payment systems are eventually linked to CB money via the banking system. However spectacular recent innovations in payment systems are depicted, a world without CB money is not in sight. Nevertheless, it is important for policy makers as well as for researchers to investigate the implications of such an evolution, even though it is deemed unlikely at the moment.

Institutional change in the payments system and monetary policy

The formulation, conduct and implementation of monetary policy take place in an institutional environment, of which the economy-wide payments system forms an integral part. In principle, central banks implement monetary policy by manipulating the short-term interest rate, that is, the overnight interest rate in the interbank market. Despite the small size of their repurchasing operations on interbank markets relative to total turnover, their impact is sufficient to steer the market. This is mainly due to their ability to issue the generally accepted medium of exchange at zero marginal cost. But central banks have additional instruments at their discretion which increase their grip on the money market by imposing a structural liquidity deficit. They can influence demand for their own liabilities by minimum reserve requirements (MRR) and by legal restrictions concerning the issuance of banknotes, as well as by (in some countries) 'moral suasion'. The main instruments of monetary policy implementation are open market operations (OMO), minimum reserve requirements (MRR) and standing facilities (lending and deposit facility). Today central banks also routinely employ announcements of levels of their main operating target in monetary policy implementation. These instruments can be adapted to cope with institutional change in the payment system. But they also have an impact on the institutional characteristics of payment systems, and can, therefore, be employed by central banks to proactively shape institutional change in payment systems.[36]

The impact of the institutional characteristics of the payments system on monetary policy can be categorised along three dimensions.

First, institutional characteristics of the payments system affect the level of demand for CB money as well as its structure, predictability, velocity and its sensitivity with respect to CBs' instruments (i.e. the interest elasticity of demand for CB money). Deutsche Bundesbank (1997) points out that the substitution of sight deposits for cash – due to decreasing costs of access to accounts by debit cards, electronic banking and ATMs – might change the information content of monetary aggregates. The velocity of circulation of sight deposits is supposed to be higher than that of cash, so that the velocity of circulation of monetary aggregates might increase, too. On the other hand, improved payment instruments might enable individuals to separate transaction holdings from store-of-value holdings more effectively. This might lead partly to a shift of funds from high velocity low-interest bearing deposits to low velocity higher-interest investments. The Bundesbank (1997) reports that the overall decline in the velocity of M3 experienced over previous decades was not caused by innovations in payment instruments. The interest rate sensitivity of monetary aggregates has increased, and this trend is expected to continue. It is mainly driven by the 'asset acquisition behaviour' of investors. The Bundesbank conjectures that a gradual change in the velocity and composition of monetary aggregates will not undermine monetary targeting in principle, as the central bank will be able to take trend velocity change into account in setting the growth rate of monetary aggregates. In addition, new payment instruments (i.e. eMoney) are included in the definition of M1.

Second, the operational efficiency of the payment system is a precondition for the emergence of deep and liquid interbank markets. These, in turn, are prerequisites for the effective implementation of monetary policy, as a large and unstable float can lead to higher and more volatile reserves on the level of individual banks as well as at the aggregate level. That leads to more volatile intraday and overnight interest rates, and can make it harder for central banks to judge the liquidity stance of the system.[37] In addition, the estimation of autonomous factors in reserve demand will become harder for central banks; this estimation is a necessary precondition for determining the maximum operational volume of refinancing operations at given interest rates. In the short run, central banks can impose accounting standards (i.e. either the payer's or the payee's account has to be debited/credited before the transaction is completed) to deal with float, albeit at the expense of distributional side effects. In the long run, more efficient procedures (e.g. electronification of procedures) will reduce float. Efficient pricing of payment services in the interbank payment system, with respect to the implicit credit entailed in float, will increase incentives for banks to implement more sophisticated treasury management practices, procedures and systems. Fry *et al.* (1999) point out that an efficient payment system, that is available and accessible throughout the monetary area, will enhance the effectiveness of the implementation of monetary policy in all financial centres throughout the monetary area by reducing transaction costs on the money market. Consequently, the fragmentation of the money market is prevented and the implementation of monetary policy can focus on a single and centralised money market. (A special case is the point Cagan (1958) made in his classic paper 'Why do we use money in open market operations'?) The implementation of TARGET was motivated by this objective.

Third, the payment system should not be a source of unforeseen and unpredictable shocks to the quantity and costs of liquidity with ensuing direct and indirect ramifications for monetary policy. Central banks are the sole providers of liquidity to the market at zero marginal costs. In addition, they are not considered competitors by payment system participants, operate under a 'public interest' prerogative[38] and are entrusted with the role of lender of last resort (LLR). This role is nowadays often accompanied by the responsibility for operation and/or oversight of payment systems and their participants. The failure of a large debtor in a DNS system and the consequential liquidity shortage could motivate the central bank – in its responsibility as an LLR – to inject liquidity, which could spill over into the overnight market. The potential conflict of interest between these functions of central banks as monetary authority and LLR led to a discussion of their institutional separation.[39] At the same time, central banks often bear legal and/or statutory responsibilities for the stability of the financial system and the payment system,[40] so that the market would expect them to act as LLR even in the absence of an official and explicit LLR mandate. The operation of the large value payment system and the oversight of other payment systems could imply an informational advantage for the central bank that would greatly enhance its position to put in place effective policies to prevent liquidity problems of individual participants to threaten systemic stability (e.g. through the operation of RTGS systems), to detect potential liquidity problems of individual participants early, distinguish liquidity from solvency problems as well as to act as LLR efficiently and effectively.

In short, the institutional characteristics of payment systems affect the demand for CB money, the environment in which monetary policy is implemented and the efficacy of different instruments of monetary policy implementation.

Central bank payment system policies

In addition to participation in shaping and implementing government initiatives regarding payment systems policies, central banks have a number of instruments at their discretion to influence institutional change in payment systems. Central banks' policies concerning payment systems can be distinguished according to the relevant addressees, which can be payment systems or their participants. The most important policy instruments available to central banks are: settlement policy and access policy to CB accounts,[41] as well as to intraday credit at the central bank. In addition, central banks often assume an active role in payment system oversight, operation, and regulation. CPSS (2002) provides an overview of relevant CB policies:

First, many central banks encourage systemically important payment systems to settle in CB money in order to reduce systemic, credit and liquidity risk as well as to ensure service continuity (settlement policy).[42] In some cases, the requirement to settle in CB money is restricted to the funding and defunding of end-of-day transactions, although settlement during the day is allowed to take place in alternative high-quality assets. Furthermore, the central bank is often, for competitive reasons, preferred over competitors as the settlement institution. Central banks often act as LLR and participate in banking supervision. Continuous involvement in the payment system provides central banks with access to valuable information which helps in fulfilling both roles successfully. Involvement can incur costs in addition to the resource costs of oversight, as central banks usually grant intraday credit when they act as settlement institutions. Thus, they have to bear certain risks, namely, credit risk and the risk of spill-over of intraday credit to overnight credit.

Second, central banks' access policies to CB money (in the form of CB accounts) are the core instrument of their payment system policy with respect to payment system participants. Access is usually granted to institutions, whose role in the payment system is considered to be important enough for financial stability, so that the associated risks for central banks can be justified. These are usually resident banks. The drivers of institutional change in the payment system, in particular liberalisation and globalisation, have led to the blurring of boundaries between different financial sectors and to an increase in the demand for cross-border and multicurrency clearing and settlement services. Consequently, some central banks have broadened the range of financial and non-financial institutions that are granted access to CB money, such as security firms, security settlement systems, foreign exchange settlement institutions and insurance companies. In many cases access to CB money and (limited) banking regulation is extended to non-banks that provide payment services. In order to facilitate cross-border foreign exchange and multicurrency settlement, some central banks adapted their policies to allow remote access to CB money, that is, access for institutions that have no offices in the country under consideration.

Third, CPSS (2002) reports that, in general, access to CB accounts also implies access to intraday credit at the central bank and the underlying considerations are very similar. In order to limit their risk exposure, central banks require collateral or third-party guarantees, charge fees and set limits, which provide further instruments to fine-tune CB policies with respect to institutions. Technological standardisation (acceptance of international standards for message protocols) can reduce the costs of direct access to interbank payment systems and can have an impact on central banks' access policies.

The Red Book and the Blue Book provide overviews of access criteria to selected large value payment systems in the Euro area, the UK, and the US and document-wide variations between different systems. Neither central banks' settlement nor their access policies at large are by any means homogenous, according to CPSS (2002). Central banks have a number of instruments from their tool-box of payment systems policies at hand to react to – but also to play a more proactive role in shaping – institutional change in the payments system.

The chapters of the book build on a common framework, which consists of diverse but complementary methodological approaches. Policy initiatives and changing demand by banks and final customers turn out to be the main drivers of recent and long-term institutional change. Recent institutional change in the payments systems results from the interaction between opposing interests as well as changing incentives and costs underlying a particular institutional structure: central bank's objective to control the monetary system – in order to ensure the effective implementation of monetary policy, the maintenance of financial stability, the smooth operation of the payment system and the collection of seigniorage – is in general thought to require commercial banks to hold some reserve of CB money. Commercial banks' objective to maximise profits requires them to economise on such reserves. The design of the payment system involves a trade-off between settlement risk and liquidity costs. The analysis of recent developments indicates that central banks and commercial banks as well as final customers have diverging preferences with respect to the optimal risk/cost combination in payment systems, due to the divergence between social and private costs of disruptions of the payments system. Institutional change in the payments system is driven by the politico-economic interaction of central banks' and commercial banks' interests, as well as their respective power resources, rather than by technological innovations. New technologies are rarely drivers in their own right; more often they have an impact on institutional change by enabling the development of new products, new markets and new governance structures by changing the incentive and costs structure underlying particular institutional arrangements in payment systems. In recent history, central banks have demonstrated their determination and their political ability to maintain control of the monetary system in the face of and in order to actively shape institutional change in the payments system.

The analysis of data concerning retail and wholesale payment systems in the Euro area, the UK and the US shows pronounced institutional variation. Policy initiatives and changing demand by banks and final customers are seen as the main drivers of institutional change. The latter lead to strong growth in the values and numbers of transactions in wholesale as well as retail and small value interbank payment systems. This in turn not only leads to calls for higher efficiency of payment systems, but also serves as motivation for many policy initiatives. New payment instruments and payment service providers, the move to RTGS and increasing electronification, are the most visible signs of institutional change. Electronification, and alternative means of payment are expected to lead to a steeper payment pyramid: the ratio of CB money to total value of payments decreases. This development gives rise to concerns about the future role of money in general and CB money in particular in the economy-wide payments system. The institutional and organisational structures of the economy-wide payments system differ across time and across economies. But they all have in common that CB money serves as the generally accepted medium of exchange and the unit of account and all economically relevant payment systems are eventually linked to CB money via the banking system. Institutional change affects monetary policy by its impact on demand for CB money and on the efficacy of monetary policy implementation at a given demand for CB money. Central banks not only have a large range of instruments at their discretion to react to but also to influence institutional change in the economy-wide payments system. They are heavily involved in the legal and political process shaping the broad legislative framework concerning payment instruments and they are transferred substantial regulatory power within this framework. In addition, central banks can adapt the instruments of monetary policy implementation and their own payment system policies to cope with and also to bring about institutional change in the payment system.

The chapters

In this section, the chapters of the book are discussed in the order they appear in the book. Each paper, starting with that by Lawrence H. White, is followed by a paper or comment written in response to it.

Lawrence H. White's sterling point in 'Payments system innovations in the United States since 1945 and their implications for monetary policy' is that the central bank's monetary liabilities consist of paper currency (in the US, Federal Reserve notes) and commercial bank deposit balances held at the central bank (which the banks use for interbank settlements). Payment system innovations have potential consequences for monetary policy, if they provide such close substitutes that they significantly reduce the scale or increase the price-elasticity of demand for CB-issued currency or CB-issued settlement deposits. His chapter analyses the structure of recent innovations that may provide close substitutes for paper currency and for CB settlement balances. He investigates the effects of these on the institutional structure of the economy-wide payment system and the response of US monetary policy. He also compares the more recent developments with the diffusion of credit and debit cards and their impact on US monetary policy.

His discussants, Ulrich Bindseil and Flemming Würtz, also take a historical perspective in 'Payment systems from the monetary policy implementation perspective' They recall that there was little doubt before 1914 that CB policy implementation meant first of all control of short-term interest rates. This changed dramatically in the early 1920s with the birth of 'reserve position doctrine' (RPD) in the US, according to which a central bank should, via open market operations, steer some reserve concept, which would impact via the money multiplier on monetary aggregates and ultimate goals. While the Fed returned to an unambiguous steering of short-term interest rates only in the 1990s, the Bank of England, for example, never adopted RPD. After discussing various possible influences of payment systems on monetary policy implementation technique, the authors eventually conclude that these factors do not help to explain the changes in implementation doctrine that were observed in particular in the US. On the contrary, the fact that today's implementation technique is again closer to that of 1900, despite dramatic institutional change in payment systems in the twentieth century, suggests that short-term interest rate control is the appropriate approach.

Forrest H. Capie, Dimitrios P. Tsomocos and Geoffrey E. Wood ('Modelling institutional change in the payments system, and its implications for monetary policy') appraise one possible technological development, namely the evolution of electronic barter, and model both it and money as transactions technologies. Their method is in the tradition of Shubik's approach to modelling monetary institutions. By comparing the models, they appraise the future of fiat money.

First an outline of the technology that may replace money is set out. This is followed by an informal description of the model used to appraise both this technology and fiat money as means of conducting exchanges. This is in turn followed by the development of a formal model, and the implications of the analysis for the survival (or otherwise) of fiat money. This leads to a discussion of economic policy, and then to a concluding overview.

Sujit Chakravorti's 'The evolving payments landscape and its implications for monetary policy' prompted by Capie, Tsomocos and Wood, focuses on the economics of payment systems. The literature largely builds on the economics of networks and he interprets money and payment systems as networks. The associated theoretical insights are applied to analyse the slow diffusion of stored-value cards in the US, to study the underlying incentives in credit card networks, and to investigate whether existing payment networks can meet future needs. Conclusions are drawn for modelling institutional change in payment networks, for incentives to invest in innovation in payment systems and for monetary policy.

In his paper 'eMoney and monetary policy: the role of the inter-eMoney-institution-market for settlement media and the unit of account', Stefan W. Schmitz presents a critical assessment of the literature on eMoney and monetary policy. After briefly summarising his own previous results on eMoney, redeemability, the unit of account and monetary policy, he arranges the alternative models of eMoney and monetary policy in three categories. First come models which assume that CB money will be replaced by another medium of exchange. Second is a review of models that argue that the residual demand for base money will remain positive; and, third, of those that propose payments systems with a publicly sanctioned unit of account, but without a generally accepted medium of exchange, in which net balances are either settled by privately issued fiat-type monies or the transfer of wealth. In the case of the last, he discusses the implicit models of the market for media of settlement between eMoney-institutions and the role of the unit of account. Emphasised is the relationship between the function of money as the generally accepted medium of exchange and its function as the unit of account, in doing so. His conclusion is that the alternative models of a world without money are inconsistent and incomplete, thus confirming his previous results on eMoney, redeemability, the unit of account and monetary policy by rejecting the alternatives.

Cornelia Holthausen ('What drives demand for and supply of electronic money? Theoretical background and lessons from history') highlights the critical role of carefully modelling the demand for money. The literature on the subject has grown rapidly over the past decade and she provides an overview of the main concepts and results. The role of frictions, such as limited enforcement of contracts and informational asymmetry, is emphasised. Discussed is whether equilibria with several monies are possible. Institutional change is interpreted as transition between equilibria and she asks whether such transitions are feasible and desirable. In addition, she relates the results to historical evidence of private clearinghouses and the demand for money in institutional arrangements, which was different from the current monopoly provision of money by central banks. Finally, she discusses the implications of the demand for CB money and for monetary policy.

Stefan W. Schmitz ('Monetary policy in a world without central bank money') sets out the prospects for monetary policy in such a world. The role of CB money as generally accepted medium of exchange is a precondition for the implementation of monetary policy in the current institutional set-up. In the paper, it is shown that conferring certain regulatory competencies (including the power to impose financial obligations on third parties) on central banks enables them to implement an equivalent to monetary policy in a world without CB money. The analysis is based on the conceptualisation of a payments system that does not settle in CB money; in which the demand for CB money is actually zero. As shown by an analysis of the legal foundations of the operations of the ECB and the Fed, central banks do in fact already possess the necessary regulatory powers to manipulate the demand for the generally accepted medium of exchange. Politico-economic objections to granting central banks the necessary regulatory competencies also apply to the institutional frameworks currently in place in the Euro area and the US.

The final paper, by Angelo Baglioni, is on 'The organisation of interbank settlement systems: current trends and implications for central banking'. Starting from the main features of the evolution of interbank payment systems in the 1990s, Baglioni analyses the choice of commercial banks among alternative interbank payment systems. The strategic interests of participants are interpreted as strategic games. Banks have a collective interest in synchronising and anticipating payment orders. But each individual bank has an individual interest in delaying payments. He discusses the potential consequences for the economy (efficiency) and for customers, and the potential role of central banks in providing intraday liquidity and in coordinating banks. This chapter also presents evidence describing the key changes in the institutional structure of payment systems, that is, the shift from net- to gross-settlement systems and the evolution of hybrid systems. Then he asks to what extent these are driven by regulatory changes (e.g. Lamfalussy standards and SEPA). In addressing the implications for monetary policy, he analyses the question of whether payment systems need to settle in CB money and how payment systems affect the demand for CB money and the equilibrium of the money market. Finally, he discusses the role of reserve requirements imposed by central banks in the implementation of monetary policy.

Overview

It is hard to avoid ending such an introductory chapter with a plea for further research, and a recommendation to study the papers that follow. Both of these should be taken as a lead. A little more, however, is worth saying. In particular, by whatever mode of analysis was used it emerged that fiat CB money would not be wholly replaced by any form of electronic money currently envisaged. Second, it was also clear that developments – which have in the past, and may in the future, improve the robustness or the efficiency of payments systems – have not had fundamentally damaging effects on the ability of central banks to control monetary conditions.

In sum, the tension between the central bank's goal and that of the commercial banks, which was alluded to in the opening of this introduction, has so far been creative rather than destructive, and shows signs of remaining so.

The research project, on which this book is based, was initiated by the principal researcher Stefan W. Schmitz at the Austrian Academy of Sciences and conducted under the project chair of Michael Latzer. Financial support by the OeNB Jubiläumsfond[43] is gratefully acknowledged.

References

Allen, H. (2003) 'Innovations in Retail Payments: E-payments', *Bank of England Quarterly Bulletin*, 428–38.

Board of Governors of the Federal Reserve System (2002) *The Future of Retail Electronic Payments Systems: Industry Interviews and Analysis*, Staff Study 175, Washington, D. C.

Boston Consulting Group (2004) *Global Payment Report 2003*, London.

Bradford, T., Davies, M. and Weiner, S. E. (2003) *Nonbanks in the Payments System*, Federal Reserve Bank of Kansas, Kansas City.

Cagan, P. (1958) 'Why do We Use Money in Open Market Operations?' *Journal of Political Economy,* 66: 34–46.

Committee on Interbank Netting Schemes (1990) *Report of the Committee on Interbank Netting Schemes of the Central Banks of the Group of Ten Countries*, Basel: Bank for International Settlements. [Lamfalussy Report]

Committee on the Federal Reserve in the Payments Mechanism (1998) *The Federal Reserve in the Payment Mechanism*, Washington, D.C.

Cowen, T. and Kroszner, R. (1994) *The New Monetary Economics*, London: Basil Blackwell Publishers.

CPSS – Committee for Payment and Settlement Systems (2000) *Clearing and Settlement Arrangements for Retail Payments in Selected Countries*, Basel: Bank for International Settlements.

CPSS – Committee for Payment and Settlement Systems (2001a) *Core Principles for Systemically Important Payment Systems*, Basel: Bank for International Settlements.

CPSS – Committee for Payment and Settlement Systems (2001b) *Recommendations for Securities Settlement Systems*, Basel: Bank for International Settlements.

CPSS – Committee for Payment and Settlement Systems (2002) *Policy Issues for Central Banks in Retail Payments*, Basel: Bank for International Settlements.

CPSS – Committee for Payment and Settlement Systems (2003) *The Role of Central Bank Money in Payment Systems*, Basel: Bank for International Settlements.

CPSS – Committee for Payment and Settlement Systems (2005) *Statistics on Payment and Settlement Systems in Selected Countries – Figures for 2003*, Basel: Bank for International Settlements. [Red Book]

Deutsche Bundesbank (1997) 'Monetary Policy and Payment Systems', *Deutsche Bundesbank Monthly Report (March)*: 33-46.

Edwards, C. L. (1997) 'Open Market Operations in the 1990', *Federal Reserve Bulletin*, 859–74.

European Central Bank (2003a) *Towards a Single Euro Payments Area – Progress Report*, Frankfurt/Main.

European Central Bank (2003b) *Oversight Standards for Euro Retail Payment Systems*, Frankfurt/Main.

European Central Bank (2004a) *Assessment of Euro Large-Value-Payment Systems against the Core Principles*, Frankfurt/Main.

European Central Bank (2004b) *The Implementation of Monetary Policy in the Euro Area*, Frankfurt/Main.

European Central Bank (2004c) *Payment and Securities Settlement Systems in the European Union*, Frankfurt/Main. [Blue Book]

European Central Bank (2004d) 'Future Developments in the TARGET System', *ECB Monthly Bulletin (April)*: 59-65.

European Central Bank (2005) *Assessment of Euro Retail Payment Systems against the Core Principles*, Frankfurt/Main.

European Commission (2004) 'Financial Integration Monitor 2004 – Background Document', Internal Market DG Working Paper, Brussels.

European Union (1992a) *Treaty Establishing the European Union*, Official Journal of the European Communities C 191, Brussels.

European Union (1992b) *Protocol on the Statute of the European System of Central Banks and the European Central Bank* (annexed to the Treaty establishing the European Union), Official Journal of the European Communities C 191, Brussels.

FBE (1999) *Guidelines on Liquidity Management*, Brussels: Federation Bancaire De L'Union Europèene.

Federal Reserve System (2002) *Alternative Instruments for Open Markets and Discount Window Operations*, Washington, D. C.: Federal Reserve System.

Federal Reserve System (2004a) *The 2004 Federal Reserve System Payments Study*, Washington, D. C.: Federal Reserve System.

Federal Reserve System (2004b) *Reserve Maintenance Manual*, Washington, D. C.: Federal Reserve System.

Freedman, C. (2000) 'Monetary Policy Implementation: Past, Present, and Future – Will the Advent of Electronic Money Lead to the Demise of Central Banking?' *International Finance,* 3: 211–27.

Freixas, X., Holthausen, C., Terol, I. and Thygesen, C. (2001) 'Settlement in Commercial Bank Money versus Central Bank Money', mimeo Universitat Pompeu Fabra, Barcelona.

Fry, M. (1999) 'Risk, Cost and Liquidity in Alternative Payment Systems', *Bank of England Bulletin (February)*: 78–86.

Fry, M. J., Kilato, I., Roger, S., Senderowicz, K., Sheppard, D., Solis, F. and Trundle, J. (1999) *Payment Systems in Global Perspective*, London: Routledge.

Goodhart, C. A. E. and Schoenmaker, D. (1995) 'Should the Functions of Monetary Policy and Banking Supervision Be Separated?', *Oxford Economic Papers,* 47: 539–60.

Group of Ten (2001) *Report on Consolidation in the Financial Sector*, Basel: Bank for International Settlements. [Ferguson Report]

Holthausen, C. (1997) 'Systemic Risk, Interbank Relationships, and Monetary Policy: A Literature Review', working paper, University Pompeu Fabra, Department of Economics, Barcelona.

Holthausen, C. and Monnet, C. (2003) 'Money and Payments: A Modern Perspective', working paper European Central Bank 245, Frankfurt/Main.

Humphrey, D. B., Sato, S., Tsurumi, M. and Vesala, J. M. (1996) 'The Evolution of Payments in Europe, Japan, and the United States – Lessons for Emerging Market Economies', policy research working paper 1676, The World Bank Financial Sector Development Department, Washington, D. C.

Johnson, O. E. G. (1998) 'The Payment System and Monetary Policy', IMF Paper on Policy Analysis and Assessment, Washington, D. C.

Lacker, J. M. (1997) 'Clearing, Settlement, and Monetary Policy', working paper 97–1, Research Department Federal Reserve Bank of Richmond.

Lacker, J. M. and Weinberg, J. A. (2003) 'Payment Economics: Studying the Mechanics of Exchange', *Journal of Monetary Economics*, 50: 381–7.

Lacker, J. M., Walker, J. D. and Weinberg, J. A. (1999) 'The Fed's Entry into Check Clearing Reconsidered,' *Federal Reserve Bank of Richmond Economic Quarterly*, 85: 1–31.

Latzer, M. and Schmitz, S. W. (eds) (2002) *Carl Menger and the Evolution of Payment Systems: From Barter to Electronic Money*, Cheltenham: Edward Elgar.

Madigan, B. F. and Nelson, W. R. (2002) 'Proposed Revision to the Federal Reserve's Discount Window Lending Programs', *Federal Reserve Bulletin* (December): 313–319.

McAndrews, J. and Trundle, J. (2001) 'New Payment System Designs: Causes and Consequences', *Bank of England Financial Stability Review* (December): 127–36.

Payment Systems Policy Working Group (2004) Comments on the Communication from the Commission to the Council and the European Parliament concerning a 'New Legal Framework for Payments in the Internal Market' (Consultative Document), Frankfurt/Main: ECB.

PRC – Payments Risk Committee (2003) *Managing Payment Liquidity in Global Markets: Risk Issues and Solutions*, New York.

Prescott, E. S. and Weinberg, J. A. (2003) 'Incentives, Communication, and Payment Instruments, '*Journal of Monetary Economics*, 50: 433–54.

Rip, A. and Kemp, R. (1998) 'Technological Change', in S. Rayner and E. L. Malone (eds), *Human Choice and Climate Change*, Vol. 2, Columbus: Batelle Press, 327–99.

Schmitz, S. W. (2002a) 'Carl Menger's "Money" and Current Neoclassical Models of Money', in M. Latzer and S. W. Schmitz (eds) *Carl Menger and the Evolution of Payment Systems: From Barter to Electronic Money*, Cheltenham: Edward Elgar, 111–32.

Schmitz, S. W. (2002b) 'The Institutional Character of Electronic Money Schemes: Redeemability and the Unit of Account', in M. Latzer and S. W. Schmitz (eds), *Carl Menger and the Evolution of Payment Systems: From Barter to Electronic Money*, Cheltenham: Edward Elgar, 159–83.

Schmitz, S. W. (2004) 'John Wheatley', *Biographical Dictionary of British Economists*, Bristol: Thoemmes Continnum, 1281-86.

Selgin, G. A. (2005) 'Wholesale Payments: Questioning the Market-Failure Hypothesis', *International Review of Law and Economics,* 24: 333–50.

Selgin, G. A. and White, L. H. (1994) 'How Would the Invisible Hand Handle Money?' *Journal of Economic Literature,* 32: 1718–49.

Sheppard, D. (1996) *Payment Systems*, Handbooks in Central Banking No. 8, Centre for Central Banking Studies, London: Bank of England.

Wood, G. E. (2000) 'The Lender of Last Resort Reconsidered', *Journal of Financial Services Research,* 18: 203–27.

Notes

1 The authors thank the participants of the project workshop at the Austrian Academy of Sciences and, in particular, Robert Lindley, for helpful comments and suggestions.

2 The field of payment economics emerged in the 1990s. It merges monetary economics and banking theory with the study of the mechanics of exchange (Lacker/Weinberg 2003 and the special issues of the *Journal of Money, Credit, and Banking* 31 (3) Part 2 and the *Journal of Monetary Economics* 50 (2)).

3 For a discussion of Wheatley's contribution, see Schmitz (2004).

4 Humphrey *et al.* 1996.

5 In addition to policy initiatives directly addressing payment systems privacy, consumer protection and anti-money-laundering laws, to name but a few, also affect payment system and can influence institutional change in payment systems.

6 CPSS 2000, McAndrews and Trundle 2001.

7 CPSS (2001a) defines a system to be systemically important, if disruptions in the respective settlement process can have a severe impact on other financial system participants or lead to systemic implications.

8 ECB 2003b, 2004a.

9 Federal Reserve System Docket No. OP-1191.

10 Communication from the Commission to the Council and the European Parliament concerning a New Legal Framework for Payments in the Internal Market (Consultative Document) COM (2003) 718.

11 Settlement finality refers to an unconditional and irrevocable payment (EU Final Settlement Directive 98/26/EC). For a discussion of the parameters influencing the choice of medium of final settlement in the CLS system, see Freixas *et al.* (2001).

12 For a discussion, see Schmitz (2002b).

13 The Reserve Bank of Australia introduced exchange settlement accounts, which provide access to CB settlement services for non-banks. Payment service providers, which are in a position to maintain liquid even during seasonal peaks as well as during periods of stress, are eligible. The only service the accounts permit are settlement services related to a clearing process that the account holder participates in.

14 See inter alia Selgin and White 1994, Holthausen and Monnet 2003.

15 See Wood 2000.

16 ECB 2004a.

17 European Commission 2004.

18 ECB 2004d.

19 Belgium, Canada, France, Germany, Hong Kong, Italy, Japan, Netherlands, Singapore, Sweden, Switzerland, United Kingdom, United States.

20 CPSS 2003, 21, Table 1. Data refer to 2002 with a few exceptions.

21 CPSS 2003, 21, Table 1. Data refer to 2002 with a few exceptions.

22 Data sources: Blue Book (ECB 2004c) and Red Book (CPSS 2005).

23 CPSS 2002.

24 CPSS 2002.

25 CPSS 2002 and BCG 2004.

26 CPSS 2002.

27 Committee on the Federal Reserve in the Payments Mechanism (1998). For a discussion of the evolution of the US ACH market, the role of the Fed, and the role of regulation (i.e., the Monetary Control Act of 1980) see White (chapter 1 in this volume).

28 Bradford, Davies and Weiner 2003.

29 Allen 2003.

30 ECB 2005.

31 CPSS 2003.

32 CPSS 2000.

33 Lacker (1997) formalises the decision problem for banks to join a private multilateral net clearing arrangement – once it is introduced exogenously in the model – based on similar considerations, namely that banks want to economise on central bank reserves. Interest on intraday credit encourages private clearing arrangements.

34 See Rip and Kemp (1998) for a discussion of sociological, philosophical and economic concepts and theories of technological change.

35 Prescott and Weinberg (2003) argue that the transition from bank drafts to cheques in the late nineteenth century was due to technological advances (i.e. development of the telegraph) and institutional innovations (i.e. credit reporting services), which enabled merchants to evaluate the quality of cheques offered by previously unknown counterparties. With the growth of interregional trade with previously unknown counterparties, the demand for a more cost-effective means of payment than prepaid bank drafts picked up as well. As a result, new technology and institutional innovations enabled customers to spur institutional change in the payment system to economise on CB money.

36 Descriptions of the monetary policy instruments of the ECB and the Fed can be found in: ECB 2004b, Edwards 1997, Madigan and Nelson 2002, Federal Reserve System 2002 and 2004b.

37 Fry *et al.* 1999.

38 Arguments for the public interest motive go beyond the role of payment systems for monetary policy implementation. An efficient and stable payment system is a necessary part of the infrastructure for both an efficient economy of intra-temporal production and exchange as well as for a stable financial system of inter-temporal allocation. However, seigniorage provides a private interest motive for central banks' involvement in large value payment systems.

39 See Goodhart and Schoenmaker (1995) and Wood (2000) for a discussion.

40 Article 105 (2) of the Treaty establishing the European Union and Article 3.1. of the ECB Statutes explicitly state that the promotion of the smooth operation of the payment system is a basic task of the ESCB. The Federal Reserve Act (1913), the Monetary Control Act (1980), and the Electronic Funds Transfer Act (1978, 1996) are the basis for the Fed's task to promote an efficient nationwide payment system.

41 Access to CB accounts influences the costs and the legal barriers that non-bank entrants to the payments market face and, thus, affects efficiency, concentration and stability of the payment system.

42 'Core Principle VI: Assets used for settlement should preferably be a claim on the central bank; where other assets are used, they should carry little or no credit risk and little or no liquidity risk.' (CPSS 2001a, 34).

43 The project proposal was submitted and financial funds were allocated to the project before Stefan W. Schmitz joined OeNB. The views expressed in this book are solely those of the authors of the respective chapters and do not necessarily reflect those of the institutions they are affiliated with.

1 Payments system innovations in the United States since 1945 and their implications for monetary policy

Lawrence H. White

The revolutions that haven't yet happened

Monetary policy works through its control over the monetary base, the volume of the central bank's monetary liabilities. (Central bankers typically prefer to think and talk about monetary policy working through changes in a targeted interest rate, but the central bank's balance sheet holds the key to understanding what the central bank can do to influence interest rates and other variables.) The central bank's monetary liabilities consist of paper currency (in the US, Federal Reserve notes) and commercial bank deposit balances held at the central bank (used for interbank settlements).[1] Payment system innovations have potential consequences for the conduct of monetary policy if they provide such close substitutes that they significantly reduce the scale or increase the interest-elasticity of demand for central-bank-issued currency or central-bank-issued settlement deposits.

Recent innovations that may provide close substitutes for paper currency include such electronic money devices as card-based, mobile-phone-based, and personal-computer-based means for consumers to hold and transfer spendable balances. Innovations that may provide close substitutes for central-bank settlement balances include deposit-transfer systems that settle outside the central bank's books, such as PayPal, e-gold and deposit transfers cleared and settled by private systems (private automated clearinghouses and ATM networks).

In a 1996 interview banker Walter Wriston declared that digital currency carried on smart cards was 'the revolution that's waiting in the woods' and a 'technology … on the verge of exploding' (Bass 1996). The predicted explosion has yet to happen.

Monetary economists (Cronin and Dowd 2001; Friedman 1999) and central bankers (BIS 1996; King 1999) have envisioned serious consequences for – perhaps the complete disappearance of – monetary policy should privately issued electronic money completely displace central bank liabilities. The literature on e-money in this respect resembles the earlier literature on the 'legal restrictions theory' of money demand,[2] which envisioned the complete displacement of central bank liabilities by higher-yielding bonds in the absence of legal restrictions. Cronin and Dowd (2001, 227) foresee that

> the demand for central bank money will not only drastically fall, but also probably disappear altogether, over a foreseeable horizon. Prospective technological progress with electronic payments and settlements systems is likely to combine with ongoing institutional changes — such as shifts toward private-sector settlements systems — to eliminate the demand for central bank money.

One BIS (1996, 2) report posits that e-money innovations 'have the potential to challenge the predominant role of cash for making small-value payments' by dint of their greater convenience, but worries that therefore 'they also raise a number of policy issues for central banks because of the possible implications for central bank seigniorage revenues and monetary policy and because of central banks' general interest in payment systems'. To date, the displacement of paper currency by e-money has been a non-event for US monetary policy makers.

At the 1999 Jackson Hole conference on 'New Challenges for Monetary Policy', sponsored by the Federal Reserve Bank of Kansas City, the Bank of England's Deputy Governor Mervyn King (1999, 49) declared that, with enough computing power,

> There is no reason, in principle, why final settlements could not be carried out by the private sector without the need for clearing through the central bank. … [T]he key to a central bank's ability to implement monetary policy is that it remains, by law or regulation, the only entity which is allowed to corner the market for settlement balances … Without such a role in settlements, central banks, in their present form, would no longer exist, nor would money.

The Federal Reserve System's role in clearing and settlement has, if anything, grown since 1999. At the 2003 Jackson Hole conference, where the topic was 'Monetary Policy and Uncertainty: Adapting to a Changing Economy', the changes and uncertainty posed by e-money and private settlement were never mentioned as a concern.[3]

Credit and debit cards

Between 1945 and 2000, the proliferations of credit cards and later debit cards were the most visible developments in US retail payments. Credit card systems grew to handle nearly one-fourth of US retail payments. The effects that these developments had on monetary policy, through their effects on the demand for central bank money, may give us some hint as to what we might expect from payment innovations now in prospect.

Sellers have extended credit to their customers for centuries. The growth of multi-outlet retail chains (most notably of gasoline stations and department stores) in the early twentieth century led to the formalisation of standing credit authorisations and their representation by company 'charge cards' that could be used for charging purchases at any of the company's outlets. Such single-company cards were supplemented by 'travel and entertainment' cards beginning in 1950. The first of these was the Diners Club card, initially accepted by 14 restaurants in New York City. American Express, then a leading issuer of traveler's cheques, launched a more widely accepted T&E card in 1958. Unlike some retail chains, Diners Club and American Express expected the consumer to pay his charge balance in full at the end of each month.

Meanwhile various banks, the first of which may have been Franklin National Bank in New York in 1951, began issuing their own 'universal' credit cards combining widespread acceptance with the opportunity to defer repayment beyond the end of the month. Because US laws at the time restricted each bank to operating in a single state or city, each bank card was similarly limited at first, accepted only by the local retailers that the bank had signed up. Bank of America, then the largest bank in California with branches throughout the state, launched its Bank Americard in 1958. It took the card nationwide through licensing agreements with banks in other states beginning in 1966. An alliance of other California banks, seeking to build a network large enough to challenge the BankAmericard, formed a reciprocal bankcard-acceptance arrangement called the Interbank Card Association in 1966, and quickly began signing up banks in other states. The association adopted the 'Master Charge' brand in 1969. Bank of America responded to the challenge by transferring ownership of its card brand to a similar association of issuing banks in 1970. The association licensed the card internationally, renaming it Visa in 1976. Master Charge became MasterCard in 1979.[4]

A third universal card, the Discover Card, was introduced by the nationwide Sears retail chain through a financial services subsidiary in 1985. American Express introduced its own universal credit card, the Optima Card, in 1987.

Credit card penetration became high in the 1970s and has continued to rise at an even pace, as measured by the share of US households having at least one credit card. According to the Federal Reserve System's Surveys of Consumer Finances (Yoo 1998, 21), the share stood at 64 per cent in 1983, 70 per cent in 1989, 72 per cent in 1992, and 75 per cent in 1995.

Some economists in the 1970s extrapolated from the growth of credit card use to the notion that credit cards would soon almost completely supplant cash and cheque payments, making the monetary aggregates irrelevant. Brunner and Meltzer (1990, 358 n. 1) later commented:

> in the US following the introduction of credit cards and a wider range of substitutes for money in the 1970s [a] common claim was that the demand for conventional money – currency and demand deposits – would go to zero and monetary velocity would approach infinity. Shortly after these predictions, monetary velocity declined.

Cross-sectionally, as one would expect, credit card ownership is associated with smaller holdings of demand deposits (Duca and Whitesell 1995). But in time series the velocity of US$ M1, as Bruner and Meltzer indicated, declined after 1980

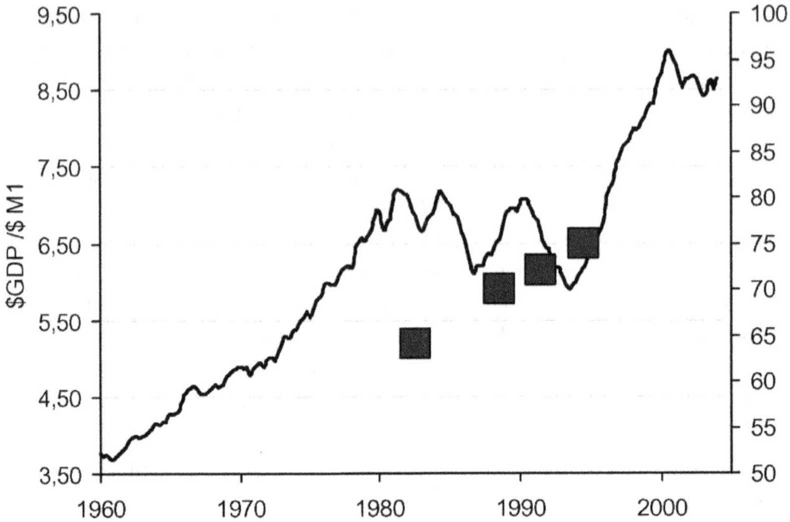

Figure 1.1 Velocity of US Ml, 1960–2004, and credit card use

despite the continued growth in the use of credit cards (see Figure 1.1). The leading explanations for the post-1980 break in the path of M1 velocity are (1) the corresponding break in the path of nominal interest rates (Rasche 1993), caused by disinflationary Federal Reserve policy, and (2) the deregulation of interest rates on M1 deposits (Rotemberg 1993).[5] Given that the spread of credit cards was gradual and steady, there is no reason to link the use of credit cards to the sudden unsteadiness of M1 velocity and the corresponding challenge for monetary policy-makers.

Eletronic payments in the US today

Wholesale wire transfer

The largest flows of electronic payments in the US are large-value ('wholesale') interbank payments over Fedwire and the National Settlement Service, both owned and operated by the Federal Reserve System, and over CHIPS, owned by an association of 54 commercial banks from 22 countries and operated by The Clearing House, an association of the US affiliates of 11 major banks.[6]

Fedwire is a real-time gross settlement system (with intraday overdrafts) that transfers funds among commercial banks' reserve accounts at Federal Reserve Banks. Banks use Fedwire to transmit interbank loans of reserves ('federal funds') and, on behalf of customers, to transmit immediate final payment for securities and real estate transactions. The National Settlement System (NSS) is a mechanism for private-sector clearing networks (that handle paper cheques, automated clearinghouse payments, ATM and debit cards, and credit cards) to settle end-of-day net obligations among participating banks by transferring funds among the banks' reserve accounts at Federal Reserve Banks.[7] According to the Federal Reserve, about 9,500 institutions can send or receive funds over Fedwire. In the year 2000, *daily* Fedwire activity approached 430,000 payments with a total dollar value around $1.5 trillion. The mean payment was around $3.5 million, the median around $25,000.[8]

CHIPS (Clearing House Interbank Payments System) handles a comparable daily volume of payments: 257,000 payments a day with a total dollar value around $1.4 trillion. Banks principally use CHIPS to transmit payment for foreign exchange transactions and cross-border payments. Rather than real-time gross settlement for each transaction, CHIPS uses what it calls 'a combination of prefunding and bilateral or multi-lateral netting', with the netting continuously conducted during the day by its 'patented balanced release algorithm'. The netting reduces gross payment flows and thereby reduces participants' liquidity needs. The 'prefunding' of settlement accounts (i.e. the pledging of liquid reserve balances, the equivalent of an escrow arrangement), in the amount of some $2.8 billion at start of each day (with provisions for intraday topping-up when necessary), allows CHIPS to provide real-time finality for payments up to the value of the paying bank's available liquid funds. CHIPS declares that 'Payments are matched, netted and settled usually in a matter of seconds. Over 85 per cent of payments are cleared before [noon]'. Settlement of interbank net obligations takes place through transfers among the banks' reserve deposits held on the books of the Federal Reserve Bank of New York.[9] CHIPS advertises that it is less costly for its participants than Fedwire, but one industry observer has said that CHIPS 'competes with Fedwire chiefly on the basis of service innovation and quality' (McGuire 2001, 4).

CHIPS introduced real-time finality only in 2001. Previously it had used end-of-day net settlement with a contingency plan for 'unwinding' of payments in the event of end-of-day participant default. (The plan never had to be put into practice because no participant has ever defaulted.) The move to real-time finality might seem to have improved the competitive position of CHIPS as against Fedwire/NSS, but volume on CHIPS has not been growing any faster than volume on Fedwire/NSS.

Even if CHIPS were to completely displace Fedwire and NSS, the implications for base money demand – and therefore for monetary policy – would seem to be minor. As noted previously in Selgin and White (2002, 145–46), CHIPS makes final settlement using base money in the form of bank deposits at the Federal Reserve Bank of New York. CHIPS could in principle settle off the Fed's books, as all clearinghouses did before the advent of the Federal Reserve. If it were to settle by physical transfer of Federal Reserve Notes, the banks' demand for base money would merely be changing form, not size or elasticity. If it were to settle by transfer of claims on the clearinghouse association's own depository, that depository would need to own base money. (In pre-Fed days, the NYCHA normally held 100 per cent gold reserves.) As long as base money remains a part of central bank liabilities, the central bank retains a foothold sufficient for conducting monetary policy.

Table 1.1 Activity in Federal Reserve priced services (2003, 2002 and 2001, in millions of items)

	2003	*2002*	*2001*	*Percent change*	
Service				2002 to 2003	2001 to 2002
Commercial check	15,806	16,587	16,905	–4.7	–1.9
15,806 16,587					
Funds transfer (Fedwire)	126	117	115	7.5	1.6
Commercial FedACH	5,588	4,986	4,448	12.1	12.1

Source: Federal Reserve System (2003, p. 118).

Table 1.2 Estimated volume and Dollar value of US electronic retail payments (2000)

	Transaction volume (millions)	*Dollar value (US$ millions)*	*Average payment value (US$)*
Payment instrument			
Credit cards	15,048	$1,235,374	$ 82.10
Debit cards	8,278	$ 348,131	$ 42.05
Automated clearing house*	5,622	$5,674,851	$1,009.40
Electronic benefits transfer	537	$ 13,744	$ 25.56
Total	29,487	$7,272,100	$ 246.62

Source: Federal Reserve System (2002b, p. 58) and author's calculations based thereon. Credit cards are the sum of general-purpose and private-label cards. Debit cards are the sum of 'offline' (signature-based, routed through Visa and MasterCard networks) and 'online' (PIN-based, routed through ATM networks) cards. EBT here counts only consumer payments using funds in special government-benefit accounts (representing food aid, welfare, Social Security, Veterans' pensions); government transfers into the accounts are included under ACH.

*Table 1.2 ACH volume exceeds Table 1.1 ACH volume because Table 1.1 includes only payments routed through the Fed's ACH system. Table 1.2 includes privately cleared ACH payments.

Retail electronic payments

Perhaps the most prominent recent development in retail payments systems in the US has been the steady progress in switching from paper cheques to electronic deposit transfers cleared through the automated clearinghouse system. The Federal Reserve (see Table 1.1) reports that the volume of paper cheques peaked in 1999 and has declined each year since. The Fed processed 15.8 billion paper cheques in 2003, a volume 4.7 per cent smaller than in the previous year.[10] At the same time, the Fed processed 5.6 billion commercial electronic payments in 2003 through its FedACH (Automated Clearing House) system, a volume 12.1 per cent greater than in the previous year (see Table 1.2). These commercial FedACH payments exclude large-value wire transfers. At present the lion's share of ACH payments are pre-arranged 'direct deposit' of payroll and 'direct payment' of monthly bills, but a growth area is payments that the consumer individually authorises via internet banking.

The Federal Reserve continues to study the status and evolution of the US payments system. The Fed's 2001 'Survey of Consumer Finances' found approximately 88 per cent of US families in that year using electronic funds transfer services in one or more of four forms: ATM cards, debit cards, direct deposit (into a consumer's bank account, typically of pay or government benefits), or direct payment (electronically deducted from a consumer's bank account). About 70 per cent used ATMs, 67 per cent direct deposit, 47 per cent debit cards, 40 per cent direct payments.[11]

The Fed's 2000 'Electronic Payment Instruments Study', in addition to measuring the volume of these four established payment techniques, noted the following 'emerging payment technologies' (Federal Reserve 2002b, 70):

- Electronic Bill Payment and Presentment
- Person-to-Person (P2P) payment
- Stored Value (prepaid) cards
- Internet Currencies

Each of these emerging payment technologies merits some discussion comment as to its character and potential implications for monetary policy. In addition, we consider the mobile phone payment systems that are now in development.

The Fed study also mentions, as payment technologies in the test-marketing stage,

- internet platforms for debit/ATM cards
- an 'ACH debit card'
- internet platforms for debit/ATM cards, routing the payment through the Electronic Funds Transfer networks (i.e. through ATM clearing systems such as Star and NYCE). Like PayPal, but unlike internet bill payment via ACH (which typically takes two or more days to deliver the payment), the EFT networks transmit the payment near-instantly[12]
- an 'ACH debit card', which in contrast to an ordinary debit card 'routes transactions through the ACH system rather than an EFT network'
- point-of-sale conversion of paper cheques to electronic transactions which are then routed through the ACH system.

We will consider these technologies in connection with electronic bill payment and presentment, because all are devices for facilitating deposit transfer.

Electronic Bill Payment and Presentment (*EBPP*) refers to 'online services that enable customers to receive, review and execute payment of their bills over the Internet' by transfer of bank deposits. EBPP is a small but rapidly growing category of ACH payments. Previously the ACH system focused on pre-authorised recurring payments (e.g. payroll, monthly mortgage). EBPP allows consumers to make one-time payments using telephone or internet bankng. As such, EBPP provides a close substitute for paper cheques rather than for paper currency. The same applies to point-of-sale conversion of paper cheques to electronic transactions which are then routed through the ACH system.

An internet platform for debit cards that would route the payment through the Electronic Funds Transfer networks (i.e. through ATM clearing systems such as Star and NYCE), rather than through ACH, would provide yet another close substitute for paper cheques rather than for paper currency. Its potential advantage over internet bill payment via ACH, which typically takes two or more days to deliver the payment, is that the EFT networks transmit payment near-instantly.[13] Thus online EFT debit would combine the convenience of online payment from an existing bank account with the immediacy of PayPal.

The replacement of paper cheques with EBPP (or online EFT debit) would reduce the use of central bank settlement balances only if ACH (or EFT) payments were more commonly cleared and settled outside the Fed's books than are cheque payments. In practice, the Fed is even more predominant in ACH than in cheque clearing. The Federal Reserve Banks clear about 69 per cent of interbank paper cheques, but more than 80 per cent of commercial interbank ACH payments and 100 per cent of government-to-recipient ACH payments (Electronic Payments Network 2002, 2).

The Fed's dominance of ACH processing has actually increased in the past decade. The ACH system was launched in 1974. The Depository Institutions Deregulation and Monetary Control Act of 1980 directed the Fed to price its payment services (both cheque and ACH processing) on a 'market-competitive' and cost-recovering basis, with the intention that private-sector payment providers would no longer face subsidised competition. In 1994 the three existing private-sector ACH operators – American Clearing House, Visa and the New York Automated Clearing House (NYACH) – formed a private exchange system, labelled PAX, allowing them to exchange transactions without going through the Fed and paying the Fed's interregional fees. Gowrisankaran and Stavins (2004, 262) estimate that in 1996 the FedACH system 'handled approximately 75 per cent of the roughly 3.3 billion on-others (between two different banks) commercial ACH transactions processed'. In 2001 and 2002 the Federal Reserve Banks substantially reduced the prices of their ACH services, and announced plans for a third price cut, driving the American Clearing House and Visa out of the business.[14] Today the NYACH, renamed the Electronic Payments Network, is the only remaining private ACH operator.[15] The EPN has publicly complained about the Fed's 'unfair' and 'anti-competitive' pricing policies, but Fed officials have argued that its reduced prices reflect its reduced unit costs for ACH transactions.[16]

In any event the settlement for all private clearing systems (paper cheques, ACH, EFT) takes place on the Fed's books through the National Settlement System. Even the complete displacement of Fed clearing by private clearing would therefore not affect the demand for base money (except to the extent that greater netting takes place before settlement) or the potency of monetary policy.

Person-to-Person (P2P) payment 'involves an electronically initiated transfer of value from one individual to another' to 'send money to family members, settle debts with friends and pay for items purchased through online auctions' (Federal

Reserve 2002b, 70). The Fed study does not name specific providers but clearly refers here to the PayPal service (purchased in October 2002 by the auction Web site eBay) and its less successful rivals (Citibank's c2it, which closed down in November 2003, and Yahoo! PayDirect). PayPal currently has about 40 million US-dollar-denominated accounts, and a total of slightly more than 45 million accounts world-wide. It does not report the US dollar stock of funds in those accounts. The Wells Fargo Bank, the payment processor for PayPal, reported US$ 12 billion in Internet payments flow during 2003. PayPal's reported payment flow for the first quarter of 2004 was US$ 4.3 billion. Compared to the previous year's first quarter, PayPal's nominal revenue grew 68 per cent.[17]

PayPal combines a credit card and deposit transfer forwarding service with the functional equivalent of an online bank with instantaneous on-us settlement. If Smith has a positive PayPal account balance, he pays Jones by transferring part of that balance. If Smith's account balance is zero, he pays by charging a pre-registered credit card or making an ACH transfer from a pre-registered bank account. Jones receives a demandable debt claim on PayPal in the form of a PayPal account balance. A positive PayPal account balance can be withdrawn (transferred to an ordinary bank account) by check or ACH transfer. Though it has deposit-like liabilities, PayPal denies that it is a bank: when opening a new PayPal account, a customer must agree to the statement 'that (i) PayPal is not a bank and the Service is a payment processing service rather than a banking service, and (ii) PayPal is not acting as a trustee, fiduciary or escrow with respect to your funds, but is acting only as an agent and custodian'.[18]

The core of PayPal's business is not in fact best described as person-to-person payment, but rather as person-to-micromerchant payment, where a 'micromerchant' is a seller whose business is too casual or too small to justify the cost of signing up with Visa or MasterCard (if they would even accept him). One journalist (Sisk 2004) notes that PayPal

> essentially invented the micromerchant category through a combination of prescience and luck: prescience in realizing early that its emphasis on person-to-person payments would not pay the rent, and luck that it was the early favorite by buyers and sellers on the Internet's iconographic success story, eBay.

'We started as P-to-P, but that ended up never being a big part of our business, and now it's less than 5 per cent', says PayPal's Todd Pearson, managing director for merchant services. 'Those who followed in our footsteps mistakenly thought that P-to-P was the main thing'.

PayPal 'gained critical mass quickly on eBay' because it offered buyers the convenience and speed of online payment with immediate confirmation, and because it offered sellers easy sign-up and fees that are a 'fraction of the cost of [accepting] credit cards' (Sisk 2004).

Does the growth of PayPal have any implications for monetary policy? For each dollar of a customer's PayPal account balance, PayPal holds a matching deposit balance in Wells Fargo Bank, unless the customer elects to have PayPal invest the funds in shares of a PayPal money-market mutual fund (MMMF). The movement of balances from other commercial bank deposits to PayPal balances of the first type does not alter the banking system's total stock of demand deposits, but merely redistributes it among banks. It poses no difficulty for US monetary policy. The movement of spendable balances into the PayPal MMMF shares poses no greater difficulty for monetary policy than the growth of other MMMFs has posed since the mid-1970s. MMMF shares are not counted in M1, so their increasing use as a means of payment (relative to M1 deposits) increases the ratio of spending to M1 (the velocity of M1). Because the growth of MMMFs has been gradual, and their transactions are limited, the growth in M1 velocity over the period has likewise been gradual (again see Figure 1.1). MMMF shares *are* counted in M2, so the Fed can track their volume and estimate its effect on M1 velocity. The amount of spending per dollar of PayPal fund shares may be greater than that of other MMMF shares: unlike the typical checkable money-market mutual fund, PayPal imposes no minimum size on out-payments. If this difference in spending is great, and PayPal were to become sizable among MMMFs, the Fed might want to track PayPal MMMF balances separately from other MMMF balances.

Whether PayPal ought to be considered a bank for regulatory purposes is an entirely separate question. It might be noted that a 'bank' is defined in US law as an intermediary that both takes deposits and makes loans. PayPal does not make loans. In the 1980s, when US banks established subsidiaries to gather deposits (but not to make loans) in locations where they were not allowed open full-fledged branch offices, such subsidiaries were known as 'non-bank banks'. PayPal might accordingly be called a combination of 'non-bank bank' and checkable money-market mutual fund.[19]

Stored Value (prepaid) cards have garnered academic attention in the past decade for their potential to reintroduce private currency. At least in the form of MasterCard's Mondex device, which permits card-to-card transfers, card balances have been seen as the twenty-first century version of the nineteenth century banknote: bearer claims that circulate without engaging any interbank clearing system. Such balances could be a very close substitute for central-bank-issued currency *if* issuing them were a profitable undertaking.

The Fed study comments that stored-value cards are 'best known for their gift card application, as a replacement for a gift certificate', and are 'also being used for payroll, incentives, insurance, refunds and other purposes' (Federal Reserve 2002b, 70). Gift-certificate cards spendable only at a single retail chain are, however, quite different from general-use cards like Visa Cash and MasterCard's Mondex.

Godschalk and Krueger (2000, 6) have argued persuasively that issuing digital bearer balances (e.g. to be carried on 'smart' microchip-embedded cards) does not yet appear to be profitable. The firm DigiCash, a pioneer in encryption software for bearer e-money, went bankrupt in 1998; the firm CyberCash did likewise in 2001.[20] German banks have given away millions of cards capable of carrying currency balances, only to find that the public has little use for them. Nor have other technical platforms like personal computers proven popular as electronic purses:

> No e-money issuer has a clear business case. There is a morning-after feeling for most e-purse roll-outs in Europe. Even in Germany with a free mass distribution of e-purses on chipcards by the banks (more than 50 million GeldKarten) the volume loaded is stagnating at a level of a negligible 0.01 per cent of the total money supply M1. For software-based e-money products like ecash we see, in spite of booming e-commerce worldwide, only a few pilot projects (e.g. Deutsche Bank).

As Kevin P. Sheehan (1998, 4) has commented: 'electronic-cash pilots have shown that the technology is effective, but they have also shown that, for the most part, consumer demand is lacking'.

For consumers, credit and debit cards already provide convenient noncash payments without explicit transaction fees. The credit card allows the consumer to borrow or enjoy float; the debit card allows him to pay from a deposit balance that earns interest up to the moment it is spent.[21] To date, the most successful niche for prepaid chip card balances has been used as a substitute for coins in unmanned point-of-sale transactions: e.g. transit systems, parking meters, laundromats.[22] Nonbanks, such as transit systems, have been the most successful issuers. Such use implies small balances per card, which implies little 'float' to the issuer. For example, an average card balance of US$10 would, at a 4 per cent interest rate, generate only US$0.40 per year per card in float for the issuer, not enough to cover the average costs of launching and maintaining the card scheme. The cards alone reportedly cost about US$2.50 each.[23] A transit system can find a smart farecard worth issuing even with near-zero float if it replaces a more costly fare-collection system,[24] but a bank will not find a currency-like card profitable with near-zero float unless it can collect sufficient per-use transaction fees. The higher the transaction fees, however, the less attractive is the card to the consumer as a cash substitute.

Lack of apparent profitability is presumably why, after test-marketing trials in the late 1990s (e.g. Visa Cash at the Atlanta Olympic Games of 1996; Mondex at Burger King restaurants on Long Island, NY in 1998; a joint trial in Manhattan's Upper West Side in 1997–98), little has been heard from Visa Cash or Mondex. MasterCard was reportedly pursuing 'more than 400 smart card projects' in late 2003, but many if not most involved storing information other than money balances, such as loyalty points, event tickets, and personal data.[25]

Internet Currencies, characterized by the Fed study as 'intended to be spent on the Web', presumably refer to such now-abandoned schemes as Beenz and Flooz. Current startups that may belong in this category include the Peppercoin (http://corp.peppercoin.com/) and BitPass (http://www.bitpass.com/learn/) 'micro-payment' systems. Promoters of these systems are hoping that pay-per-download music sites will be a 'killer application' for micro-payments. Unlike Beenz and Flooz, Peppercoin and BitPass do not involve proprietary units of account, but denominate their payments in dollars. Thus they might alternatively be categorized as P2P systems (akin to PayPal, except that they emulate bearer currency rather than deposit transfer) or as the online equivalent of prepaid card balances. As in the case of prepaid cards, internet currencies limited to small payments should not be expected to pose a challenge to monetary policy.

There also exist 'internet currencies' today that are not dollar-based: the gold-based systems as e-gold.com and GoldMoney.com. Both offer gold ownership accounts, denominated in gold grams, with account balances transferable online. (As PayPal does, the services allow transfer to anyone with an email address and will create an account for the recipient if he does not already have an account.) E-gold currently claims 732,000 gold-denominated accounts (contrast PayPal's 45 million accounts), and processed 25,000 spending transactions on a recent day totaling 136kg, which at $12.815/g amounts to $1.74 million (compare PayPal's $47 million per day). The marketplace has not stampeded to e-gold, or to bricks-and-mortar gold banks, because of the well-known network property of a monetary standard (or 'critical mass' problem, from the point of view of a potential competitor): customers who try to spend gold-denominated account balances around the Internet (or around town) will discover relatively few stores willing to accept them in payment. The incentive to join the network of those who accept e-gold is weak so long as the network is small, so smallness of the network is self-perpetuating.[26]

The inertial barrier to a new monetary standard can be overcome by high inflation that makes the incumbent standard costly to use: in recent decades chronic high inflation in countries with peso and ruble standards has led to spontaneous 'dollarization', the displacement of local currencies by US dollars. The most plausible scenario for spontaneous displacement of dollars by gold-based payments is likewise the advent of a high dollar inflation that is expected to persist. *In the event* of high inflation, the availability of a gold-based (or Euro-based, or Swiss-Franc-based) substitute for dollar-based payments will amplify the price-elasticity of demand to hold dollars and thereby compound the Fed's problems. But this correspondingly means that the availability plays the salutary role (from the public's perspective) of increasing the Fed's incentive to avoid high inflation. So long as the Fed does responsibly avoid high inflation, the availability of gold-based payment systems will not seriously weaken the demand to hold base dollars and therefore will not threaten the Fed's ability to conduct monetary policy.

Phone-based payments have taken over much of the new-technology 'buzz factor' that card-based payments have lost. A number of different models are being discussed and test-marketed, mostly outside the US. Although there are no apparent legal barriers to their development within the US, mobile phone penetration is slightly lower in the US.

Visa International and Philips Electronics have a joint venture to equip mobile phones with chips allowing them to conduct micropayment and credit-card transactions at unmanned points-of-sale.[27] Similarly the Hungary-based consortium SEMOPS (www.semops.com), for Secure Mobile Payment System, is developing a system for mobile point-of-sale payment, eliminating the consumer's need to wait in a line when the store is busy. These schemes offer new 'front-end' access to established credit card systems rather than any fundamentally new payment system (the 'back end' remains the same).

PhonePaid is a UK-based service, accessible either via the web *or* by calling a toll-free number and following the prompts, that appears to be closely modelled on PayPal. To pay someone, you need his mobile phone number (rather than his email address, as with PayPal).[28] As an alternative P2P system, the monetary policy implications of PhonePaid appear identical to those of PayPal.

The British telecom firm Vodafone has launched 'm-pay', a system that 'allows Vodafone consumers to make remote micropayments [5p to £5] by charging to their phone account'. Merchants need m-pay hardware in order to accept m-payments. A consumer's payments during the month appear on his monthly phone bill.[29] Such systems represent a potentially important innovation, because they turn phone companies into direct competitors with banks and credit card networks as payment service providers. They provide a substitute not only for deposit transfer and credit card, but also for cash payment.

In parallel with the historical emergence of par acceptance among private banknote issuers, mobile payment providers are already discussing hardware interoperability agreements in order to widen acceptance.[30] Should they provide any payment recipient the option to credit his own mobile account with whichever telecom (which would be more useful to him that a claim on the payer's telecom, thereby further widening acceptance), the participating telecoms would find it convenient to form an inter-telecom clearinghouse for mobile payments. To the extent that customers with net payment inflow choose to carry positive mobile account balances (rather than demand a transfer to their bank accounts at month-end), the phone billing system has become a parallel deposit-transfer system.

Conclusion

Payment system innovations, in the US as in Europe, continue (as they have for centuries) to promote the substitution of alternative payment media for direct use of base money. Though no revolution is evident, the real demand for central-bank-issued currency may shrink relative to transactions volume and to demand for broader monetary aggregates. In some respects, though no trend is evident in the US, central-bank-issued deposit liabilities may be challenged as a medium for settling interbank flows. As argued elsewhere (Selgin and White 2002, 147–54), the central bank's power to influence nominal variables is not proportional to the size of its balance sheet. Shrinkage of the central bank's balance sheet will therefore *not* usher in a new era in which monetary policy has no effect, either for good or for ill.

References

Anderson, R. G. and Rasche, R. H. (2001) 'Retail Sweep Programs and Bank Reserves, 1994–1999', *Federal Reserve Bank of St. Louis Review* (January/February): 51–72.

Bass, T. A. (1996) 'The Future of Money', *Wired* 4.10. http://www.wired.com/wired/archive/4.10/wriston.html (accessed 5 November 1996).

Bank of International Settlements (1996) *Implications for Central Banks of the Development of Digital Money*, Basel: Bank of International Settlements.

Brunner, K. and Meltzer, A. H. (1990) Money Supply', in B. M. Friedman, F. Hahn (eds) *Handbook of Monetary Economics*, Vol. 1, Amsterdam: North-Holland, 357–98.

Cronin, D. and Dowd, K. D. (2001) 'Does Monetary Policy Have a Future?' *Cato Journal,* 21: 227–44.

Davis, C. (2002) 'EFT Networks Push for Debit on the Internet', *Electronic Payments International* (27 November). http://www.cashedge.com/ce/about/news_112702_epi .html. (accessed 30 November 2004).

Duca, J. V. and Whitesell, W. C. (1995) 'Credit Cards and Money Demand: A Cross Sectional Study', *Journal of Money, Credit, and Banking,* 27: 604–23.

Electronic Payments Network (2002) 'Fair Competition in the Automated Clearing House Payments System: A Private Sector ACH Operator Perspective' (18 December) http://www.epaynetwork.com/infofiles/EPN_Fair_Competition_in_ACH_12_2002.pdf (accessed 30 November 2004).

Federal Reserve System (2002b) 'Retail Payments Research Project: A Snapshot of the U.S. Payments Landscape', http://www.frbservices.org/Retail/pdf/RetailPayments ResearchProject.pdf (accessed 30 November 2004).

Federal Reserve System (2003) *90th Annual Report to Congress*, Washington, D. C. http://www.federalreserve.gov/ boarddocs/rptcongress/annual03/ar03.pdf (accessed 30 November 2004).

Friedman, B. (1999) 'The Future of Monetary Policy', *International Finance,* 2: 321–28.

Godschalk, H. and Krueger, M. (2000) 'Why E-money Still Fails: Chances of E-Money Within a Competitive Payment Instrument Market', paper prepared for the Third Berlin Internet Economics Workshop, May, Berlin.

Gowrisankaran, G. and Stavins, J. (2004) 'Network Externalities and Technology Adoption: Lessons from Electronic Payments', *RAND Journal of Economics,* 35: 260–76.

Hafer, R. W. and Wheelock, D. C. (2001) 'The Rise and Fall of a Policy Rule: Monetarism at the St. Louis Fed, 1968–1986', *St. Louis Federal Reserve Bank Review* (January/February): 1–24.

Herd, M. (2001) 'Federal Reserve Check Volume Decreases, ACH Volume Continues to Rise', NACHA news release (2 August), http://www.nacha.org/ news/Stats/ Federal_Reserve_ Check_Volume_Decreases_-_2000.doc (accessed 30 November 2004).

King, M. (1999) 'Challenges for Monetary Policy: New and Old,' in *New Challenges for Monetary Policy*, Kansas City: Federal Reserve Bank of Kansas City: 11–57.

Lonie, S. (2003) 'A Year in the Life of M-Pay', http://www.chyp.com/PubWebFiles/ DigMoney/6_2003/SusieLonie.pdf (accessed 30 November 2004).

MasterCard International (2004) 'Building a Global Brand.' http://www.mastercardbrand-center.com/mcbrand/index.jsp?screen_name=aboutOurBrandsHistoryGlobal (accessed 30 November 2004).

McCullagh, D. (2001) 'Digging Those Digicash Blues', Wired News (14 June). http:// www.wired.com/news/exec/0,1370,44507,00.html (accessed 30 November 2004).

McGuire, B. (2004) 'Delivering Payments Value Online: CHIPS Ventures into Web-Based Management Services', Tower Group ViewPoint 73 (January) http://www.chips.org/ infofiles/CHIPS_Tower_Group_Jan_2004.pdf (accessed 30 November 2004).

Mobile Payment Forum (2002) 'Enabling Secure, Interoperable, and User-friendly Mobile Payments', White Paper http://www.mobilepaymentforum.org/pdfs/mpf_whitepaper. pdf (accessed 30 November 2004).

Rasche, R. H. (1993) 'Monetary Aggregates, Monetary Policy and Economic Activity', *Federal Reserve Bank of St. Louis Review,* 75: 1–35.

Roseman, L. (2003) 'Letter to George Thomas of EPN' (17 January) http://www.epaynetwork.com/infofiles/EPN_FRB_Response.pdf (accessed 30 November 2004).

Rotemberg, J. J. (1993) 'Commentary [on Rasche 1993]', *Federal Reserve Bank of St. Louis Review,* 75: 36–41.

Schmitz, S. W. (2002) 'The Institutional Character of Electronic Money Schemes: Redeemability and the Unit of Account', in M. Latzer and S. W. Schmitz (eds) *Carl Menger and the Evolution of Payment Systems: From Barter to Electronic Money,* Cheltenham: Edward Elgar, 159–83.

Selgin, G. and White, L. H. (2002) 'Mengerian Perspectives on the Future of Money', in M. Latzer and Schmitz, S. W. (eds) *Carl Menger and the Evolution of Payment Systems: From Barter to Electronic Money,* Cheltenham: Edward Elgar, 133–58.

Sheehan, K. P. (1998) 'Electronic Cash', *FDIC Banking Review,* (Summer): 1–8.

Sisk, M. (2004) 'The Rush to Fill c2it's Void', *Bank Technology News* (February). http://www.electronicbanker.com/cgi-bin/readstory.pl?story=20040202BTNB311.xml %0D%0A (accessed 30 November 2004).

Visa USA (2004), 'Who We Are: History', http://usa.visa.com/personal/about_visa/who/who_we_are_history.html (accessed 30 November 2004).

Wallace, N. (1983) 'A Legal Restrictions Theory of the Demand for "Money" and the Role of Monetary Policy', *Federal Reserve Bank of Minneapolis Quarterly Review,* 7: 1–7.

White, L. H. (1987) 'Accounting for Non-Interest-Bearing Currency: A Critique of the Legal Restrictions Theory', *Journal of Money, Credit, and Banking,* 19: 448–56.

Yoo, P. S. (1998) 'Still Charging: The Growth of Credit Card Debt Between 1992 and 1995', *Federal Reserve Bank of St. Louis Review* (January/February): 19–27.

Notes

1 In the US, Federal Reserve liabilities of both types also serve to satisfy a commercial bank's statutory reserve requirements against demand deposits. By computerised "sweeping" of demand deposits into other liabilities without reserve requirements, US banks have reduced their statutory requirements so dramatically in the past ten years that the requirements have effectively become non-binding (Anderson and Rasche 2001). Many banks now more than satisfy their requirements simply with the Federal Reserve notes they hold to meet customer cheque-cashing and automatic teller machine withdrawals.

2 Wallace 1983 and White 1987.

3 The uncertainty that seemed of the greatest concern to the 2003 Jackson Hole policymakers was uncertainty about the size of the gap between actual output and 'potential output'.

4 MasterCard International (2004), Visa USA (2004).

5 For discussion of the impact of the velocity trend break on monetary policy thinking, see Hafer and Wheelock (2001).

6 The Clearing House, formerly known as the New York Clearing House Association (NYCHA), is jointly owned by The Bank of New York, ABN AMRO, Bank of America, Deutsche Bank, HSBC, Citigroup, Wells Fargo, Bank One, JP Morgan Chase, Wachovia, and Fleet.

7 http://www.federalreserve.gov/paymentsystems/fedwire/default.htm

8 http://www.federalreserve.gov/paymentsystems/coreprinciples/default.htm

9 See McGuire (2004, 1) and http://www.chips.org/about.php.

10 The Federal Reserve System (2002b, 12) estimates that it clears 41 per cent of the paper cheques written in the US; total cheques thus numbered close to 40 billion. The other clearing routes are 'on-us', that is, within-bank (29 per cent), through private

clearinghouses (18 per cent), same-day settlement (6 per cent), Treasury/postal money order (1 per cent), and other (5 per cent).

11 Federal Reserve System 2003, 73.
12 See Davis (2002).
13 See Davis (2002).
14 Electronic Payments Network 2002, 7.
15 Regional payments associations – for example, Western Payments Alliance, South Western Automated Clearing House Association, Southern Payments Exchange – support and represent commercial banks in their ACH business but do not themselves process payments.
16 Herd 2001 and Roseman 2003.
17 http://www.epaynews.com/statistics/transactions.html; www.epaynews.com archive (04 May 2004 and 23 April 2004).
18 http://www.paypal.com/cgi-bin/webscr?cmd=p/gen/ua/ua-outside
19 In a 2001 interview (at http://www.efinanceinsider.com/email31501.html), PayPal's 'co-founder and CEO' Peter Thiel said that PayPal had deliberately avoided becoming a bank in order to avoid bank regulation: 'We're 90 per cent a payments company, and maybe 10 per cent bank-like. We are not regulated like a bank because we don't offer FDIC insurance, but correspondingly we also have much less of a regulatory load. We are pretty determined to stay on that side of the banking rules. We've spent a lot of time looking at whether we should become a bank — we even had the option to acquire a bank charter in the fall — but we decided to avoid that track because of the regulatory cost issues and the sense that the payment piece is most valuable to people'.
20 See also McCullagh (2001).
21 Retailers face higher transaction processing fees for credit and debit cards (typically around 3 per cent) than for prepaid cards (typically less than 1 per cent), but for some reason retailers seldom offer consumers a discount for paying by the cheaper method. As a result consumers have little incentive to prefer prepaid cards.
22 Godschalk and Krueger 2000, 17.
23 http://www.cardtechnology.com/cgi-bin/readstory.pl?story=20040301CTDN623.xml
24 As a replacement for collecting paper notes and coins from fare card vending machines, the Chicago Transit Authority now offers a 'prepaid smart fare card' with an 'automatic replenishment' feature whereby the commuter authorizes the CTA to reload the card balance when necessary by charging the commuter's credit card or debiting his bank account. http://www.cardtechnology.com/cgi-bin/readstory.pl?story=20040108CTDN004.xml
25 http://www.cardtechnology.com/cgi-bin/readstory.pl?story=20040303CTDN652.xml
26 Schmitz (2002) discusses how network effects reinforce the dominant unit of account in the context of electronic money systems._
27 http://www.cardtechnology.com/cgi-bin/readstory.pl?story=20040109CTDN020.xml
28 http://www.phonepaid.com/home/home.htm
29 Lonie 2003, 5.
30 Mobile Payment Forum 2002.

2 Payment systems from the monetary policy implementation perspective*

Ulrich Bindseil and Flemming Würtz

When we first saw the title of Larry White's paper we would be invited to discuss, 'Impact of Changes in Payment Systems on US Monetary Policy, 1945-today' we were eager to get the first draft of the paper to see what arguments he would have found to indeed substantiate such an impact. Being convinced that such an impact did not exist, we were preparing ourselves to a heated debate. When we then saw the paper, we were nearly disappointed to see that Larry White did not at all seek to prove such a relationship, but 'only' has written an excellent survey of recent payment system developments and speculates, on that basis, on what future impacts may arise on monetary policy. We learned a great deal from this survey, and are not really in a position to comment on it. We will thus instead try to elaborate on the arguments we would have brought forward if Larry White would have written the paper once announced in his title; that is, we will explain in detail why we think that payment system innovations in at least the last 60 years did not have a relevant impact on monetary policy in the US (or in other industrialised countries). After the second section has done so, the third will look at how payment systems do impact on the day-to-day implementation practice, without however justifying one or the other fundamental approach to monetary policy. The fourth section revisits briefly a popular topic, namely what would happen to central banks if banknotes in circulation would vanish. The last section concludes briefly.

The irrelevance of change of payment systems for changes of US monetary policy in the twentieth century

Bindseil (2004a), (2004b) has argued that the history of the official US monetary policy implementation doctrine between 1920 and around 1990 suffered from the idea, unheard before 1920, and rejected by all central banks again today, that some quantity, and not the short-term interest rate, constitute the operational, that is, day-to-day target of monetary policy. According to this quantity focussed view, monetary policy would start with open market operations, which impact on reserve holdings of banks (or the monetary base), via the money multiplier on monetary aggregates, and so on. Interest rates have no role in this scheme. Goodfriend (2003) and Bindseil (2004a) argue that the origin of this mistaken view lies in the Fed's desire to mask its responsibility for the inflation during the Second World War, and for the following deflationary recession of 1920. The Fed at that time lacked independence towards the Treasury, and like most other central banks during war times, did not raise interest rates as strict monetary policy considerations would have suggested. What makes the episode extraordinary in the case of the Fed and distinguishes it from other national monetary histories of First World War and the early 1920s, was the ex post rationalisation given to it, namely that the reasons for the inflation in the first six years of the Fed had not been the failure of the monetary authorities, under Treasury pressure, to hike short term interest rates, but excessive borrowing by the banks through the discount window, that is, not too low policy rates were the problem, but quantities per se, as if the latter were not influenced by rates. This switch of paradigm seems to take place rather precisely around 1920. Two main events seem to explain the switch exactly in 1920 namely (i) the above-mentioned start of the tightening of monetary policy in November 1919 and its substantial impact on economic activity, and (ii) an academic event, namely the invention of the money multiplier by the American C. A. Philipps (1920). One can thus trace back the birth of 'Reserve Position Doctrine'('RPD') rather precisely to that year.

The main episodes in official US monetary policy implementation technique during the twentieth century can be structured as follows:[1]

1920–1930: This period appears to be characterised by a relatively un-dogmatic application of RPD in its 'borrowed reserves targeting' variant. After completely banning a discussion of the appropriate level of the discount rate from the early 1920s' annual reports of the Fed, open market operations and discount rate setting are again presented in the annual reports jointly as main policy measures. Still, no explicit responsibility for short term rates is taken, and changes of discount rates are often presented as *following* changes in market rates.

1931–1952: During this period, the Fed tended to leave the market with substantial excess reserves, such that money market rates were mostly close to zero (and reflected to a significant degree credit risk). According to Friedman and Schwartz (1963), the Fed would have been too restrictive in its excess reserves policy during the 1930s. According to this view, the Fed would have contributed to shrink monetary aggregates, and had it paid attention to the money multiplier and RPD, it could have easily avoided that mistake.

1952–1970: The official approach of the Fed during this period was 'free reserves targeting', that is, targeting of excess reserves minus borrowed reserves. The practical approach was eclectic both with regard to the measurement of the monetary conditions, and with regard to the use of instruments. Annual reports provide evidence that changes of reserve requirements, open market operations, and changes of the discount rate were all actively used, whereby the latter was again normally presented as following market rates, instead of guiding them.

1970–1979: Towards the end of the 1960s, the federal funds rate was becoming more important as an indicator of monetary policy. Especially in the period 1974–1979, the Fed implicitly targeted a federal funds rate level, intervening in the market whenever the Fed funds rate moved out of a very narrow band.[2]

1979-1982: In 1979, Paul Volcker became chairman of the Board of Governors and felt that inflation, which had two-digit levels during most of the 1970s, needed eventually to be stopped. The Fed concluded that the moment had come for taking a monetarist approach also serious in day-to-day monetary policy implementation, by substituting interest rate targeting by an RPD target, which this time was defined as *non-borrowed reserves*, that is, reserves held by banks minus borrowed reserves, the recourse to the discount window. Although Axilrod and Lindsey (1981) provided an official scientific motivation for the 1979–82 approach, it seems difficult today to reconstruct what was exactly done. According to Strongin (1995, 475):

> Non-borrowed reserves targeting was the most complicated of the reserves operating procedures that the Federal Reserve has ever used and it lasted the shortest length of time.... Considerable debate within the Federal Reserve system about how these procedures actually worked is still going on.

Today's views on the Volcker episode are split. Some, as for instance Goodhart (2001) and Mishkin (2004), argue that the whole approach was just about avoiding the Fed to take responsibility for the necessary strong hiking of interest rates to bring down inflation, and the associated economic effects such as a strong rise in unemployment. In the words of Goodhart (2001), the episode, 'if properly analysed, reveals that the Fed continued to use interest rates as its fundamental modus operandi, even if it dressed up its activities under the mask of monetary base control ... there was a degree of play-acting, even deception ...'. The 'smokescreen' created by Volcker would thus have been simply a necessary condition for bringing inflation to an end under conditions of imperfect central bank independence.

1982–1989: This episode of 'borrowed reserves targeting' was most likely an attempt to retreat from quantity-oriented operational targets without needing to admit it too openly. It probably means in practice focussing again quite unambiguously on rates. Attempts made by the Fed to justify borrowed reserves targeting within a coherent RPD framework indeed seem to be missing.

1994–today: In 1994, the gradual move to federal funds rate targeting is completed by announcing, after each FOMC meeting, the decision with regard to the Fed funds target rate. This had not even been practice in the 1974–79's episode of interest rate targeting. In 1998, for the first time, the 'Domestic Policy Directive', which is part of the minutes of the FOMC, again contained a reference to the Fed funds target rate, instead of a reference to the vague concept of 'reserve pressure'.

We would not see any of these changes being motivated by changes in payment systems, or financial markets in general. We also follow Goodhart that the Fed in practice never really disregarded short term interest rates in its day-to-day operations – also because this would have led to extreme volatility of short term interest rates, which cannot be in the interest of any central bank that wants to influence economic decisions in a controlled way.[3]

Obviously, the Fed has at several occasions justified these changes. Consider just two examples:

Already Goldenweiser (1925, 46), to explain why the Fed had not copied the Bank of England's well-developed, interest rate focussed system, appeals to rather unspecified financial and institutional difference:

> The conclusion … is, that while there are many analogies between banking conditions and practices in this country and in England, there are sufficient differences in the nature of the money market and in the character of services rendered by the Bank of England, to make it impossible to follow British precedents in American banking.

And still after the quantity-focussed episode had come to an end, the Fed in 1994 explained (Board of Governors 1994):

> In general, no one approach to implementing monetary policy is likely to be satisfactory under all economic circumstances. … When economic and financial conditions warrant close control of monetary aggregate, more emphasis may be placed on guiding open market operations by a fairly strict targeting of reserves. In other circumstances, a more flexible approach to managing reserves may be required.

Detailed explanations of such relationships, maybe also elaborating on a possible role of payment systems, were however never given, to our knowledge. Also the fact that controlling short term interest rates as operational targets has been appropriate for all central banks before 1914, that it is used again by all central banks today, regardless of the financial and economic environment (with very few exceptions!), and that also the Fed has used it consistently since 1990 under ever-changing economic conditions, leaves us sceptical on this explanation. Needless to say that, in particular, payment systems have been extremely heterogeneous across time and countries.

Payment systems' impact on day-to-day monetary policy implementation

While having just argued that payment system issues cannot explain the changes in the US Fed's (or other central banks') monetary policy implementation approach, we will now look more closely at how in practice payment systems *do* matter, at a technical level. For that, we first need to have a short look at how monetary policy works in practice.

Table 2.1 Definition of variables employed in the model

M	Outstanding volume of open market operations, netted as a central bank balance sheet *asset*
A	Autonomous liquidity factors, netted as a central bank balance sheet *liability* (in fact all central bank balance sheet items other than M, B, D, R)
B,D	Recourse to borrowing and deposit facility, respectively.
R	Reserve holdings of banks with the central bank
RR	The level of required reserves which banks need to hold on *average* with the central bank in the course of a maintenance period.
$\overline{X}$	For any central bank balance sheet quantity *X*, the average over a reserve maintenance period with *T* days.
i_t	Overnight interbank interest rate on day *t* of the reserve maintenance period, with $t = 1 \ldots T$
i_B	Rate of the borrowing facility (e.g. discount facility) at the end of the reserve maintenance period.
i_D	Rate of the deposit facility at the end of the reserve maintenance period ($i_D < i_B$). Absence of a deposit facility is equivalent to a deposit facility rate of zero, $i_D = 0$.

Table 2.2 Stylised central bank balance sheet

M (open market operations	*A (autonomous factors)*
B (use of borrowing facility)	D (use of deposit facility) R (reserve holdings)

Monetary policy implementation in practice

Assume the notation in Table 2.1 for a simple model of monetary policy implementation.[4]

In terms of above-indicated quantities, the stylised central bank balance sheet can be drawn as in Table 2.2.

The central bank's balance sheet identity ('Assets = Liabilities') can be expressed accordingly as $M + B = A + D + R$. Assume for a moment that there is *no uncertainty* regarding autonomous factors or regarding the liquidity supply through open market operations in the remainder of the reserve maintenance period, and thus that no news would emerge in its course on any of the factors relevant for the overnight interest rate. Assume also, for the sake of simplicity, that interbank markets are perfect, that 'averaging' in the course of a maintenance period is perfectly functioning and that there is no demand for working balances (i.e. $\overline{R} = \overline{RR}$). In this case reserve holdings on different days within the maintenance period are perfect substitutes, and it follows from the central bank balance sheet identity over the reserve maintenance period that $\overline{B} - \overline{D} = \overline{RR} - \overline{M} + \overline{A}$, with either $\overline{B} > 0$, $\overline{D} = 0$, or $\overline{D} > 0$, $\overline{B} = 0$, that is, there will normally be an aggregate recourse to either one of the two standing facilities. A deterministic aggregate recourse to one standing facility at the end of the reserve maintenance period however implies that the competitive price in the market should correspond to the respective standing facility rate, since this rate represents the marginal value of reserves at the end of the maintenance period. The property that market rates will correspond in the entire reserve maintenance period to one or the other standing facility rate may then be expressed as follows:

$$\begin{aligned} &\overline{M} > \overline{A} + \overline{RR} \Rightarrow (\overline{B} = 0; \overline{D} = \overline{M} - \overline{A} - \overline{RR}; i_1 = i_2 = \ldots i_T = i_D) \\ &\overline{M} < \overline{A} + \overline{RR} \Rightarrow (\overline{B} = \overline{A} + \overline{RR} - \overline{M}; \overline{D} = 0; i_1 = i_2 = \ldots i_T = i_B) \end{aligned} \quad (1)$$

Now, one may consider the more interesting and relevant case in which the liquidity supply and the rates of the standing facilities are subject to *uncertainty*. It is assumed that the money market participants have a homogenous information set I_t at the time of each market session $t = 1 \ldots$T. The basic relationship between quantities and prices (overnight rates) under the assumptions made above (especially the one of perfect interbank markets and averaging) is then described by the following equation, in which $f_{(\overline{M}-\overline{A}-\overline{RR}|It)}$ is the probability density function the money market participants assign during the trading session t to the random variable $\overline{M} - \overline{A} - \overline{RR}$:

$$\begin{aligned} \forall t = 1 \ldots T : i_t &= E[i_B | I_t] P(\bar{M} - \bar{A} - \overline{RR} < 0 | I_t) \\ &\quad + E[i_D | I_t] P(\bar{M} - \bar{A} - \overline{RR} > 0 | I_t) \\ &= E[i_B | I_t] \int_{-\infty}^{0} f_{(\bar{M}-\bar{A}-\overline{RR}|It)}(x)dx + E[i_D | I_t] \left(1 - \int_{0}^{\infty} f_{(\bar{M}-\bar{A}-\overline{RR}|It)}(x)dx\right) \end{aligned} \quad (2)$$

In words: the overnight rate on any day will correspond to the weighted expected rate of the two standing facilities, the weights being the respective probabilities that the market will be 'short' or 'long' of reserves at the end of the maintenance period before having recourse to standing facilities. This expression may be considered as *the fundamental equation* of monetary policy implementation. It follows from the model that payment systems only affect the overnight rate to the extent that they affect banks' accumulated reserve position with the central bank in the course of a maintenance period. Accordingly, the central bank can perfectly steer the overnight rate, through its control over reserves via open market operations (M).

Where do now payment systems come into play? Consider four issues one by one.

1. Payment systems and autonomous factors: banknotes and float

First, payment systems directly impact on two autonomous factors in the central bank balance sheet: banknotes and the float.

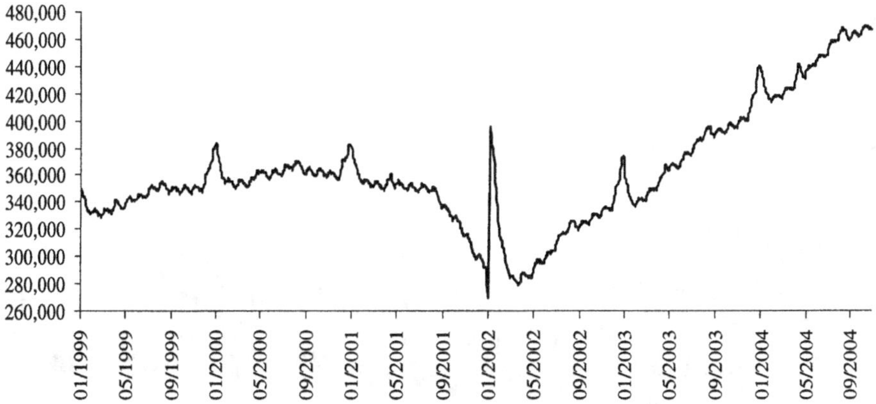

Figure 2.1 Banknotes of the Eurosystem from January 1999 to October 2004, in millions of euros

Banknotes are typically one of the largest single items in the central bank balance sheet. For a long time, economists have speculated about what the vanishing of banknotes would mean for monetary policy (see last section). Figure 2.1, which displays euro banknotes in circulation from 1 January 1999 to 30 October 2004, suggests that such considerations remain little relevant – for the foreseeable future. Banknotes exhibit a rather regular weekly, monthly and seasonal pattern. These patterns reflect social regularities such as the withdrawal of cash before the weekend, the payment of salaries, the summer holiday season and Christmas shopping. Moreover, this series displays a general upward trend, which temporarily reversed only when the euro banknotes were introduced at the beginning of 2002.

The regularities in the banknote time series suggest an *econometric* forecasting approach. Traditionally, central banks have used both informal methods (charts, looking for similar situations in the past, simple calculus) and econometric forecasts. The forecast level of banknotes, like the forecast of any other autonomous factor, impacts on the appropriate volume of open market operations, and mistakes in forecasting banknotes may imply temporary disequilibria in the money market with the short term rate moving away from the target rate.

Items in course of settlement ('float' of the payment system): Payment system float is created whenever the crediting and the debiting of the accounts of banks with the central bank related to interbank payments do not occur simultaneously. It can be both liquidity-providing (appearing on the asset side of the central bank balance sheet) or liquidity-withdrawing (appearing on the liability side of the balance sheet). For instance, cheques which are credited before being debited inject liquidity (create an asset-side float). In contrast, *transfers* have, if any, the opposite effect. The relevance of float thus depends on the specification of the payment system. In the euro area, a majority of national central banks do not exhibit any float, and the overall volatility created by the float is limited (see Figure 2.2). In

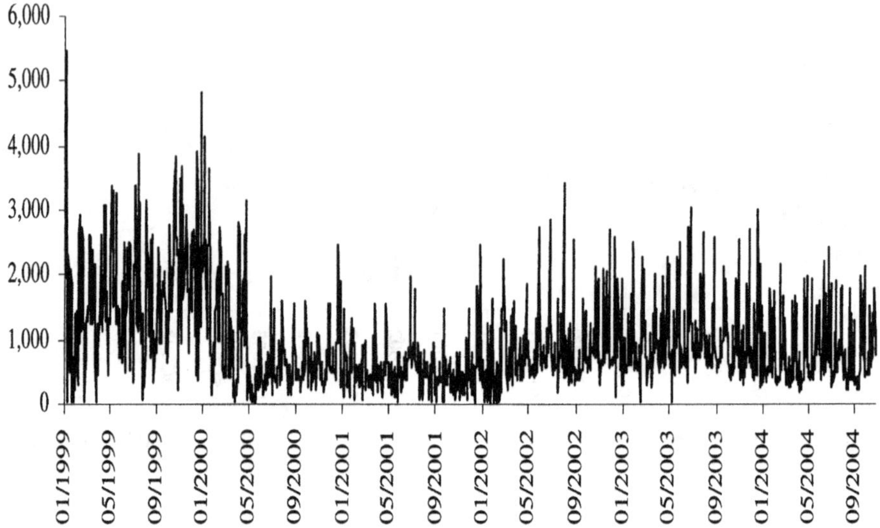

Figure 2.2 Items in course of settlement in the Eurosystem from January 1999 to October 2004, in millions of euros

the US, the float is still a considerably more important source of shocks to the supply of reserves, due to the persisting popularity of payment by cheques.[5] Again, like any other autonomous factor, the forecast of the float will be reflected in the calibration of open market operations, and forecasting errors may have an effect on short term interest rates.

2. *Uncertainties stemming from payment systems*

In the simplistic model given earlier, we had assumed perfect interbank markets and no demand for working balances. This is the same as saying that banks should face no uncertainty about their own end-of-day reserve position with the central bank. The only uncertainty we assumed to exist was about the *aggregate* level of autonomous factors in the central banks' balance sheet. This is of course an unrealistic assumption. In practice, individual banks are exposed to significant uncertainty about their own end-of-day reserve position. Such uncertainties to a large extent derive from the structure of payment systems. Banks do not know precisely their net position in these systems, the development of which have moreover enhanced the possibility of banks to offer their customers the possibility to withdraw and deposit liquidity with same day value, thereby further increasing banks' uncertainty about their end-of-day reserve position. Banks' uncertainty about their end-of-day reserves implies that they in praxis prefer to hold working balances with the central bank such that they can 'buffer out' unforeseen payments. This can be regarded as an exogenous factor affecting the central banks' steering of the overnight interest rates in several ways, which are shortly discussed below.

First, it affects the optimal layout of the central banks' operational framework for monetary policy implementation; second, it implies another liquidity need, so-called excess reserves, which the central bank also needs to take into account in its calibration of the aggregate liquidity conditions; and third, it affects the dynamics of the overnight rate.

LAYOUT OF THE CENTRAL BANKS' OPERATIONAL FRAMEWORK

Commercial banks' demand for working balances is normally facilitated through the averaging provision of the central bank's reserve requirement system. With an averaging scheme in place, commercial banks can, to a large extent, without incurring any costs, buffer out liquidity shocks by replacing reserve holdings on one day with reserve holdings on another day. However, if on one day within a reserve maintenance period the aggregate availability of reserves is below the aggregate need for working balances, the overnight rate would increase towards the rate of the borrowing facility, unless the central bank would intervene. The larger the level of reserve requirements and the lower the daily fluctuations of reserves, the less likely is this situation of course to occur. Hence, banks' uncertainty about their end-of-day position affects how frequently the central bank has to intervene for a given level of reserve requirements (and vice versa). In this regard, the Eurosystem has chosen a relatively high level of required reserves – about ten times as high as that of the Federal Reserve System. As a result of this and the one-month averaging period, the ECB only needs to adjust the banking systems reserve position rather infrequently, normally only once per week, whereas the FED intervenes on a daily basis since, in its case, buffers provided by reserve requirements are too low to smooth out autonomous factor shocks and fluctuations in the demand for working balances.[6]

EXCESS RESERVES

On the last day of the maintenance period, it is no longer possible for banks, at a zero cost, to buffer out liquidity shocks via their reserve holdings, because their reserve requirements are binding on that day. Nevertheless, also on the last day of the maintenance period, banks are of course still exposed to uncertainties about their end-of-day liquidity positions, and in order to avoid the penalties associated with a non-compliance with their reserve requirements, they prefer to suffer the costs of holding non-remunerated excess reserves, that is, reserve holdings in excess of their required reserves. In the case of the Eurosystem,[7] Figure 2.3 reveals the average amounts of excess reserves per reserve maintenance period during the first three and a half years of the euro.

Excess reserves' averages per maintenance period had an expected value of €707 million and a standard deviation of €34 million. The minimum value within the period considered was €437 million (in the maintenance period ending on 23 September 1999), while the maximum was €1,668 million. Another pattern that emerges is that maintenance periods ending on weekends also exhibit above-average

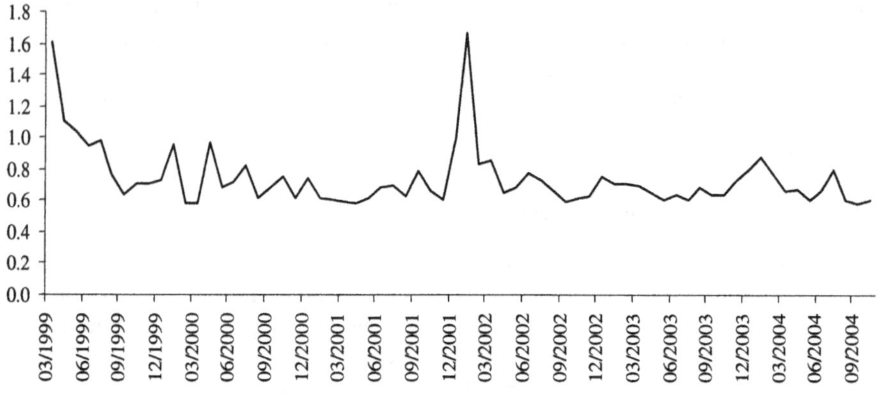

Figure 2.3 Average excess reserves per maintenance period from March 1999 to October 2004, in billions of euros

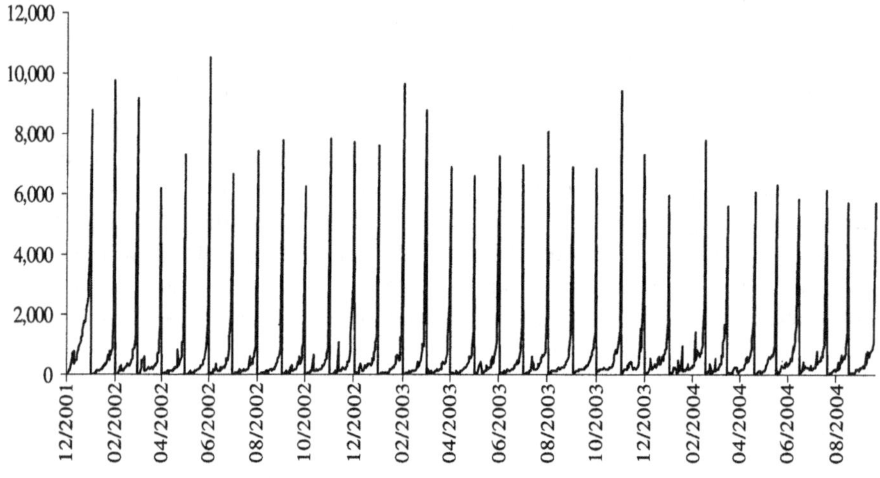

Figure 2.4 Excess reserves in the euro area from 24 December 2001 to 22 October 2004, in millions of euros

levels of excess reserves. Indeed, from the start of monetary union until May 2002, the average amount of daily excess reserves in reserve maintenance periods ending on Sundays was €877 million, against €674 million in all other reserve maintenance periods (excluding the first three in 1999). As Figure 2.4 reveals, the intra-reserve maintenance period evolution of daily excess reserves exhibits a similar pattern in every maintenance period, with a low level at the start of the period and then a rapid build-up during the last few days.

The increasing trend of daily excess reserves within each maintenance period obviously stems from the fact that the number of banks which have already fulfilled their required reserves and which may hence generate excess reserves if they are exposed to a positive liquidity shock at the end of the day (and do not have recourse to the deposit facility) increases steadily. Bindseil *et al.* (2004) show that there are no indications from euro area data that excess reserves would depend on liquidity conditions or on short term interest rates. Therefore, in the calibration of open market operations, they can effectively be treated as an *exogenous demand factor*, which needs to be forecast similarly to autonomous factors.

DYNAMICS OF THE OVERNIGHT RATE

The final, somewhat more technical, implication of banks' uncertainty about their end-of-day reserve position is that it affects the dynamics of the overnight rate, which, in principle can no longer be fully explained by equation 2. As already mentioned earlier, the model presented in the first part of the third section assumes that banks are only uncertain about the aggregate liquidity conditions. Whenever the overnight rate deviates from the weighted average of standing facilities expected for the last moment of the maintenance period, banks would perform intertemporal arbitrage, thereby re-aligning the current with the expected future overnight rate. However, given the fact that banks do not precisely know their end-of-day position, they will, whenever the overnight rate falls sufficiently, demand more working balances, which then becomes a cheap insurance against unexpected outgoing payments. Likewise, if the overnight rate increases, the demand for working balances will decline.[8] This implies that the overnight rate should, ceteris paribus, be less responsive to a given expected aggregate liquidity imbalance at the end of the maintenance period. The relevance of this effect obviously depends on the amount of individual banks' uncertainty about their own end-of-day position, which in turn largely depends on payment systems. Moreover, it is mostly relevant towards the end of the maintenance period, since the averaging provision of reserve requirements earlier than that normally gives banks sufficient flexibility in their liquidity management, as discussed earlier.

For the case of the euro area, where, as mentioned earlier, excess reserves are found to be inelastic with respect to the level of the overnight rate, this effect appears irrelevant in practice. Even though the euro area overnight rate appears to be less responsive to an expected aggregate liquidity imbalance than what follows from the uncertainty about the latter, there are, as argued in Würtz and Krylova (2004), several other possible explanations for this.

Another possible impact of banks' uncertainty about their end-of-day position is that they want to avoid fulfilling their reserve requirements before the end of the maintenance period, such that they would lose the possibility to buffer out unexpected liquidity shocks via their reserve holdings. This should, ceteris paribus, imply that banks have a preference for fulfilling their reserve requirements late in the maintenance period. To the extent that the central bank does not accommodate these preferences in its supply of liquidity, the overnight rate will be comparatively low in the beginning of the maintenance period as banks will pay a premium to avoid holding reserves at this stage.[9] For the case of the euro area, there is little evidence, however, of such an effect.[10] In the US, Hamilton

(1996) found evidence that the overnight rate in fact tends to increase towards the end of the maintenance period. There seems, however, to be evidence that this is no longer the case.

In sum, even though there is evidence of some shortcomings of equation 2 in describing the overnight rate, these are normally very minor.[11] If reserve requirements are indeed sufficiently large, as it is the case in the euro area, equation 2 normally provides a sufficient basis for policy makers and market participants for judging and steering the overnight rate. Normally, payment system related issues do not play a role.

3. Intra-day interbank money market issues

The simplistic model in the first part of the third section only models end-of-day positions, assuming implicitly that intra-day liquidity of the money market is never an issue. This is indeed normally the case, at least for the euro area. The amount of collateral available to banks in the RTGS systems is sufficient to avoid any impact of intra-day payment flows on short term interest rates, that is, intra-day liquidity is always sufficient. Exceptions to this arose on a few occasions nevertheless: during the first days of the euro, for instance, in January 1999; after 22 September 2001, during the cash-change-over in January 2002. However, these exceptions had their origins in the uncertainties surrounding payments during these periods, and not in technical limitations or failures of payment systems. In any case, at least for the euro area, one could conclude that the efficiency of payment systems is so high that monetary policy implementation can focus almost always solely on end-of-day positions, that is, on what is reflected in the central bank's end-of-day balance sheet. There, payment systems have an impact as described in the previous section.

4. Payment systems and the conduct of open market operations

In the previous two sections, it was argued that payment systems impact on monetary policy implementation in practice by influencing the need of the central bank to supply reserves via open market operations. When forecasts of these factors are not perfect, transitory money market disturbances may arise. Indeed, in the euro area, excess reserves and banknotes in circulation are, right after government deposits, the second and third largest source of liquidity imbalances.

Furthermore, payment and security settlement systems are directly relevant for open market operations as these operations obviously need to be settled. Liquidity supplying reverse operations, today's standard for open market operations, are secured (collateralised), such that in fact two legs of the operations need to be settled, the security leg being clearly the more complex one. The efficiency of the payment and settlement infrastructure thus may create constraints in particular for the conduct of open market operations with same day settlement late in the day. Also the set of counterparties with access to open market operations may be restricted by the need to have certain types of payment and security accounts.

Table 2.3 Stylised central bank balance sheet with zero demand for banknotes

Net autonomous factors	100	Banknotes	0
Borrowing facility	0	Deposit facility	0
		Open market operations	100

Table 2.4 Stylised central bank balance sheet with positive demand for banknotes and large net foreign reserve holdings

Net autonomous factors	200	Banknotes	100
Borrowing facility	0	Deposit facility	0
		Open market operations	100

Outlook: What if the demand for banknotes vanishes?

Of course, it is true that, in the future, payment system innovations could one day lead to more fundamental challenges to monetary policy. The most popular scenario, the shrinkage of banknotes in circulation, does not appear today any more likely than it appeared 10, 20 or 30 years ago. Still, it remains a scenario that economists have continuously speculated about.[12]

Assume that banknotes would be substituted more and more by electronic payments, denominated in the currency units of the (previously used) banknotes. Assume also that reserve requirements would be zero (reserve requirements are another solution to the problem). The central bank balance sheet could then look as in Table 2.3.

Thus, the central bank would have to absorb constantly through open market operations reserves from the banking system to keep the money market balanced and control interest rates (e.g. at a level suggested by a kind of Taylor rule). Otherwise there would be excess reserves in the interbank market (of 100 in the example given earlier) and money market rates would fall to zero. Such a situation is in fact not at all special for central banks, many of which have operated in such a context for years. For example, all ten central banks of EU member states which joined on 1 May 2004 operate in a so-called surplus of the banking system vis-à-vis the central bank – not because banknote demand is zero, but because they hold large net foreign assets, as reflected in the stylised balance sheet in Table 2.4.

From the strict monetary policy implementation point of view, the two balance sheet structures require exactly the same action – namely absorption of 100 units of account through open market operations. There are various ways to do so, like repo operations, collection of fixed term deposits, and issuance of debt certificates. While monetary policy implementation in the sense of interest rate steering is thus not confronted by really new challenges when banknotes vanish, the profitability of central banks would obviously suffer. This would need to be reflected by an adequate equipment of central banks with capital, or alternatively guaranteed transfers by the government (the latter always appearing to be less favourable for central bank independence).

Conclusions

Changes in payment systems do not help in explaining changes in monetary policy implementation approaches during the twentieth century. They are also not likely to cause important changes in the foreseeable or even distant future. Still, payment system issues have some well-defined technical implications for monetary policy implementation: banknotes in circulation, the payment system float and excess reserves need to be forecast in a similar way as autonomous factors. In case of forecast errors, the control of short term interest rates normally only suffers temporarily without having any macro-economic impact.

References

Axilrod, S. H. and Lindsey, D. E. (1981) 'Federal Reserve System Implementation of monetary policy: Analytical foundations of the new approach', *American Economic Review*, 71: 246–52.

Bindseil, U. (2004a) 'The operational target of monetary policy and the rise and fall of reserve position doctrine', European Central Bank Working Paper no. 372, Frankfurt/Main.

Bindseil, U. (2004b) *Monetary Policy Implementation: Theory, Past, Present*, Oxford: Oxford University Press.

Bindseil, U., Camba-Mendez, G. Hirsch, A. and Weller, B. (2004), 'Excess reserves and the implementation of monetary policy of the ECB', European Central Bank Working Paper no. 361, Frankfurt/Main.

Blenck, D., Hasko, H., Hilton, S. and Masaki, K. (2002) 'The main features of the monetary policy frameworks of the bank of Japan, the Federal Reserve and the Eurosystem', in Bank for International Settlements (ed.) 'Comparing monetary policy operating procedures across the United States, Japan, and the euro area', *BIS Paper New Series,* 9: 23–47.

Board of Governors (1994) *The Federal Reserve System: Purposes and Functions,* various editions, Washington, D.C.: Board of Governors of the Federal Reserve System.

Cook, T. C. and Hahn, T. (1989) 'The effect of changes in the Federal Funds rate target on market interest rate in the 1970s', *Journal of Monetary Economics*, 24: 331–51.

Dow, J. P (2001) 'The demand for excess reserves', *Southern Economic Journal*, 67: 685–700.

Fama, E. G. (1980) 'Banking in the theory of finance', *Journal of Monetary Economics*, 6: 39–57.

Friedman, M. and A. Schwartz (1963) *A Monetary History of the United States, 1867–1960*, Princeton: Princeton University Press.

Goldenweiser, E. A. (1925) *The Federal Reserve System in operation*, New York: McGrawHill.

Goodfriend, M. (2003) 'Review of Allan Meltzer's A history of the Federal reserve, Volume 1: 1913–1951', *The Region (December),* Minnesota: Federal Reserve Bank of Minneapolis.

Goodhart C. A. E. (2001) 'The endogeneity of money', in P. Arestis, M. Desai, and S. Dow (eds) *Money, Macroeconomics and Keynes*, London: Routledge.

Hamilton, J. D. (1996) 'The Daily Market for Federal Funds', *Journal of Political Economy*, 104: 25–56.

Meltzer, A. H. (2003) *A History of the Federal Reserve*, Vol. 1, 1913–1951, Chicago: University of Chicago Press.

Meulendyke, A.-M. (1998) *US Monetary Policy and Financial Markets*, New York: Federal Reserve Bank of New York.

Mishkin, F. (2004) *The Economics of Money, Banking and Financial Markets*, 7th edition, Boston: Pearson-Addison Wesley.

Perez-Quirós, G. and Mendizábal, H. R. (2000) 'The daily market for funds in Europe: Has something changed with EMU?' European Central Bank Working Paper no. 67, Frankfurt/Main.

Phillips, C. A. (1920) *Bank Credit*, New York: Macmillan.

Prati, A., Bartolini, L., and Bertola, G. (2003) 'The overnight interbank market: evidence from the G7', *Journal of Banking and Finance*, 27: 2045–83.

Strongin, S. (1995) 'The identification of monetary policy disturbances. Explaining the liquidity puzzle', *Journal of Monetary Economics*, 35: 463–97.

Woodford, M. (2001) 'Monetary policy in the information economy', Paper prepared for the 'Symposium on Economic Policy for the Information Economy', 30 August–1 September, Federal Reserve Bank of Kansas City, Jackson Hole, Wyoming.

Woodford, M. (2003), *Interest and Prices: Foundations of a Theory of Monetary Policy*, Princeton: Princeton University Press.

Würtz, F. (2003), 'A comprehensive model on the euro overnight rate', European Central Bank Working Paper no. 207, Frankfurt/Main.

Würtz, F. and Krylova, E. (2004) 'The liquidity effect in the euro area', paper presented at a workshop on 'Monetary Policy Implementation: Lessons from the Past and Challenges Ahead', 20–21 January, European Central Bank, Frankfurt/Main.

Notes

* Views expressed are those of the authors, and not related to views of the ECB. Authors' address: European Central Bank, Directorate General Operations, Kaiserstrasse 29, 60311 Frankfurt am Main, Germany. We wish to thank Soizic Lewicke-Frin and participants to the Seminar at the Austrian Academy of Sciences, 26 June 2004, for helpful input and comments.

1 See e.g. Meulendyke (1998) for a detailed overview.

2 See e.g. Cook and Hahn (1989).

3 See also Bindseil (2004a, 19–20) and Bindseil (2004b, 235–8)

4 See e.g. Bindseil (2004b) for a more detailed explanation of this model.

5 See e.g. Blenck *et al.* (2001, 44).

6 See e.g. Blenck *et al.* (2001). The fact that reserve requirements are comparatively low in the US as compared to Europe does not reflect a deliberate choice of the Fed, but rather the fact that statutory limitations prevent the FED from increasing their (non-remunerated) reserve requirements. Reserve ratios are higher in the US than in the euro area, but as reserve requirements are not remunerated, banks made substantial efforts to shrink their liabilities to which the reserve ratios apply. They were so successful in doing so that, eventually, the reserve base is much lower in the US than in the euro area, where required reserves are remunerated, eliminating incentives for circumventing reserve requirements.

7 The US case is described inter alia by Dow (2001).

8 See Woodford (2001).

9 See Perez-Quirós and Mendizábal (2000).

10 See Würtz (2003).

11 See also Prati *et al* (2003).

12 See e.g. Fama (1980) and Woodford (2001).

3 Modelling institutional change in the payments system, and its implications for monetary policy

Forrest H. Capie, Dimitrios P. Tsomocos and Geoffrey E. Wood[1]

Many institutional changes have taken place to payments systems. Indeed, they have been in continual change ever since money first emerged as the dominant technology for conducting transactions. Means of settlement between banks have changed: cheques replaced cash in many transactions, and they have in their turn been replaced partially (much more in some countries than others) by cards. Technology is even developing whereby mobile telephones can be used to effect instantaneous settlement of transactions. These have all affected the relationship between the quantity of money demanded and income. But none of the innovations has threatened to move us from a money-using society to one which transacts by some other means.

The implications for monetary policy have therefore been, in theory at least, trivial. And this has also been true in practice. Central banks have remained able to use monetary policy to influence, and to control within surprisingly narrow limits, the course of the price level. Indeed, as the short-to-medium relationship between money and income has become looser (as evidenced by increasing difficulty in fitting well-behaved money demand functions), central bank control of inflation has improved. The changed constitutional relationship between central bank and government that has occurred in many countries appears to have produced benefits which have more than offset the increasing difficulty of using monetary policy to control inflation.

But how long can that benign outcome last? It would be too much to expect still further improvements to inflation control; that would be an excessive demand on monetary policy and central banks. Our concern is whether the *present* benign situation can persist. Will developments which appear to be on the horizon loosen the money-income relationship still further, or even end it by eliminating money as a transactions technology?

The aim of this paper is to appraise one such possible technological development, and to model both it and money as transactions technologies. By comparing the models, we shall be able to appraise the future of fiat money.

The structure of the paper is as follows. We first set out an outline of the technology that may replace money. Then we provide an informal description of the model we use to appraise both this technology and fiat money as means of conducting exchanges. This is followed by the development of our formal model.

We then develop the implications of our analysis for the survival (or otherwise) of fiat money. This leads to a discussion of economic policy, and then to a concluding overview of our findings and policy conclusions.

One preliminary remains: definition. McCallum (1985, 2003) distinguishes very clearly between a monetary system of exchange, a barter system of exchange and an accounting system of exchange. The first is one which uses a 'tangible mechanism of exchange'; a 'monetary system of exchange', he goes on, is '... one in which the vast majority of transactions involve money on one side'. This he contrasts with barter, '... in which commodities are directly exchanged without any intermediate conversion into money'. The third type of system is one in which '... there is no money [by which McCallum means at this point a medium of exchange] but exchanges are conducted by means of signals to an accounting network, with debits and credits to the wealth accounts of buyers and sellers being effected with each exchange'. McCallum goes on to say that he regards that system as non-monetary, as a 'highly efficient form of barter'.

In the present paper we follow him in that. It must be noted, though, that whether such a system would dominate barter conducted electronically but *without* an agreed medium and unit of account should be demonstrated rather than assumed. We do, however, leave for another paper whether electronic barter with a mechanism and a unit of account would dominate electronic barter without these two features. The question is interesting, for only if the former does dominate is the concept and controllability of a price level a logically possible subject for discussion in an electronic barter world. But making the comparison would require detailed modelling of transactions costs in the two systems, and the results would not be relevant to the present paper's conclusions.

Technology and exchange

The development of electronic, and in particular of computer, technology has led to speculation that electronic technology will replace fiat money in facilitating exchange. Just as barter was supplanted first by commodity money and then by fiat money because these were superior transactions technologies, so, it is argued, information storage and transmission will be so facilitated by computer technology that in its turn fiat money will be displaced.

Central to analysis of this proposition is the medium-of-exchange function of money. The crucial distinction is between a money-using economy and a barter economy; whether it is one of primitive or of electronic barter, is that in the former a medium of exchange is used. Our aim in this paper is to establish a simple formal framework which will let us examine the crucial determinants of whether or not a medium of exchange will be used. To do this, we construct a model of exchange with costs of transacting an intrinsic part of it; for if there are no costs of transacting then there are no transactions costs on which a medium of exchange can economise.

As was observed some years ago by George Stigler (1972), a world without transactions costs would seem a very strange place. There would be no firms – and therefore no banks, insurance companies, or other financial institutions. And further, there would be no money. The essence of our argument is that so long as there are transactions costs there will be money, and that even electronic barter will not, except under very special circumstances which we set out later in this chapter, be able to replace 'fiat' money because it will not be as effective in reducing transactions costs. To develop the economic intuition underlying our model, we first argue informally why some form of money to mediate trade in mass anonymous markets evolved as a device to reduce the costs of transacting. Then, we go on to show that once the *concept* of using money had developed, still further cost reductions were achieved by a further development – convergence to a very small number of commodities which were used as money. Indeed, a single money is, subject to certain constraints on its issuance, the optimal outcome. We would remark at this point that, while all the subsequent arguments are set implicitly or explicitly in an exchange economy, the conclusions would be expected to hold *a fortiori* in an economy with production, for if there is production then the *number* of exchanges will exceed these in an exchange economy with the endowment that our production economy produces.

Barter, whether with or without electronic accounting, involves the double coincidence of wants. The buyer must want what the seller is selling – and vice versa. That could be eliminated by what Meltzer (1998) calls 'barter credit' – supplying goods now in exchange for a promise of goods later. But such transactions are rare even in economies with developed and reliable legal systems. Why? The reason is that there is a cheaper way of transacting. Credit, whether barter credit or not, requires the seller to know about the buyer – about his or her creditworthiness, and the features (such as income) which contribute to that. If a money which is widely accepted and recognised is available, then the personal attributes of the buyer become irrelevant. All that matters is what he is offering. *Less information has to be gathered, so trade becomes cheaper.* This expands the possibilities for trade, so both buyer and seller gain. (The analogy with a tariff reduction is clear.)

For something to *evolve* as the *sole* medium of exchange of a society, rather than be imposed as such, two conditions have to be satisfied. These are as follows. First, not all goods are equally suitable for use as money; the costs of acquiring information must depend on the good selected. Second, the marginal cost of acquiring information about whatever is used in exchange falls the more frequently it is used. These two features let us explain the once widespread use of precious metals as a means of payment. Such metals can be assayed for fineness, are divisible, can be readily quantified by weighing, and are homogeneous – an ounce of gold of a certain fineness is identical to another ounce of that fineness. Alternative monies – cattle, stones and tablets of salt – did not possess these attributes to anything like the same extent. These are the attributes that guide us towards the monetary commodity. But, it should be emphasised, the information-economising attribute is crucial. Precious metals are not always available. If they are not, something else is used. Cigarettes were used as money in German prisoner-of-war camps in the Second World War.[2] They were used because everyone could recognise them, and knew that everyone would accept them in any exchange.

We can thus see that a society will tend to evolve towards the use of a very few commodities as money, given the assumption that not all commodities are equally good at satisfying the medium of exchange function; and that one good will come to dominate if the marginal cost of acquiring information about that good falls the more it is used.

Not only does the use of money eliminate the need to know about the buyer in a transaction. When it has evolved into use as a unit of account, another saving is achieved. Without a medium of account and unit of account, any transactor must know the bilateral exchange value of each commodity for every other commodity.[3]

> If there are n commodities, there are at least $(n(n\text{-}1))/2$ separate values. The number of bilateral exchange ratios (prices) rises quickly. With $n = 100$ commodities, there are at least 4,950 prices to know. At $n = 500$, the number is 124,750, and with 1,000 commodities there are at least 499,500 prices. Without a unit of account, trade would be very limited by costs of information. Use of a unit of account to express value reduces the number of prices from $(n(n\text{-}1)/ 2$ to n (Meltzer 1998, 12).

So far we have argued that evolution to the use of a few commodities and subsequently to one commodity as money, is beneficial. Subject to certain constraints going beyond that brings still further benefits. Paper money, so long as there is not overissue that leads to inflation, brings a resource saving if it substitutes in whole or in part for the commodities which heretofore had served as money.

To summarise, we have argued that the concept and use of money emerged through a process of search and discovery. Its advantage over barter credit, which has some advantages over simple barter, is that it reduces transaction costs still further by shifting attention from the qualities of the prospective purchaser of a good to the qualities of what he is offering to pay for it. From (in Allan Meltzer's (1998) words) '... a unique and possibly obscure set of attributes to a common and widely known set of attributes'. A money-using society requires less information than a bartering society.

Before going on to develop a formal demonstration of these conclusions, and then to show their relevance to the future of electronic barter and paper money, it is useful to place the arguments in their historical context, for the view of the development and role of money set out earlier is not new. A thorough exposition of it was provided over 100 years ago by Carl Menger (1892).[4] He maintained that money was a 'social' creation, a product of the invisible hand. His was an example of an invisible hand explanation – in contrast to a government-based explanation – of a social institution.[5] The basic point was not original to Menger, either. (It is a bold writer who asserts that he has found the original inventor of any economic concept!) Adam Smith had made the point in the *Wealth of Nations*.

> In order to avoid the inconvenience of such situations [where the would-be seller of a good does not want what the would-be buyer offers] every prudent man in every period of society, after the first establishment of the division of

> labour, must naturally have endeavoured to manage his affairs in such a manner, as to have at all times by him, besides the peculiar product of his own industry, a certain quantity of some one commodity or other, such as he imagined few people would be likely to refuse in exchange for the product of their industry (Smith 1776/1981 edition, 37–38).

And that money was originally a social institution, although it had subsequently become a government one, was also noted by Keynes (1935, 4–5).

> Thus the Age of Money had succeeded to the Age of Barter as soon as men had adopted a money-of-account. And the Age of State money was reached when the state claimed the right to declare what thing should answer as money to the current money of account – when it claimed the right not only to enforce the dictionary but also to write the dictionary.[6]

Now, it is not logically necessary for the medium of exchange to serve also as the medium of account. But as several authors have emphasised, if they do not coincide, the 'computational benefits' of having a medium of account are incomplete unless the simple step of having it coincide with the medium of exchange is taken.[7] Severe inflation can disrupt this, but it does need to be severe; the two seem to continue to coincide even at inflation rates well into three figures per annum.

Strategic market games: A bird's eye view

Strategic market games provide a framework rigorously to introduce money, other financial instruments as well as financial intermediaries to closed models. The need for accounting clarity, institutional detail and the criterion of 'playability' is such that minimal institutions (e.g. clearing houses, central banks and other financial intermediaries, credit, default, etc.) and well-defined price formation mechanisms (sell-all, bid-offer, double auction) naturally emerge as logical necessities in the rules of the game and the equilibrium concept used. Ultimately, this class of games contributes to the development of formal micro foundations to money, financial economics and macroeconomics.

Strategic market games are related to the design of resource allocation methods introduced by Hurwicz (1960, 1973). They were introduced formally by Dubey and Shubik (1978, 1980), Shapley (1976), Shapley and Shubik (1977), Shubik (1973) and Shubik and Wilson (1977). Three main price formation mechanisms were introduced: one-sided Cournot type of model, a two-sided Cournot type and a double auction (or two-sided Bertrand-Edgeworth model). Fiat or commodity money is used and other market structures are also modelled. For example, foreign exchange markets whereby no natural *numéraire* or fiat money is a medium of exchange, then one can employ a modified price formation where trading posts between any two instruments or commodities are set and consistent prices that clear all markets are determined via a giant clearinghouse.

Endogenous default, credit, financial intermediaries and incomplete asset markets are introduced and, therefore, one can formally model and analyse payment systems, monetary, fiscal and regulatory policies. For an excellent presentation of these models one can consult Shubik (1990, 1999), and for a more technical analysis Giraud (2003). In principle, inefficiency in this class of models arises due to insufficient liquidity, or oligopolistic effects, or institutional restrictions. Hence, active policy has non-neutral effects and possibly, but not always, ameliorates welfare losses because of the transactions technology present in the models. Last but not least, abstracting from the oligopolistic effects, there exists a large literature on monetary general equilibrium models which is akin to the strategic market games one, since money and institutions are introduced into the standard Arrow-Debreu model.[8]

In sum, since the institutions of society in general, and the financial institutions in particular, are the carriers of economic process, a *mathematical institutional economics* is needed as it has been argued by Martin Shubik. This is what strategic market games attempt so as to achieve a better understanding of production, distribution, policy and, more generally, of political economy.

Formal model

We use the strategic market game developed in Shubik and Tsomocos (2002). Money depreciates (i.e. it wears out through deterioration of notes' and coins' quality) when used in exchange, and its replacement is costly.[9] The stipulated means of exchange is fiat money and all transactions need cash in advance (see endnote 15 for the motivation of this constraint). Thus, agents borrow fiat money to make their transactions. The government extracts seigniorage costs from the players in the form of interest rate payments. In order to do so, it participates in exchange and bids to provide for its inputs of production. The objective function of the government for the purposes of our argument, without loss of generality, is to minimise the interest rate subject to the requirement to replace worn out fiat money used in exchange, and the interest rate which is a choice variable of the government determines its revenues. We assume that the initial money supply enters exogenously. Figure 3.1 shows the extensive form of the game. The exchange game is a one-period game with four subperiods. At each subperiod, as we explain below, an agent or a group of agents move. We first modify the game to admit both fiat money and electronic barter. We conceptualise electronic barter mediated as through a giant clearing house run by an institution, perhaps the government. We then analyse the condition under which fiat money dominates electronic barter.

At the first move the government, P_g, determines the interest rate. At the second move, individuals, $P_1,\ldots,P_H$, obtain fiat money in the money market at the predetermined interest rate. At the third move, individuals exchange commodities and the government buys inputs of production to be used in the replacement of depreciated fiat money. We maintain simplicity of strategy sets by assuming a

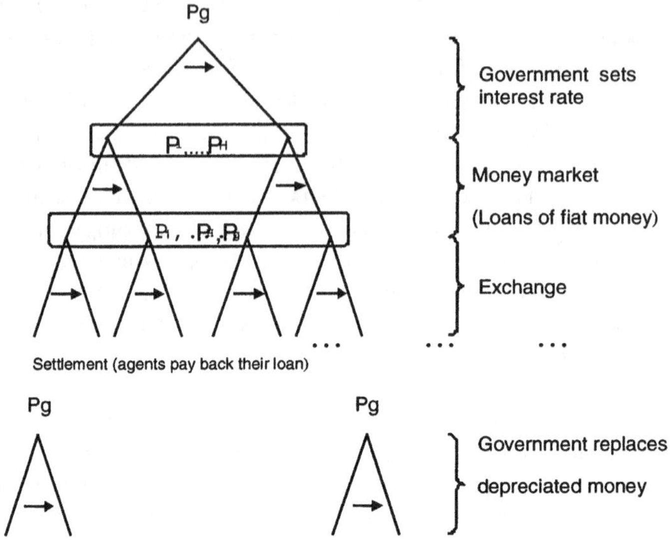

Figure 3.1 Trade with seigniorage cost of fiat money

continuum of traders, simultaneous moves, and a minimum of information at the second and the third stage. Then traders pay back their loans, and finally the government replaces depreciated money.

The government levies seigniorage costs to replenish depreciated money and also participates in exchange.[10]

Let $h \in H = \{1,\ldots,H\}$ be the set of agents and $l \in L = \{1,\ldots,L\}$ be the set of tradable commodities. Each agent is endowed with a vector of commodities $e^h \in \mathfrak{R}^L_+$. The utility functions of agents are of the form $u^h\colon \mathfrak{R}^L \to \mathfrak{R}$.

The following assumptions hold:

(i) $\sum_{h\in H} e^h \gg 0$
(i.e. every commodity is present in the economy)

(ii) $e^h \neq 0, \forall\, h \in H$
(i.e. no agent has the null endowment of commodities)

(iii) u^h is continuous, concave and strictly monotonic $\forall\, h \in H$
(i.e. the more consumption the better)

Agents maximise their utility of consumption subject to the following constraints:

$$\sum_{l\in L} b_l^h \leq v^h \tag{1}$$

(i.e. expenditures in commodities $\leq$ borrowed money)

$$q_l^h \leq e_l^h, \forall l \in L \tag{2}$$

(i.e. sales of commodities $\leq$ endowment of commodities)

$$(1+r)v^h \leq \sum_{l \in L} p_l q_l^h + \Delta(1) \tag{3}$$

(i.e. loan repayment $\leq$ receipts from sales of commodities + money at hand)
where, $b_l^h \equiv$ money bid of h for the purchase of commodity $l \in L$,
$q_l^h \equiv$ quantity of commodity $l \in L$ offered by h,
$v^h \equiv$ loans contracted by h,
$r \equiv$ loan interest rate,
$p_l \equiv$ commodity price of $l \in L$ and
$\Delta(1)$ is the difference between the right- and left-hand sides of equation (1).

As can be seen from the budget constraints (1) and (3), receipts from sales of commodities cannot be used contemporaneously for financing purchases of other commodities. This is the essence of the cash-in-advance constraint which can also be thought as a liquidity constraint.

The exogenously fixed money supply M depreciates at a rate η. Thus, if the total amount of fiat money borrowed by the agents from the government (or central bank) is $\sum_{h \in H} v^h = \mu$ and the expenditure of the government for the purchase of inputs of production is $\bar{g}$ then $\eta[\mu + \bar{g}]$ is the depreciated amount of money, since $[\bar{\mu} + \bar{g}]$is the total amount of money in circulation.

The government's production function for money exhibits decreasing returns to scale in order to generate a unique optimum.[11]

$$z_{L+1} = F(x_1^g, \ldots, x_L^g) \tag{4}$$

with
$z_{L+1} \equiv$ amount of fiat money produced,
x_l^g inputs of production.

We impose the standard technical assumptions on the government's production set, $y^g \in \Re_+^L$, that guarantee feasibility and the existence of a solution to the government's maximisation problem.

(iv) $0 \in y^g$,
(v) y^g is convex and closed
(vi) $\exists B > 0 \ni if (x_1^g,\ldots,x_L^g; Z_{L+1}) \in y^g$ then $x_l^g \in B, \forall\, l \in L$ and $Z_{L+1} \leq B$

The government seeks to minimise interest rates because it simply aims to levy the necessary seigniorage to replace depreciated fiat money. Thus the government's optimisation problem becomes,[12]

$$\max_{r,b_l^g,l\in L}{}^{13} -r$$

$$\text{s.t.} \quad z_{L+1} = \eta \left[\sum_{h\in H} v^h + \sum_{l\in L} b_l^g \right] \tag{5}$$

$$\sum_{l\in L} b_l^g = r \sum_{h\in H} v^h \tag{6}$$

Where (5) is the amount of depreciated money that needs to be replaced, and (6) is the budget constraint of the government (i.e. its expenditures to finance the cost of production come from seigniorage).

The final allocations for the agents and the government are:

$$x_l^h = e_l^h - q_l^h + \frac{b_l^h}{p_l}, \forall l \in L \tag{7}$$

(i.e. consumption = initial endowment – sales + purchases)
and

$$x_l^g = \frac{b_l^g}{p_l} \tag{8}$$

(government's inputs of production = money offered/prices).

Note that the relation between η and r is a complicated one and depends on gains from trade that in turn determine the volume of transactions. The interest rate r is set by the government to raise seigniorage revenue for the financing of fiat money production so as to replace depreciated money.

Finally, a Nash equilibrium (NE) or $\Gamma(H, u^h, e^h, \eta, M, x^h, x^g)$ is a set of strategy choices, $s = (s^h, s^g) = (b_l^h, q_l^h, x_l^h, b_l^g, p)$; $\forall\ h \in H$ and the government, and $\alpha = (\alpha^h, \alpha^g) \in \sum = \underset{h\in H}{\mathrm{X}} B^h \times B^g$, $\ni$

$$\Pi(s/\alpha) \leq \Pi(s) \tag{9}$$

where B^h, B^g are the choice sets of the agents and the government (i.e. $B^h = \langle (b_l^h, q_l^h, v^h)_{l\in L}$: (1)–(2)hold$\rangle$ and $B^g = \langle (r, b_l^g)_{l\in L}$: (5)–(6)hold$\rangle$), and (s/α) is s with either s^t or s^g replaced by any other strategy choice α^t or α^g.[14] Also, $\Pi(\cdot)$ represents the payoff functions of agents ($\Pi^h(\cdot) = u^h$) and of the government ($\Pi^g(\cdot) = -r$).

Prices are formed using the Dubey and Shubik (1978) price formation mechanism. Prices are by that mechanism formed as the ratio of the aggregate cash bid in a particular market to the aggregate quantity of commodities offered for sale. This is equivalent to an equilibrium condition; its accounting clarity allows for cash flows in the economy to be traced precisely.

$$\text{Thus, } p_l = \left\{ \begin{array}{ll} \dfrac{\sum_{h\in H} b_l^h + b_l^g}{\sum_{h\in H} q_l^h}, & \mathit{if} \sum_{h\in H} b_l^h + b_l^g;\ \sum_{h\in H} q_l^h > 0 \\ 0, & \mathit{otherwise} \end{array} \right\} \tag{10}$$

The existence and inefficiency theorems for these outcomes are stated and proved in Shubik and Tsomocos (2002). Here we will focus our attention on the relative efficiency of using alternative means of payments (on fiat money versus electronic barter).

Trade with fiat money versus electronic barter

We conceptualise exchange using fiat money as follows. Consider a simple case in which $L = 4$. Fiat money can be exchanged against every commodity but commodities cannot be exchanged with each other. Figure 3.2 describes the situation. The arcs connecting m with commodities 1, 2, 3 and 4 indicate that money can be exchanged against all commodities. On the other hand, commodities cannot be exchanged with each other (i.e. there are no arcs connecting them).[15]

Thus, there exist four markets. If on the other hand we want to conceptualise 'electronic barter' we assume that commodities can be exchanged with each other, perhaps via an accounting device of e-barter, which now becomes the

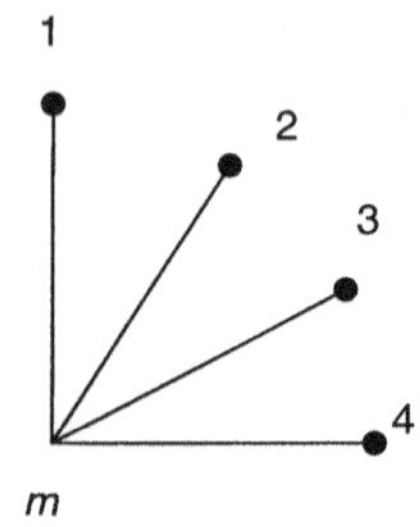

Figure 3.2 Trade with fiat money

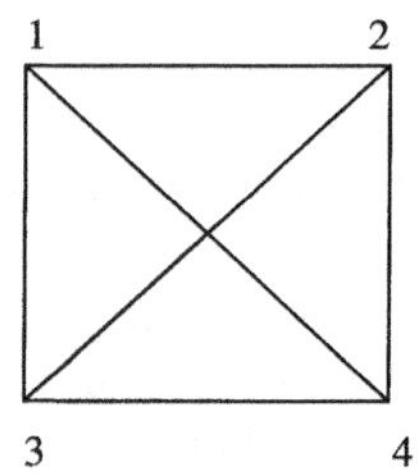

Figure 3.3 Trade via electronic barter

stipulated means of exchange, through a clearing house that matches demand and supply. In this case there will be $\frac{L(L-1)}{2}$ markets, that is, six markets altogether.[16] Thus, in Figure 3.3 arcs connect all commodities with each other indicating that exchange occurs via electronic barter.

Let us assume that the combined cost of gathering and then processing information on each transaction is c. On the other hand trade with fiat money, by virtue of its anonymity, divisibility, fungibility and its other properties does not require any additional costs except its production and replacement costs. These are covered in its production process as described in equation (4). Also, information costs concerning the creditworthiness of borrowers in a fiat money economy are dealt with by commercial banks and not by the original issuers of money (i.e. central banks) or by those who accept money in exchange for goods or services. These costs cannot be avoided by the operators of the central clearing house (or a similar transactions institution) that implements electronic barter. Then the total cost of exchange with e-barter is:

$$\overline{C} = \frac{cL(L-1)}{2}(H+1)^{17} \tag{11}$$

We note that each agent participates in only one side of the market since wash sales (i.e. the same individual participating in both sides of a particular market) are not profitable in a strategic market game without oligopolistic effects. If we assume that set-up costs for establishing either of the two market structures are negligible we have proposition 1. We also note that the total cost of fiat money and of electronic barter is endogenously determined; both depend on the volume of transactions; see equations (6) and (11).

Proposition 1:
The cost of exchange with fiat money is lower than exchange with e-barter provided that,

$$\frac{L(L-1)}{2}c(H+1) - rM > 0, \text{ where } M = \sum\nolimits_{h\in H} v^h$$

Proof:
The cost of exchange with fiat money is $r\sum_{h\in H} v^h$ (*), since replacement of depreciated money is financed by seigniorage which is levied by interest rates. Hence, (11) – (*) $= \frac{L(L-1)}{2}c(H+1) - r\sum_{h\in H} v^h$ represents the cost difference of exchange with electronic barter versus fiat money. □

One point can usefully be made here about this relationship. If we imagine technical progress lowering c, the very same process is likely to increase the number of commodities, L. Indeed, over time we have seen a proliferation of traded commodities most of them being associated with technical progress. Note also that while the lower bound of r is zero, that of c is inevitably above zero.[18]

Proposition 1 underlines the fact that fiat money is a decoupling device that economises on transaction costs regardless from where they emanate (i.e. processing, information acquisition etc.). On the other hand, electronic barter is a centralised accounting mechanism that requires detailed knowledge of every transaction. Thus, it inevitably entails higher aggregate costs in complicated market systems with multiple markets and commodities. It is not a coincidence that the advent of money (or equivalently the decline of barter) occurred contemporaneously with the development of the market system.

Proposition 2:
The equilibria of $\Gamma(H, u^h, e^h, \eta, x^h, x^g)$ with trade with fiat money coincide with those of the corresponding game with e-barter only if $r = 0$ and $c = 0$.

Proof:
If $r = 0$ and $c = 0$ the two alternative methods of financing trade produce the same commodity allocations. To get the same prices and allocations set

$$\frac{\sum\limits_{h\in H} b_l^h}{\sum\limits_{h\in H} q_l^h} = p_l \text{ and } x_l^h = e_l^h - q_l^h + \frac{b_l^h}{p_l} \forall l \in L, h \in H.$$

Then, regardless whether trade is conducted with fiat or through electronic barter, the same equilibrium obtains. □

Proposition 2 underlines the fact that alternative methods of financing become distinct only when transactions costs are present in the economy. Unless one introduces process and the organisational details of market transactions, it is difficult to delineate the differences between alternative media of exchange. Both of them, without transactions costs, are identical units of account. Money is both neutral and super-neutral. Trade, no matter how organised, generates the same allocations. Whenever $r = 0$ and $c = 0$ then money is a 'veil'.[19] Even in the case of bimetallism or multiple means of exchange, as long as there are determinate conversion rates among the media of exchange, the analysis can be conducted in terms of a 'primary' means of payment. However, the allocations generated by the two methods of financing trade are not unambiguously Pareto ranked whenever r, $c \neq 0$. It remains an open question to determine the conditions on r and c that allow one method to generate Pareto superior allocations over the other.

A natural question that emerges from this analysis is whether it is possible for fiat money and electronic barter to coexist in equilibrium; in particular, whether fiat money can be used for a subset of commodities and electronic barter for the rest. This issue is complicated and beyond the scope of our present analysis, since the volume of transactions with each medium of exchange is endogenously determined and in turn determines the subset of commodities whose trade might occur with each medium of exchange. Also, the gains from trade of each commodity influence the marginal benefit and cost using different methods of financing trade. For example, if there exist big gains from trade in a specific commodity, the government may reduce the marginal cost of trading in that market by introducing electronic barter and thus avoiding depreciation of fiat money used in this particular very liquid market. We plan to explore this question in future research.

The price level – meaningful and determinate

The intrinsic informational superiority of central bank issued base money will ensure that demand for it is not extinguished by the growth of e-barter. Demand will remain from the non-bank public, and, because of that, derived demand will remain from the banking sector. The central bank will thus retain control of short-term interest rates.[20] This might seem at first glance sufficient for it to retain control of the price level; for in many models a short rate is the sole transmitter of monetary policy actions. For example, much recent work on monetary policy uses small macroeconomic models which include an IS function analogous to that in a basic IS-LM model. These can be backward looking, and thus very close to the traditional specification,[21] or forward looking, embodying rational expectations.[22] But whatever the specification, a common feature is that demand for current output is a function of the real rate of interest, and that rate in turn is typically assumed to be a short-term nominal rate. There is a crucial assumption of slow price level adjustment; monetary policy in such models affects output and inflation only through its effects on the real rate of interest. This is surely a somewhat hazardous assumption in the present context. Sluggish price adjustment is a result of price adjustment being costly. In a world where transaction costs have been drastically reduced by technical progress, it would be strange to assume that the costs of price adjustment remained unaffected. Accordingly, it also seems strange to continue to argue that monetary policy depends crucially for its effectiveness on prices being statutory.

It is all the stranger since no such dependence is necessary. Viewing the short rate as the sole transmitter of monetary policy is unnecessarily restrictive both theoretically and empirically. Allan Meltzer (1999a) has recently summarised the body of theory and evidence which considers that specification to be inadequate. He argued that, while so long as prices are sticky the real interest rate is indeed affected by central bank operations, so too is the real monetary base, and changes in the latter affect aggregate demand in ways additional to the effect of changes in the real interest rate. Meltzer (1999b) reports empirical results for the United States which support this argument, as does Nelson (2000) for the United Kingdom,[23] who provides a clear summary of his results as follows:

> The common feature of the regressions is that for the United States and the United Kingdom, real money growth enters output regressions sizeably, positively, and significantly. The real interest rate generally enters with a negative sign, though both the sign and the significance of the real interest rate term appear to be less consistent across sub-samples than those of the money growth terms?' (Nelson 2000, 13; emphasis added).

These empirical results are consistent with two quite distinct bodies of analysis. One is on an approach which assumes utility is non-separable in consumption and real money holdings. This justifies a real money balance term in the IS function as a result of optimising behaviour. Koenig (1990) reports results which support this; but others suggest that the coefficient on real balances is likely to be small.[24]

A *direct* role for money is perhaps better defended and explained by an approach with much earlier origins. David Hume (1752) thought that money affected the economy through a wide variety of channels, and expressed this thought in a metaphor – water flowing from one place to another – that frequently recurs in the discussions of the money transmission process.[25]

> Money always finds its way back again by a hundred canals, of which we have not notion or suspicion. … For above a thousand years, the money of Europe has been flowing to Rome, by one open and sensible current; but it has been emptied by many secret and insensible canals (Hume 1752/1955 reprint, 48).

The many channels view is also articulated by Friedman and Schwartz (1962, 486–87).

> …The attempt to correct portfolio imbalances (resulting from an increase in the money stock) raises the prices of the sources of service flows relative to

> the flows themselves which leads to an increase in spending both on the service flows and then produce a new source of service flows. ... Sooner or later the acceleration in nominal income will have to take the form of rising prices, since the initial position was assumed to be one of equilibrium and we have introduced nothing to change the long-run trend of nominal income.

This argument is also expressed in Brunner and Meltzer (1993) and was stated very succinctly in Meltzer (1999b, 10), as follows:

> Monetary policy works by changing relative prices. There are many, many, such prices. Some economists erroneously believe....monetary policy works only by changing a single short-term interest rate.

He also argues (1999a, 10-11) that money balances are crucial in the transmission mechanism. He sees '... the gap between desired and actual real balances as a measure of the relative price adjustment required to restore full equilibrium'.

Our formal model, which compared fiat money with e-barter, also yields the result that control of the issue of fiat money controls the price level without any intermediation through an interest rate channel. Our model manifests *real* as well as *nominal* determinacy as has been shown in Tsomocos (1996, 2003a, 2003b). This is unlike the classical competitive model which possesses a 'finite' number of equilibria with respect to real allocations; only relative prices can be determined. Our model resolves nominal indeterminacy through the presence of *private liquid wealth.*[26] By liquid wealth we mean a commodity or a monetary instrument which can be used interchangeably with money in real, financial or bank transactions, and its conversion rate is institutionally predetermined. The essence of the determinacy argument and consequently of the non-neutrality result is that monetary policy affects nominal variables, yet if private liquid wealth is non-zero then monetary changes directly affect the endowments of agents, resulting in different optimisation choices and consequently different real consumption. The issues of determinacy and money non-neutrality are intimately connected and are analytically equivalent.

Finally, if a model does not possess equilibria that are nominally determinate then any discussion of exchange with a particular means of payment (either fiat or e-barter) is not legitimate. If multiple price levels support the same equilibrium real allocations then it is impossible to compare the relative virtues of exchange with different means of payment.[27]

Conclusion

In this paper we first set out the argument (a very traditional one) that money evolved to reduce transaction costs by economising on information.

A formal model in which money existed by virtue of that property was then developed and the costs of operating a fiat money system were compared with the costs of operating a system of e-barter. The key cost parameters were identified. It was shown that within this framework fiat money dominates – is cheaper than – e-barter, unless inflation drives up the nominal interest rate. Second, increases in the number of commodities increase the costs of e-barter faster than they do the costs of using fiat money; and finally that the lower bound to the cost of using fiat money is always below that of e-barter. Thus fiat money is a superior transaction technology to e-barter; transaction chains that use it have intrinsically lower information requirements. The resulting demand for fiat money by the non-bank public will in turn give rise to demand by the banking sector. Their joint demands will ensure both that central banks survive and that they will retain control of a price level measured in the money they issue. Institutional change in the payments system will no doubt have quantitative implications for central bank operations, but it will not have qualitative implications for them.

References

Alchian, A. A. (1977) 'Why money?' *Journal of Money, Credit and Banking*, 9: 133–40.

Brunner, K. and Meltzer, M. (1971) 'The uses of money: money in the theory of an exchange economy', *American Economic Review*, 61: 784–805.

Brunner, K. and Meltzer, A. (1993) *Money and the economy: issues in monetary analysis*, Cambridge: Cambridge University Press.

Capie, F. H. (1986) 'Conditions in which very rapid inflation appears', *Carnegie-Rochester Conferences on Public Policy*, 24: 115–65.

Capie, F. H. and Gomez, Y. (2002) 'Electronic money: a survey of "potential users", *Bank of Finland Economic Trends*, Helsinki.

Clower, R. W. (1969) 'Introduction', in R. W. Clower (ed.), *Readings in Monetary Theory*, London: Penguin.

Drèze, J. and Polemarchakis, H. M. (2000) 'Monetary equilibria', in G. Debreu, Neuefeind, W. and Trockel, W. (eds), *Economic Essays: a Festschrift for Werner Hildenbrand,* Heidelberg: Springer, 83–104.

Dubey, P. and Geanakoplos, J. (1992) 'The value of money in a finite-horizon economy: a role for banks', in Dasgupta, P. and Gale, D. *et al.* (eds), *Economic Analysis of Markets and Games*, Cambridge: MIT Press.

Dubey, P. and Geanakoplos, J. (2003) 'Monetary equilibrium with missing markets', *Journal of Mathematical Economics*, 39: 585–618.

Dubey, P. and Shubik, M. (1978) 'The non-cooperative equilibria of a closed trading economy with market supply and bidding strategies', *Journal of Economic Theory*, 17: 1–20.

Dubey, P. and Shubik, M. (1980) 'A strategic market game with price and quantity strategies', *Zeitschrift für Nationalokonomie*, 40: 25–34.

Friedman, M. (1956) 'The quantity theory of money: a restatement', in M. Friedman (ed.), *Studies in the Quantity Theory of Money*, Chicago: University of Chicago Press.

Friedman, M. and Schwartz, A. J. (1962) *A Monetary History of the United States*, Princeton: Princeton University Press.

Fuhrer, J. C. and Moore, G. R. (1995) 'Monetary policy trade-offs and the correlation between nominal interest rates and output', *American Economic Review*, 85: 219–39.

Giraud, G. (2003) 'Strategic market games: an introduction', *Journal of Mathematical Economics*, 39: 355–75.

Glasser, D. (1989) *Free Banking and Monetary Reform*, Cambridge: Cambridge University Press.

Gomez, Y. (2001) 'Electronic money and the monetary system', unpublished PhD thesis, City University, London.

Goodhart, C. A. E. (2000) 'Can central banking survive the IT revolution?' *International Finance*, 3: 189–202.

Grandmont, J.-M. (1983) *Money and Value*, Cambridge: Cambridge University Press.

Hume, D. (1752), 'Of money', reprinted in E. Rotwein (ed.) (1955) *Writings on Economics*, London: Nelson.

Hurwicz, L. (1960) 'Optimality and informational efficiency in resource allocation processes', in K. J. Arrow, S. Karlin and P. Puppes (eds), *Mathematical Methods in the Social Sciences,* Stanford: Stanford University Press.

Hurwicz, L. (1973) 'The design of mechanisms for resource allocation', *American Economic Review*, 63: 1–30.

Keynes, J. M. (1935) *A Treatise on Money*, Vol. 1, London: Macmillan.

King, M. (1999) 'Challenges for Monetary Policy: Old and New', paper prepared for the Symposium on "New Challenges for Monetary Policy", 27 August, sponsored by the Federal Reserve Bank of Kansas City at Jackson Hole, Wyoming.

King, M. (2002) 'No money, no inflation – the role of money in the economy', *Bank of England Quarterly Bulletin* (Summer): 162–74.

Koenig, E. F. (1990) 'Real money balances and the timing of consumption: an empirical investigation', *Quarterly Journal of Economics*, 105: 399–425.

Latzer, M. and Schmitz, S. W. (2002) *Carl Menger and the Evolution of Payment Systems: From Barter to Electronic Money*, Cheltenham: Edward Elgar.

Lucas, R. E. (1980) 'Equilibrium in a pure currency economy', in J. H. Kareken and N. Wallace (eds), *Models of Monetary Economies*, Minneapolis: Federal Reserve Bank of Minneapolis.

McCallum, B. (1985) 'Bank regulation, accounting systems of exchange, and the unit of account: a critical review', *Carnegie-Rochester Conference Series on Public Series,* 23: 13–45.

McCallum, B. (1989) *Monetary Economics: Theory and Policy,* New York: Macmillan.

McCallum, B. (1999) 'Theoretical analysis regarding a zero nominal bound for interest rates', *Journal of Monetary Economics*, 32: 163–72.

McCallum, B. (December 2003), 'Monetary policy in economies with little or no money', National Bureau of Economic Research Working Paper, Cambridge.

McCallum, B. and Nelson, E. (1999a) 'An optimising IS-LM specification for monetary policy and business cycle analysis', *Journal of Money, Credit and Banking*, 31: 296–316.

Meltzer, A. H. (1998) 'What is money?', in G. E. Wood (ed.), *Money, Prices and the Real Economy*, Cheltenham: Edward Elgar, 8–18.

Meltzer, A. H. (1999a) 'The transmission process', Working Paper, Carnegie-Mellon University.

Meltzer, A. H. (1999b) 'A liquidity trap', Working Paper, Carnegie-Mellon University.

Menger, C. (1892) 'On the origin of money', *Economic Journal*, 2: 239–55.

Mills, T. C. and Wood, G. E. (1977) 'Money substitutes and monetary policy in the UK 1922–1971', *European Economic Review*, 10: 19–36.

Mills, T. C. and Wood, G. E. (1982) 'Econometric evaluation of alternative UK money stock series, 1870-1913', *Journal of Money, Credit and Banking*, 14, 245–67.

Monnet, C. (2002) *Optimal Public Money*, Typescript, Frankfurt/Main: ECB.

Nelson, E. (2000) 'Direct effects of base money on aggregate demand: theory and evidence', Bank of England Working Paper no. 122, London.

Niebans, J. (1978) 'The Theory of Money', Baltimore: John Hopkins University Press.

Radford, R. A. (1945), 'The economic organisation of POW camp', *Economica,* 12: 189–201.

Selgin, G. A. and White, L. H. (2002) 'Mengerian perspectives on the future of money', in M. Latzer, S. W Schmitz (eds), *Carl Menger and the Evolution of Payments Systems: From Barter to Electronic Money*, Cheltenham: Edward Elgar, 133–58.

Shapley, L. (1976) 'Noncooperative general exchange', in: S. Lin, (ed.), *Theory of Measurement of Economic Externalities,* New York: Academic Press, 155–175.

Shapley, L. and Shubik, M. (1977), 'Trade using one commodity as a means of payment', *Journal of Political Economy*, 85: 937–68.

Shubik, M. (1973) 'Commodity money, oligopoly, credit and bankruptcy in a general equilibrium model', *Western Economic Journal*, 10: 24–38.

Shubik, M. (1990) 'A game theoretic approach to the theory of money and financial institutions', in B. M. Friedman and F. H. Hahn (eds), *Handbook of Monetary Economics*, Amsterdam: North Holland, 171–219.

Shubik, M. (1999) *The Theory of Money and Financial Institutions*, Cambridge: MIT Press.

Shubik, M. and Tsomocos, D. P. (2002) 'A strategic market game with seigniorage costs of fiat money', *Economic Theory,* 19: 187–201.

Shubik, M. and Wilson, C. (1977) 'The optimal bankruptcy rule in a trading economy using fiat money', *Zeitschrift für Nationalokonomie*, 37: 337–54.

Smith, A. (1776) 'The Wealth of Nations', The University of Chicago Press, 1981 edition.

Stigler, G. J. (1972) 'The law and economics of public policy: a plea to scholars', *Journal of Legal Studies*, 1:1–12.

Tsomocos, D. P. (1996) 'Essays on money, banking and general economic equilibrium', unpublished PhD thesis, Yale University.

Tsomocos, D. P. (2003a) 'Equilibrium analysis, banking, contagion, and financial fragility', Bank of England Working Paper No. 175, London.

Tsomocos, D. P. (2003b) 'Equilibrium analysis, banking and financial instability', *Journal of Mathematical Economics*, 39: 619–55.

Wicksell, J. (1935) 'Lectures in Political Economy', Vol. 2, London Routledge and Kegan Paul.

Wood, G. E. (1995) 'The quantity theory in the 1980s', in W. Eltis (ed.), *The Quantity Theory of Money: From Locke and Hume to Friedman*, Cheltenham: Edward Elgar.

Yeager, L. B. (1968) 'Essential properties of the medium of exchange', *Kyklos*, 21: 45–69.

Notes

1 The views expressed here are those of the authors and do not necessarily reflect those of the Bank of England, City University, LSE or the University of Oxford.

The authors are grateful to Peter Andrews, Willem Buiter, Charles Goodhart, Mervyn King, Andrew Liliko, Stefan W. Schmitz, Martin Shubik, seminar participants at the Austrian Academy of Sciences, the Bank of England, the European Central Bank and the 2003 International Conference of Game Theory, Mumbai, India. All remaining errors are ours.

2 Radford 1945.

3 McCallum (2003) emphasises that the choice of a *medium* of account is of great importance and that, once that choice has been made, the subsequent choice of a *unit* of account is of little significance. The example he gives is that the choice of gold or silver as a medium of account can be vital, but once that choice is made, the quantity of it which is the unit of account is unimportant. The debate over bimetallism in the US in the run-up to the Presidential Election of 1896 makes the point.

4 The complete text of this paper has recently been translated into English and is available in Latzer and Schmitz (2002).

5 See Latzer and Schmitz 2002.

6 The most fully developed modern statement of the 'transactions cost' theory of money can be found in the work of Karl Brunner and Allan Meltzer. The most detailed statement

of their view is given in Brunner and Meltzer (1971). Alchian (1977) also develops the argument and Yeager (1968) draws out the implications of it for the behaviour of the macroeconomy. The argument that money evolved as a result of private initiative of course leaves unexplained why all money is now state money. Some scholars (e.g. Goodhart (2000)) argue that state money is an inherently superior 'institutional symbol of trust' (to use Shubik's definition of money), while others (e.g. Glasser (1989)) point to the successful existence of private mints until they were extinguished by law and maintain the opposite. A formal model of an explanation for the dominance of state money can be found in Monnet (2002). An additional factor which may predispose a society to state rather than private fiat money is the comparative irrelevance of the solvency of the state. See also endnote 14.

7 Wicksell, 1935, Niehans, 1978 and McCallum, 1985.

8 See e.g. Drèze and Polemarchakis (2000), Dubey and Geanakoplos (1992, 2003), Grandmont (1983) and Lucas (1980).

9 Calculations of the rate of depreciation of various types of money can be found in Shubik and Tsomocos (2002).

10 A more extensive presentation and discussion can be found in Shubik and Tsomocos (2002).

11 For example, a Leontief production technology with coefficients γ_l, $\forall\, l \in L$, $Z_{L+1} = \min[\gamma_l x_l^g, \ldots, \gamma_L x_L^g,]$. If another technology were chosen, a unique equilibrium could be guaranteed by an exogenous institutional constraint, such as a price level target.

12 Government purchases are all used in the production process, i.e. government does not obtain utility from consumption.

13 Mathematically, minimisation of r is equivalent to maximise $-r$.

14 Without loss of generality, we consider the case of perfect competition (i.e. a continuum of agents). Thus, agents regard prices as fixed in the optimisation problems.

15 Note that the constraint that goods cannot be directly exchanged for goods is not imposed but naturally emerges as a consequence of our prior argument that trade with money dominates primitive barter.

16 Extensive discussion on various market structures and how these affect exchange is contained in Shubik (1999).

17 We implicitly assume that we are in equilibrium such that agents participate in all markets.

18 Why money is replaced by barter as a result of hyperinflation is summarised in the relationship given above. In hyperinflation, the nominal interest rate rises enormously. See Capie (1986) for a review of some such episodes.

19 For more on this, see Shubik and Tsomocos (2002) and Tsomocos (1996, 2003a, 2003b).

20 We do not imply that without such demand it would lose control of short rates. The argument in Goodhart (2000) that the central bank can control rates through its being able to sustain losses seems to us to be correct, despite objections of Selgin and White (2002).

21 See e.g. Fuhrer and Moore (1995).

22 See e.g. McCallum and Nelson (1999a).

23 The result is not novel; earlier work (e.g. Mills and Wood (1977)) found a relationship between the base and the price level over long runs of data in the United Kingdom.

24 See e.g. McCallum (1999).

25 See Wood (1995) for a discussion of the development of the quantity theory and the history of the 'water' metaphor.

26 Tsomocos 1996.

27 McCallum (2003) reaches this same conclusion by a different route. It is, however, clearly related to the above argument in that it focuses on a voluntary demand for base money on the part of banks – that is, of demand for it in the absence of reserve requirements. He, as an alternative, suggests that payment of interest in reserves could also achieve such a demand.

4 The evolving payments landscape and its implications for monetary policy

Sujit Chakravorti[1]

While the literature on the economics of exchange and the role of money is rather extensive, economists have devoted less time linking the evolution of the payment system and its potential implications for monetary policy.[2] A smooth functioning payment system is vital for effective implementation of monetary policy. The key questions that this chapter asks are: (1) How is the payment system evolving? (2) What are the economic forces driving the adoption of new payment instruments? (3) Would recent developments in the payment system limit the central bank from conducting monetary policy?

Large-value payment systems migrated to electronic systems in advanced economies many years ago and account for the bulk of the total value of payment transfers. However, large-value payments account for a small proportion of the total number of payment transactions.[3] On the other hand, the migration from paper payments to electronic substitutes has been significantly slower for small-value or retail transactions in many advanced economies. Today, more and more payments are made via payment cards that either debit a customer's transactions account at financial institutions or access a line of credit extended by a financial institution or a merchant. Transactional use of currency along with checks continues to decline in most advanced economies.

More recently, stored-value cards, usually plastic cards similar in size to credit cards, are able to mimic many characteristics of money. In this chapter, stored-value cards will be defined as cards where the monetary value is recorded on the card and online verification is not necessary for the transaction to be completed. While the adoption of general-purpose stored value cards has been slow, stored value has been successfully adopted for closed-loop systems such as university campuses, military bases, and transportation systems. Financial institutions along with merchants have started to consider expanding closed-loop payment mechanisms to a wider class of merchants.

This chapter will discuss recent trends in payment systems, study the economic forces underlying the adoption of new payment instruments, and explore the effects of these changes for monetary policy. Recent payment trends indicate a migration away from currency and checks towards electronic payment alternatives. This chapter will review the recent economics literature that builds upon the network economics literature to study the underlying factors driving the adoption

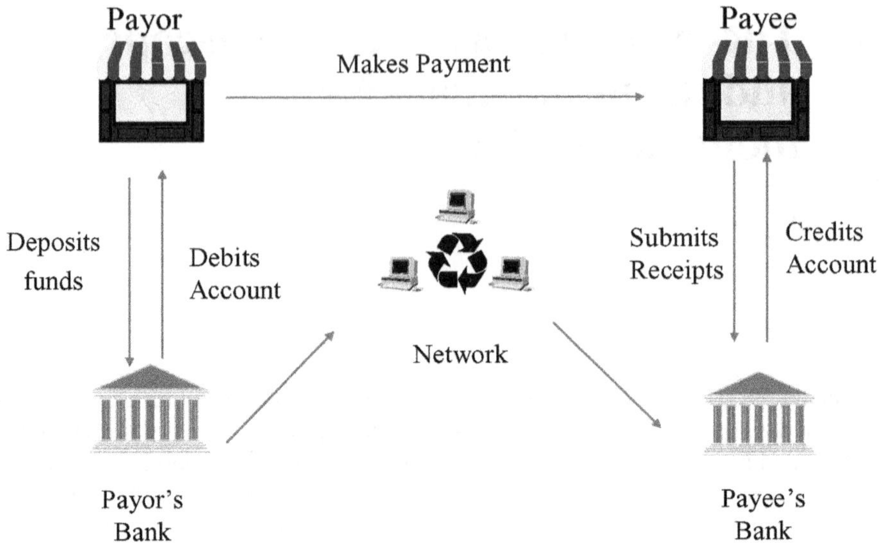

Figure 4.1 A payment transaction

of new payment instruments. While countries are at different stages in the migration to electronic alternatives, this shift has not affected the ability of central banks to conduct monetary policy. In this chapter, I argue that the migration to cash substitutes will not impact monetary policy unless final interbank settlement of most transactions occurs in non-central bank issued reserves. Furthermore, if the central bank maintains price stability and provides sufficient quantities of currency, the likelihood of its currency not being the generally accepted medium of exchange is negligible. In the next section, a description of payment systems and recent trends are discussed. In the third section, the economics of emerging payment instruments is discussed. In the fourth section, the costs and benefits of monetary exchange are investigated. In the fifth section, the impact of recent developments in payment systems and its implications for monetary policy are explored. Finally, the last section concludes the chapter.

Payment taxonomy and trends

A payment system encompasses a means for a transactor to initiate a payment; communications and computation infrastructure to carry each transactor's initiation message to its bank and also messages among banks to direct interbank payments to be made; contracts, laws, regulations, and industry standards to establish rights and responsibilities of transactors and their banks and to facilitate coordination among them, and so forth. In Figure 4.1, a non-cash payment and the corresponding settlement between a payor and payee are diagrammed for a payment transaction that accesses an account at a financial institution.[4] Payments are processed via

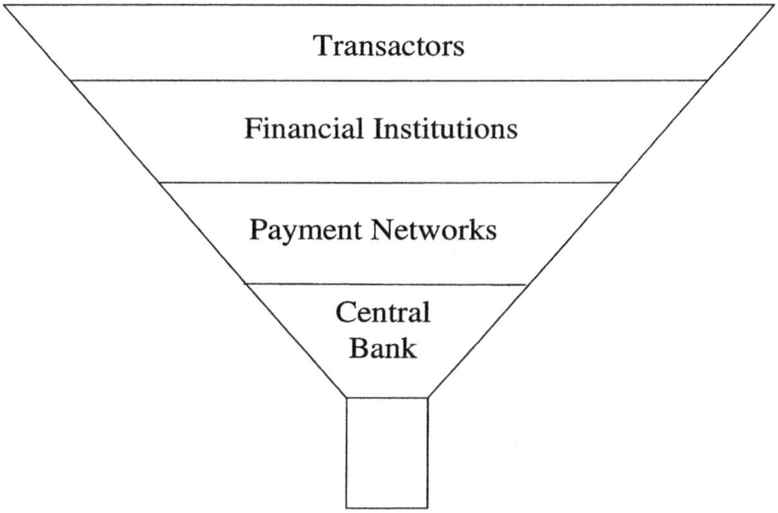

Figure 4.2 Flow of funds

financial institutions, whereby the payee's account is credited and the payor's account is debited the underlying value of the transaction. Payments that are cleared and settled electronically have extensive information networks that authorize payments and send messages to the appropriate institutions to make payment.

In most payment networks, final interbank settlement occurs with central bank reserves. Payment networks net transactions among financial institutions and settle a much smaller amount with reserves held at the central bank. In Figure 4.2, the flow of payments starting with transactors and eventually ending with the central bank issued reserves is diagrammed. For most payment transactions, payees and payors access relationships with financial institutions to initiate their payments. Financial institutions, primarily banks, process these transactions via payment networks. In most cases, the final settlement positions of financial institutions are settled via payment networks where final settlement occurs on the books of the central bank with reserves held by financial institutions. In most advanced economies, the reserves are transferred on systems operated by the central bank.

Payment transactions can be categorized into three groups: value-based, account-based, and credit-based.[5] Value-based transactions involve a transfer of monetary value at the time of exchange. Currency is an example of a value-based transaction. Payments made with prepaid cards where the monetary values are recorded on the cards are also examples of value-based transactions.[6] An account-based transaction is a transfer of monetary value from a payor's account at its financial institution to a payee's account at its financial institution. Checks and debit cards are examples of account-based transactions. Credit-based transactions involve a third-party extending credit to the purchaser of goods and services. Examples of credit-based transactions are credit and charge cards.

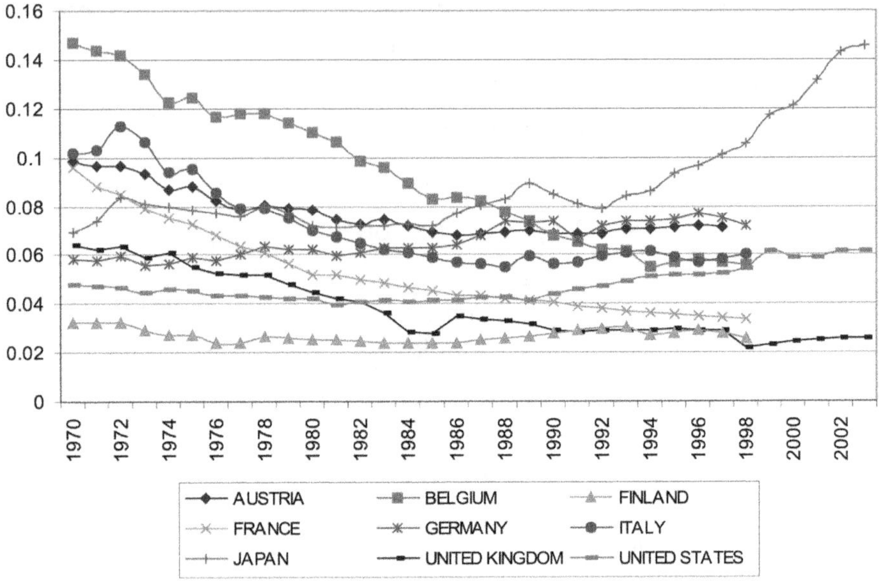

Figure 4.3 Currency holdings/GDP for 9 advanced economies

Various estimates suggest that the number of cash transactions is decreasing.[7] Cash usage differs across advanced economies. In Figure 4.3, the ratio of currency holdings to gross domestic product is plotted for the years between 1970 and 2002. With the exception of 3 countries – Japan, Germany, and the United States – this ratio has decreased. In the case of Japan, the cost of holding cash is extremely low because of an extremely low nominal rate of return on relatively safe assets and low crime rates. In the case of US dollars and the German deutsche marks, large quantities were held outside of the United States and Germany, respectively, and foreign holdings of these currencies may have been increasing during the time period considered. However, an increase in this ratio does not necessarily indicate that cash usage for transactional purposes has increased because this measure does not distinguish the store of value role of money from its medium of exchange role.

Another measure of cash usage across countries is the number of non-cash transactions. In Table 4.1, per capita annual usage of non-cash instruments for 2001 are presented. The low non-cash transaction totals for Italy (52) and Japan (29) suggest that residents of these countries are relatively heavy cash users. On the other hand, relatively high non-cash transaction totals for Finland (186), France (201), and the United States (270) suggest that residents of these countries are low cash users. However, comparing non-cash per-capita transactions across countries may be problematic given differences in the total number of payments made annually by residents of each country.

A recent survey in the United States indicates that cash usage is declining. A recent in-store payment usage survey conducted by the American Bankers

Table 4.1 2001 Non-cash per capita payments by instrument

	Checks	*Debit Cards*	*Credit Cards*	*Direct Credits*	*Direct Debits*	*Total*
Austria	1	13	4	66	34	118
Belgium	6	45	NAV	73	17	153
Finland	1	56	23	98	9	186
France	71	60	NAV	36	34	201
Germany	4	15	4	85	62	151
Italy	10	7	5	18	11	52
Japan	2	0	18	10	NAV	29
United Kingdom	43	45	26	32	36	185
United States	145	44	60	14	8	270

Source: Committee on Payment and Settlement Systems (various years) and European Central Bank (2004).

Association and Dove Consulting states that the number of cash payments is below card-based ones for in-store purchases (American Bankers Association, 2003). According to the study, the percentage of in-store cash purchases fell from 39 percent to 32 percent from 1999 to 2003, while credit and debit card payments increased from 43 percent to 52 percent. Credit card payments remained stable during the period but debit card payments increased by 10 percent. Check payments decreased by 3 percent during the same period. Prepaid cards only made up 2 percent of the in-store purchases. This evidence suggests that, while prepaid cards have started to enter the payments marketplace, consumers are primarily using debit cards as a substitute for in-store cash purchases.

Residents of countries represented in Figure 4.4 have either completely migrated or continue to migrate to account-based electronic payment alternatives from checks and other non-electronic account-based transactions. Check usage continues to decline in the industrialized countries.[8] In the three highest per capita check usage countries – France, United Kingdom, and United States – per capita check usage fell at least by 17 percent during the period of 1997 to 2002 (CPSS, various years). Credit and debit card payments account for a significant proportion of the decrease in the number of checks along with other electronic alternatives.

The economics of new payment instruments

In addition to the more mature payment instruments, several types of payment instruments are still trying to gain market penetration. For example, stored-value applications have achieved critical mass in certain closed environments such as transportation systems, universities, and military bases and ships. However, general-purpose stored value has yet to achieve significant market penetration in terms of the volume of payments vis-à-vis other more established payment instruments.

Chakravorti (2004) suggests three necessary conditions for the adoption of general-purpose stored value. First, stored value must provide superior benefits to all payment system participants for some types of transactions. Second, consumers and merchants should simultaneously benefit from stored value. Third, there should be low levels of fraud rates associated with the new payment instrument. These conditions also apply generally for the adoption of any emerging payment instrument.

Consumers, merchants, and payment providers must benefit from the migration to a different payment instrument for certain types of transactions.[9] For example, the introduction of credit cards allowed consumers to access short-term uncollateralized lines of credit at the point of sale, allowed merchants to sell goods and services to liquidity and credit-constrained customers while transferring the underlying credit risk to a third party, and allowed financial institutions to earn income from consumers and merchants. Several economic models find conditions under which credit cards improve social welfare. Chakravorti and Emmons (2003) argue that consumers benefit from consumption when they are liquidity constrained and merchants benefit from sales to liquidity-constrained individuals. Rochet and Tirole (2003) and others who extend their model construct models find conditions when non-cash alternatives improve consumer and merchant welfare.

Payment services can be viewed as network goods.[10] A good is defined as a network good when the benefits to an existing user increase with the number of new users.[11] The classic example used to illustrate a network good is a fax machine. The value of purchasing a fax machine is directly related to the number of fax machines that exist. Each additional fax machine increases the benefit of each existing owner of a fax machine. Furthermore, network goods must reach a minimum adoption threshold point. Economides and Himmelberg (1995) refer to this minimum as critical mass. They also find that the critical mass point does not depend on the market structure of the underlying good or service.

Aligning incentives for various payment system participants to establish critical mass has proven to be a very difficult task for issuers of new payment services. In addition to payment services being network goods, they are also two-sided. In the case of payments, payors would adopt a payment instrument if there is a sufficient number of payees who accept that payment form. In other words, payment network operators must be able to get both sides on board. Because there are two distinct end-users and their adoption decisions depend on each other's demand, the market for payment services is two-sided.[12] A good or service is said to be two-sided if the ratio of prices charged to each end-user affects the usage of that good or service by the other end-user and if the two end-users are unable to negotiate prices directly. Payment services such as credit and debit cards often charge different amounts to merchants and consumers.[13] Such pricing decisions are not unique to payment systems but exist in other products such as newspapers (readers and advertisers), Adobe Acrobat (readers and writers), and in bars where men are charged higher entrance fees than women to encourage a more gender-balanced patronage presumably preferred by both men and women.

A key economic factor driving adoption of new payment instruments is the level of security preventing fraudulent usage and which entity is liable for these transactions.[14] Often differences in the underlying regulatory structure will affect which entity is liable for transactions that do not settle resulting in different adoption rates for different payment instruments.[15] Reputation is often a key driver in the adoption of payment instruments because of payment providers, who may cover losses to protect their brand.

In addition to these general factors determining the adoption of new payment services, there are some key environmental factors for the adoption of stored-value payment instruments. Van Hove (2004) suggests certain key characteristics for the successful launch of stored value. Stored value is likely to penetrate markets and merchant locations that are cash intensive. In some Scandinavian countries, Van Hove states that debit cards are used for relatively small payments. He states that consumers and merchants do not pay fees for debit cards resulting in high usage of debit cards for relatively small transactions. Van Hove also suggests that some minimum comfort level with alternative electronic payment networks is necessary for stored value adoption. In other words, the relationship between debit card usage and stored value adoption is perhaps hump-shaped where a minimum level of penetration by electronic payment networks aids the adoption of stored-value products, but too much adoption of alternatives may impede it.

Stored-value products are generally successful when payments are time-critical (public transport), are associated with high cash handling costs (vending machines), or vandalism problems such as parking meters and pay phones. Van Hove argues that putting stored-value cards in the hands of consumers and arming merchants with acceptance terminals are not sufficient conditions to increase usage. While the implementation of general-purpose stored-value instruments have been tried in various countries, they have yet to gain critical mass in terms of the number of transactions although they have been extremely successful for niche applications.

A sufficient condition for the usage of stored value is the removal of alternative payment forms for certain types of purchases for which there are few close substitutes. For example, Octopus cards, the only payment form accepted for mass transportation systems in Hong Kong, has gained critical mass. The operators of the Octopus card have now expanded its use to non-transit purchases.[16] Some US transportation service providers have considered expanding their stored-value product to other merchants.

To mimic the micro payment niche for stored-value cards, some payment providers are aggregating small payments into larger payments before accessing a customer's account. Micro payments are generally costly to process for relatively small transaction sizes. In some countries, cell phone operators allow their customers to make relatively small purchases using their phone account. These are paid by the customer when the phone bill is paid.

Monetary exchange

Monetary economists agree that monetary exchange is generally welfare improving over barter exchange in most instances. Money can be defined as an asset that can be exchanged for goods repeatedly without third-party intermediation.

Money has taken many forms in history, ranging from precious metals to currency issued by the monetary authority. Today, currency issued by the central bank has become the generally accepted medium of exchange and serves as the unit of account in most countries. In addition to currency, the central bank can also create reserves that can be used to offset monetary obligations among financial institutions. The bulk of the value of payments in advanced countries is settled with central bank reserves. Thus, central bank reserves are the medium of exchange for interbank transfers.

While there are clear and documented benefits of monetary exchange, recent advances in electronic trading systems, especially via the Internet, may increase the efficiency of barter for certain types of transactions.[17] Capie, Tsomocos, and Wood (chapter 3) consider environmental factors where electronic barter may dominate monetary exchange. They find that fiat money dominates barter except when transaction costs and the prevailing interest rate is zero. In their model, the interest rate is a function of the cost to replace depreciated fiat money. In other words, the interest rate captures the cost of replacing depreciating currency and the combined cost of gathering and processing information for each transaction. The model being considered has a fixed exogenous money supply and maintains that supply at a cost r.

An interesting extension of their model would be to consider alternative media of exchange. Examples of clubs where goods are exchanged for an internal currency have existed in the United States during the Great Depression and more recently in Argentina during the market downturns.[18] While neither of these currencies circulated outside of these small circles, they did allow for exchange.

Another interesting extension of their model would be to set up a clearinghouse that settles in fiat money by netting due tos and due froms of each agent. Therefore, the necessary money holdings would be reduced. In fact, large-value settlement systems settle with a small proportion of the total gross transaction size. If agents are sellers and buyers, the clearinghouse would need fewer funds to settle. In such a model, the means of payment would change but the medium of final settlement would remain the same.

Capie, Tsomocos, and Wood present a model that suggests scenarios where barter may not be dominated by monetary exchange. Remote transactions where a majority of the transactions are on-us might result in benefits to barter. There have been companies set up to exchange excess capacity in exchange for excess capacity in other goods. Unfortunately, these clearinghouses generally did not survive. A more likely alternative to central-bank-issued currency is privately issued currency. Perhaps, frequent flyer miles can be interpreted as a medium of exchange with a unit of account function that can be used to purchase goods and services. However, in most cases, frequent flyer miles are not transferable, individual accounts cannot be combined, miles cannot be usually sold, and can be used only to purchase a small set of goods and services. Future research should explore conditions where both privately issued and central-bank-issued currency circulate side-by-side, especially when the monetary authority provides sufficient currency and keeps prices stable.[19]

Monetary policy

In this section, we discuss the impact of an alternative medium of exchange on the ability of the central bank to conduct monetary policy. The emergence of alternative media of exchange is directly influenced by the central bank's actions. While the payment system continues to evolve, the unit of account of the final settlement medium has remained constant. As discussed previously, while cash outstanding has not dropped dramatically in most industrialized countries, survey evidence suggests that cash transactions are decreasing. Furthermore, many small-value transactions are being aggregated into medium-sized payments. While there has been a migration away from currency to other payment instruments such as debit and credit cards, the volume of interbank payments has not decreased. From 1987 to 2003, the value of interbank payments (Fedwire fund transfers and CHIPS payments, the two US interbank payment networks) increased by 80 percent in real terms.

Freedman (2000) and Goodhart (2000) question Friedman's (1999) claim that the central bank would lose its ability to conduct monetary policy in a world where central banks do not issue and control the medium of exchange. Both Freedman and Goodhart discuss alternative monetary policy tools. Schmitz (chapter 5 in this volume) stresses that the central bank's role as provider of the medium of final settlement is not likely to be challenged in the near future. Given recent developments in the payment system, central banks in advanced economies are not likely to lose their monopoly status as providers of the ultimate settlement medium: central bank reserves.

There are episodes throughout history where dual currencies have circulated side-by-side. Countries that have experienced high inflation rates have witnessed foreign currencies that have circulated. However, central banks can prevent such currencies from circulating by achieving price stability and supplying sufficient currency for circulation. Kroszner (2003) argues that advancements in electronic payment systems and access to alternative fiat currencies provide pressures on domestic central banks to adhere to policies of price stability.

As long as ultimate settlement occurs in good funds denominated in the domestic currency, shifts in payment media will not impair the central bank from conducting monetary policy. However, if the central bank does not adequately maintain price stability or provide sufficient currency, other media of exchange with different units of account may circulate simultaneously.

Conclusions

Advancements in payment technologies continue to improve the efficiency of the payment system and financial markets in general. First, there is a trend towards more electronic payment instruments in the advanced economies. While the ratio of currency holdings to GDP has not decreased in all of the advanced economies, surveys indicate that currency usage for transactional purposes is decreasing. Second, there is a trend by some cash-intensive service providers to issue closed-loop stored-value instruments. While general-purpose stored-value cards are in circulation in some countries, their usage is still rather limited. However, the unit of account continues to be the fiat money issued by the central bank.

Future research should consider under what conditions the central bank issued money would be dominated by alternative currencies. From history, we have learned that if the central bank achieves price stability and supplies sufficient currency, the potential emergence of non-government issued, generally accepted, medium of exchange is negligible.

References

American Bankers Association (2003) 'Consumers Now Favor Credit and Debit over Cash and Checks as Payment for In-Store Purchases', Press Release, December 16.

Andreeff, A., Binmoeller, L. C., Boboch, E. M., Cerda, O., Chakravorti, S., Ciesielski, T. and Green, E. (2001) 'Electronic Bill Presentment and Payment — Is It Just a Click Away?' *Federal Reserve Bank of Chicago Economic Perspectives* (fourth quarter): 2–16.

Armstrong, M. (2004) 'Competition in Two-sided Markets', *Mimeo.*

Berger, A. N., Hancock, D. and Marquardt, J. C. (1996) 'A Framework for Analyzing Efficiency, Risks, Costs, and Innovations in the Payments System,' *Journal of Money, Credit, and Banking*, 28: 696–732.

Chakravorti, S. (1997) 'How Do We Pay?' *Federal Reserve Bank of Dallas Financial Industry Issues* (first quarter).

Chakravorti, S. (2004) 'Why Has Stored Value Not Caught On?', *Journal of Financial Transformation*, 12: 39–48.

Chakravorti, S. and Davis, E. (2004) 'An Electronic Supply Chain: Will Payments Follow?' *Federal Reserve Bank of Chicago Fed Letter* (September).

Chakrovorti, S. and Emmons, W. R. (2003) 'Who pays for credit cards?' *Journal of Consumer Affairs*, 37: 208–230.

Chakravorti, S. and Roson, R. (2004) 'Platform Competition in Two-Sided Markets: The Case of Payment Networks', Federal Reserve Bank of Chicago Working Paper WP-2004–09.

Colacelli, M. and Blackburn, D. (2004) 'Secondary Currency in Circulation: An Empirical Analysis', mimeo Harvard University.

Committee on Payment and Settlement Systems (CPSS) (1997), *Real-Time Gross Settlement Systems,* Bank for International Settlements: Basle.

Committee on Payment and Settlement Systems (CPSS) (various years), *Statistics on Payment and Settlement Systems in Selected Countries,* Bank for International Settlements: Basle.

Economides, N. (1996) 'The Economics of Networks', *International Journal of Industrial Organization,* 14: 673–99.

Economides, N. and Himmelberg, C. (1995) 'Critical Mass and Network Evolution in Telecommunications', in G. Brock (ed.), *Toward a Competitive Telecommunications Industry: Selected Papers from the 1994 Telecommunications Policy Research Conference*, Mahwah, NJ: Lawrence Erlbaum, 47–66.

European Central Bank (2004) *Payment and Securities and Settlement Systems in the European Union,* Frankfurt/Main: ECB.

Farrell, J. and Soloner, G. (1986) 'Installed Base and Compatibility: Innovation, Product Preannouncements, and Predation', *American Economic Review,* 76: 940–55.

Freedman, C. (2000) 'Monetary Policy Implementation: Past Present and Future – Will the Advent of Electronic Money Lead to the Demise of Central Banking?' *International Finance,* 3: 211–27.

Friedman, B. M. (1999) 'The Future of Monetary Policy: The Central Bank as an Army with Only a Signal Corps?' *International Finance,* 2: 321–38.

Goodhart, C. A. E. (2000) 'Can Central Banking Survive the IT Revolution?' *International Finance,* 3: 189–209.

Guthrie, G. and Wright, J. (2003) 'Competing Payment Schemes', Working Paper No. 0311, Department of Economics, National University of Singapore.

Hancock, D. and Humphrey D. B. (1998) 'Payment Transactions, Instruments, and Systems: A Survey', *Journal of Banking and Finance,* 21: 1573–624.

Katz, M. L. and Shapiro, C. (1985) 'Network Externalities, Competition and Compatibility', *American Economic Review,* 75: 424–44.

Kroszner, R. S. (2003) 'Currency Competition in the Digital Age', in D. Altig and B. D. Smith (eds) *Evolution and Procedures in Central Banking,* New York: Cambridge University Press, 275–99.

McAndrews, J. J. (1997) 'Network Issues and Payment Systems', *Federal Reserve Bank of Philadelphia Business Review* (November/December): 15–25.

Osterberg, W. P. and Thomson, J. B. (1998) 'Network Externalities: The Catch-22 of Retail Payments Innovations', *Federal Reserve Bank of Cleveland Economic Commentary* (February).

Poon, S. and Chau, P. Y. K. (2001) 'Octopus: The Growing e-Payment System in Hong Kong', *Electronic Markets*, 11: 97–106.

Roberds, W. (1998) 'The Impact of Fraud on New Methods of Retail Payment', *Federal Reserve Bank of Atlanta Economic Review* (first quarter): 42–52.

Rochet, J. C. and Tirole, J. (2003) 'Platform Competition in Two-Sided Markets', *Journal of European Economic Association*, 1: 990–1029.

Schmitz, S. W. (2002) 'The Institutional Character of Electronic Money Schemes: Redeemability and the Unit of Account', in M. Latzer and S. W. Schmitz (eds) (2002), *Carl Menger and the Evolution of Payment Systems: From Barter to Electronic Money,* Cheltenham: Edward Elgar, 159–83.

Van Hove, L. (2004) 'Electronic Purses in Euroland: Why do Penetration and Usage Rates Differ?' *SUERF Studies* 4, Vienna: The European Money and Finance Forum.

Notes

1 I thank Victor Lubasi for excellent research assistance. The views expressed are those of the authors and do not represent the views of the Federal Reserve Bank of Chicago or the Federal Reserve System. All remaining errors are my own.

2 Berger, Hancock, and Marquardt (1996) provide a framework to study payment systems and survey several papers of a special issue. Hancock and Humphrey (1998) survey the payments literature and suggest future areas of research.

3 For a summary and statistics of large-value settlement systems, see Committee on Payment and Settlement Systems (1997) and Committee on Payment and Settlement Systems (various years). For descriptions of the US large-value systems, see White (chapter 1 in this volume).

4 The diagram would change slightly for payments that access a credit line instead of good funds at a financial institution. Instead of depositing funds, the payor would establish a line of credit with a financial institution that would be accessed when a payment is made. At some later date, the payor would pay a portion or the full amount of the credit line.

5 For more discussion on the taxonomy of payment instruments, see Chakravorti (1997).

6 Often prepaid cards do not record the monetary value on the card but deduct the monetary value from an account located somewhere else. These types of transactions would be categorized as account-based transactions.

7 The number of cash transactions is difficult to measure because individual transactions are difficult to track unlike check and card-based payments. As a result, cash is an attractive payment instrument for illegal transactions and tax avoidance.

8 However, there are certain payment segments such as business-to-business and consumer bill payments where checks remain the preferred payment instrument in the United States (Andreff *et al.*, 2001 and Chakravorti and Davis, 2004). However, check usage is declining in these payment segments as well.

9 The case of forced adoption is not being considered here. For example, the success of coin substitution over paper bills is critically dependent on the removal of the paper bills by the monetary authority.

10 For excellent summaries on why payment services are network goods, see McAndrews (1997) and Osterberg and Thomson (1998).

11 For more on network goods, see Economides (1996), Farrell and Soloner (1986), and Katz and Shapiro (1985).

12 For more on two-sided markets, see Armstrong (2004) and Rochet and Tirole (2003).

13 Chakravorti and Roson (2004), Guthrie and Wright (2004), and Rochet and Tirole (2003) build theoretical models to study two-sided markets with applications to payments markets.

14 For a discussion on payments fraud, see Roberds (1998).

15 For example, liability limits on credit cards may have been a critical factor in their dominant market share of internet payments.

16 For a description of Octopus, see Poon and Chau (2001).

17 Even in monetized economies, there are often transactions such as carpooling that are bartered.

18 For more on secondary currency circulation, see Colacelli and Blackburn (2004).

19 Schmitz (2002) considers these issues.

5 eMoney and monetary policy: the role of the inter-eMoney-institution market for settlement media and the unit of account

A critical assessment of the literature

Stefan W. Schmitz[1]

In Schmitz (2002b) I present the arguments for the likely evolution of the institutional structure of electronic money schemes and the implications for the monopoly of the central bank (CB) to provide the generally accepted medium of exchange and the unit of account. In section 1, I briefly summarise the methodological approach, the arguments and the results on eMoney, redeemability, the unit of account and monetary policy.

In this paper I focus on the discussion of alternative models and opposing views of the ongoing institutional change in the economy-wide payments system with particular attention to electronic money. I argue that these alternatives are incomplete and inconsistent, thus, strengthening the conclusions in Schmitz (2002b) by rejecting the alternatives. The analysis focuses on the role of the inter-eMoney-institution market for settlement media (henceforth 'money market'), the existence of a generally accepted medium of exchange and its function as the unit of account.

This paper is structured along the following lines: In the first section I present a short summary of the appropriate methodological approach to the analysis of the institutional structure of eMoney-schemes and the ensuing results as derived in Schmitz (2002a, b). In the second one I classify the vast literature on eMoney and a world without money according to common approaches to the generally accepted medium of exchange and the unit of account and provide a critical assessment of each class of models in turn. The third summarises the results and concludes the paper.

eMoney redeemability, the unit of account and monetary policy

In their introduction Schmitz and Wood demonstrated that institutional change in the payments system is driven by the politico-economic interaction of central banks and commercial banks (and final customers). New technologies have an indirect impact as they can change incentives and costs underlying particular institutional arrangements in payment systems.[2] The following section, therefore, focuses on the impact of the evolution of electronic money on the incentives and costs concerning core characteristics of the institutional structure of payment systems, the choice of the generally accepted medium of exchange and the unit of account.

The evolution of payments systems is subject to ongoing institutional change, for instance, the emergence of coinage, transferable deposits and banknotes, fiat money and credit card systems. The diffusion of electronic money schemes is a further instance of institutional change. The method of institutional analysis is the appropriate concept to investigate the likely consequences of the diffusion of eMoney. The evolution of the retail payment system is path dependent, as the existence of a generally accepted medium of exchange and a uniform unit of account can be interpreted as information networks that exhibit network effects.[3] The generally accepted medium of exchange is the most liquid good in the economy, the good with the highest marketability and, thus, involves the lowest spread. Its incidental function is the unit of account function, because it is the good that embodies the unit of account. It also serves as the means of final settlement, because it is the only medium that is not a direct or indirect claim on future resources and that ensures settlement finality in the interbank payment system (in an economic sense rather than a legal sense).

In the current state of payments systems a dominant medium of exchange prevails in the respective market where it also entails the function of the uniform unit of account. The analysis of the effects of the diffusion of eMoney-schemes has (i) to derive the necessary and sufficient conditions for a transition from one generally accepted medium of exchange and the associated unit of account to another and (ii) the effects of the diffusion of new technologies on the evolution of payments systems with respect to these conditions. That is, will the diffusion of eMoney lead to a sufficient reduction in the marginal costs of adopting a potentially emerging new generally accepted medium of exchange individually?[4] How does the payments system operate in the phase of transition form one generally accepted medium of exchange to another? Is the parallel use of multiple units of account efficient and sustainable?

These questions gained increased attention due to the emergence of new technology: (i) The diffusion of the Internet could increase the costs of enforcement of national legislation. Electronic money could be issued in foreign jurisdictions, where national legal restrictions on the issue of banknotes do not apply and cannot be enforced. Electronic money can be a close substitute for banknotes and coins; (ii) The diffusion of Internet usage and advances in encryption technology reduce the costs of issuance and distribution of electronic money relative to the issuance and distribution of physical banknotes and coins; (iii) The transaction costs associated with the parallel use of multiple units of account and the exchange of real assets decrease. Relative prices of different units of account, goods and real assets in different units of account could be calculated (almost) instantaneously at low marginal costs due to continuous trading of units of account, goods and real assets, the real-time availability of price information and the low costs of computer power to conduct the necessary calculations. Furthermore, the units of account, the goods, and the real assets can be exchanged at low marginal costs due to continuous access to the online markets, where trading takes place instantaneously.[5]

An appropriate methodology to address the individual decisions at the margin – that is, the individual choice of the medium of exchange and the unit of account in a given institutional arrangement – is based on New Institutional Economics, for example, methodological individualism, transaction and information costs and an explicit analysis of the process of transition between equilibria. In Schmitz (2002a) I argued that current neoclassical models of money based on comparative static analysis are inappropriate to analyse institutional change in the payments system, as they do not account for the dynamics of transition between equilibria.[6]

Schmitz (2002b) shows that the parallel use of multiple units of account is not desirable, and in the case of fiat-type currencies, is not feasible.[7] The argument does not provide a rationale for legal barriers against potential currency competition.[8] I demonstrate that users and issuers face strong strategic incentives not to opt for an alternative unit of account in eMoney schemes under current inflation rates. On the one hand, this result is due to network effects, sunk costs,[9] information costs and switching costs which are characteristic of retail payment systems and the choice of the unit of account.[10] On the other hand, the argument rests on the findings regarding the underlying mechanism of price formation: In the case of a price matching strategy, the existence and sufficient liquidity of markets denominated in the dominant unit of account are necessary preconditions for eMoney-schemes – denominated in alternative units of account – to be able to quote prices in the alternative unit of account. Trading on markets denominated in the alternative unit of accounts involves higher prices due to a bid-ask spread in exchange between the dominant unit of account and alternative ones.[11] In the case of a price discovery strategy, the market denominated in the eMoney unit of account is less liquid relative to the one denominated in the dominant unit of account. Thus, the intensity of competition and the information content of prices are lower, the spread between bid and ask prices is higher. The institutional analysis of eMoney and monetary policy analyses the choice of unit of account in an environment of a dominant unit of account. At moderate levels of inflation, participants in the payments system have no incentive to switch from the dominant unit of account to an emerging alternative in the relevant market. Consequently, the most likely institutional structure of emerging eMoney schemes includes denomination in the dominant unit of account and redeemability, which is argued to be a necessary but not sufficient precondition for the sustainable exchange of eMonies for CB money at par.

The role of national currencies as units of account will not be diminished by the diffusion of eMoney at current moderate levels of inflation. As central banks hold on to the monopoly of the supply of the generally accepted medium of exchange at zero marginal cost, they retain control of its supply and its purchasing power, in principle.[12] The balance sheet of central banks will shorten relative to a world without eMoney, which is mainly a positive sign as institutional change in the payments system (e.g. electronification of retail payments systems, tiering in wholesale payment systems) can increase its efficiency – which implies that monetary policy becomes rather more than less effective.[13] Moreover, central banks have proven to cope well with similar changes in the past (e.g. diffusion of credit and debit cards,[14] elimination of reserve requirements in Australia, Canada, New Zealand, Sweden, United Kingdom[15]). In an economy in which CB money serves as the generally accepted medium of exchange and the unit of account, the diffusion of electronic money could have an impact on monetary policy. The nature and predictability of the relationship between the instruments of monetary policy (i.e. US federal funds rate, ECB main refinancing operations minimum bid rate), aggregate spending and the objectives of monetary policy could change.

The inconsistency and incompleteness of alternative models of eMoney and a world without money

In this section I provide a critical assessment of models of monetary policy and central banking in economies without CB money. I classify the models according to their approach to the institutional structure of the monetary system.[16] In the first part of this section I present models that assume the proliferation of alternative media of exchange and units of account that replace CB money. In the second part I review models that focus on arguments that the residual demand for CB money remains positive. In the third part I analyse models that propose payments systems with a publicly sanctioned unit of account but without a generally accepted medium of exchange, in which net balances are either settled by privately issued fiat-type electronic monies or the transfer of wealth. In the discussion I focus on the (often) implicit institutional structure of the monetary systems presented; in particular on the models of the market for media of final settlement between eMoney institutions, the existence of a generally accepted medium of exchange and a unit of account. I emphasise the relationship between the function of money as the generally accepted medium of exchange and its function as the unit of account.

Models assuming the proliferation of other media of exchange and units of account

Despite the large number of papers addressing the issue of electronic money and monetary policy dating prior to the year 1999, the current debate was strongly influenced by Friedman (1999, 2000).[17] He does not doubt that the CB retains its monopoly to influence the level of reserves in the economy denominated in CB money but he questions the relevance of that monopoly over the next quarter century. It is challenged by a potential reduction of the demand for CB reserves due to privately operated retail payment systems – namely private (electronic) monies which are not redeemable in CB reserves. Examples include issuers like the MTA (Metropolitan Transport Authority) and telephone service providers. Furthermore, currency is supposed to be of little relevance to transactions in the economy and is viewed as largely endogenous as the central bank accommodates the public's demand for currency.

He conjectures that, at the same time, institutional change in financial markets – largely driven by innovations in information and communication technology (ICT) pose a threat to the credit channel of the monetary transmission mechanism. Non-bank financial intermediaries play an increasingly important role in the provision of credit to the real sector without being subject to reserve requirements. Disintermediation and securitisation enable the real economy to allocate savings and investment on financial markets directly. 'From the perspective of the "credit view", therefore, the central bank monopoly over the supply of reserves is irrelevant' (Friedman 1999, 332).

Banks hold reserves at the central bank because CB money is the only means of payment that provides settlement finality – it is the medium of final settlement. Private competition might challenge that role of CB reserves too, as private clearinghouses can provide net settlement in terms of their own liabilities. Currently, these liabilities are denominated and redeemable in CB money such that the clearinghouse needs to hold reserves on the books of the central bank. In addition, all balances not netted out during the day continue to be settled in CB money so that the system remains ultimately anchored in CB money. If the balances on the clearinghouse's books gain settlement finality, the demand for CB reserves derived from interbank settlement might be reduced to an extent that renders CB policy instruments ineffective.

Friedman (2000) clarifies the argument in the light of critique put forward by Goodhart (2000), Freedman (2000) and Woodford (2000). Extreme events such as the elimination of demand for CB money (reserves and/or cash), he argues, are not necessary preconditions for the loss of efficacy of traditional monetary policy instruments. Monetary policy actions still affect the level of economic activity and asset prices in those parts of the economy that are directly or indirectly based on CB money. He questions, however, that these economic consequences are related in any close manner to the general price level, to aggregate output fluctuations and asset prices in the entire economy, at the margin. The monetary policy decisions of the central bank will fail to move market rates, as the market might no longer attribute the central bank the power to move the real interest rate for the entire economy at its own discretion without large market interventions. Already the volume of CB market intervention is relatively low compared to total turnover in money markets and, as the balance sheets of central banks will shrink, they will have to rely on 'Open Mouth Operations even more.

Friedman rests his discussion of the efficacy of monetary policy on the volume of CB operations in money markets. The relatively small volume of OMOs compared to daily turnover is irrelevant, as price formation works at the margin and the central bank is in the unique position to manipulate the supply at the margin at zero marginal cost.[18] Comparing the small size of OMOs and the structural liquidity deficit to turnover in interbank markets is therefore misleading, as it relates the continuous reallocation of aggregate reserves among market participants to discretionary and exogenous changes in aggregate reserves.

DISCUSSION

Although the effects of advances in ICT on the institutional foundations of financial markets and the financial system are uncertain and to some extent necessarily speculative, there are analytical instruments available to investigate the likelihood, the preconditions and the likely effects of such change.[19] Especially, the evolution of private and interbank payment systems would deserve a more detailed analysis of the institutional arrangements involved and their consequences for the role of CB money as the unit of account, and the medium of final settlement. Neither in the case of privately issued fiat-type monies and the parallel use of multiple units of account, nor in the case of privately operated wholesale payments system, does Friedman provide any details of the institutional structure of the model or of the transition between the current institutional arrangements and the envisaged monetary and financial future.[20] The different strands of reasoning in Friedman (1999) show a common structure: ongoing trends that imply the reduction of the ratio of CB money to aggregate spending – through privately operated clearing mechanisms (e.g. CHIPS) or innovations in the area of retail payment systems (credit, debit and smart cards) – are extrapolated further to the mathematical limit. The amount of CB money necessary to operate wholesale and retail payment systems finally reaches zero. Friedman implicitly assumes that the behaviour of the monetary system while approaching the limit, and once it has reached the limit, exhibits structural continuity, in principle.[21] Even though CB money is expected to become irrelevant in the limit, the monetary system does not exhibit any signs of instability or structural changes. It remains unclear whether another medium of exchange will assume the functions of the generally accepted medium of exchange and the unit of account function. The consequences for the real economy and the monetary system of neither option are considered. Structural effects of an economy approaching the limit and finally reaching it, are neither explicitly nor implicitly discussed.

Both the institutional structure of interbank settlement systems and of retail payment systems have changed considerably over the past decades due to financial innovation.[22] The economy-wide payments system has had to adapt to the interdependent trends of globalisation, liberalisation, advances in ICT and increasing financial sophistication. Friedman fails to present convincing arguments and evidence that these processes towards the limit have reduced the efficacy of monetary policy so far. Furthermore, he presents no detailed argument for the assertion that the link between monetary policy instruments and aggregate spending will loosen at the margin. The argument rests upon the claim that the market might no longer attribute the central bank the power to move the real market rate for the entire economy at its own discretion without large market interventions. Friedman claims that extreme events – such as the elimination of demand for CB money – are a sufficient but not a necessary condition for the loss of efficacy of monetary policy, but he fails to demonstrate why the market should discontinue to act upon the announcements of the central bank as long as it retains the monopoly to supply the generally accepted medium of exchange and the unit of account at zero marginal costs. He does not expand on the preconditions under which the central bank loses its monopoly before the limit is reached, nor does he discuss the institutional structure of the monetary system in the limit. If the demand for CB money remains positive in some parts of the economy, the question arises, which generally accepted medium of exchange and unit(s) of account prevail in the other parts of the economy and how they are related to CB money?

A number of papers contest the argument that the demand for CB money would eventually be eliminated by the diffusion of electronic money. Goodhart (2000), Freedman (2000) and Woodford (2000) are explicit responses to Friedman's gloomy forecast.

Models focusing on the evolution of the demand for central bank money

Goodhart (2000) focuses on the question whether the diffusion of ICT will completely eliminate the demand for currency and renders the central bank impotent in its pursuit of monetary policy. He argues that currency has two distinct advantages over electronic money: (i) Notes and coins offer anonymity to both the payer and the payee. Advocates of electronic money occasionally emphasise that the technology to ensure anonymity for the payer and the payee by strong encryption is also available.[23] But Goodhart points out that confidence in anonymity is a more complex issue and that the protection of personal data requires the decisive political will and a detailed legal framework.[24] Currency continues to have a comparative advantage relative to electronic money as individuals favour currency whenever they want to maintain their anonymity; (ii) Currency is legal tender in many countries so that it cannot be refused as a means of payment in cases where the underlying contract does not explicitly specify another form of payment. In addition to a first mover advantage, anonymity and legal tender legislation result in currency having a comparative advantage vis-à-vis electronic money. Therefore, its demand remains positive despite the diffusion of electronic money. Capie and Wood (2001) generalise the argument with respect to anonymity by pointing out that currency is the most cost effective means of payment with respect to transaction costs (i.e. information costs). Krüger (1999) provides anecdotal support from foreign exchange wholesale markets for the thesis, that even if marginal transaction costs are already very low due to advanced ICT, the transaction costs can be reduced even further by the use of a generally accepted medium of exchange.

Capie, Tsomocos and Wood (chapter 3 in this volume) model an economy in which the role of fiat money as medium of exchange is contested by advances in ICT that reduce the costs of barter. The costs of operating the monetary system are fixed costs given the quantity of money, which depends on the number of trades only indirectly via individual money demand. The costs of barter consist of transaction costs of gathering and processing information, which are incurred in each transaction by each individual. Although technological progress is likely to reduce the transaction costs of barter, they expect that it might as well raise the number of commodities and hence the number of markets and transactions. Thus, the total costs of barter – aggregated across markets and transactions – do not necessarily fall and might even increase. It should be added that technological progress might also reduce the operational costs of the monetary system, that is, the diffusion of electronic means of payment could reduce the tear and wear of cash as well as the costs of cash logistics and, thus, the costs of operating the monetary system. They conclude that the transaction costs associated with electronic barter are likely to remain so high that the demand for fiat money will not vanish. The results hold for any fiat money (e.g. foreign currency) and not just for the CB money of the national central bank. Implicitly they assume that the demand for CB money will be sufficient to maintain its role as generally accepted medium of exchange and as the unit of account.

Berentsen (1998) suggests that, due to the low transaction costs associated with electronic money, the demand for currency eventually vanishes. But as electronic money is predominantly used in small-value payments, and due to the low costs of converting interest bearing deposit balances into electronic money holdings, the stock of electronic money is expected to be small. Most liquid assets would be held as demand deposits. Even in the absence of binding reserve requirements banks would hold settlement balances to settle daily net positions in the interbank payment system. Hence, the demand for CB money would remain positive and the central bank would maintain its monopoly to provide the generally accepted medium of exchange at zero marginal costs. Berentsen implicitly assumes that electronic money is denominated in the dominant unit of account of CB money, which also remains the generally accepted medium of exchange and the medium of final settlement in the interbank payment system. However, he does not consider the case in which electronic money were denominated in a unit of account different from the dominant one in the respective market. He does not provide any arguments for the continuing role of CB money as the generally accepted medium of exchange and unit of account. Furthermore, he fails to establish a link between electronic money, the generally accepted medium of exchange and the unit of account. The institutional set-up he has in mind seems to involve the redeemability of electronic money into CB money and, thus, its denomination in the unit of account. Finally, the interbank payment system is based on CB money as the banks' settlement demand for CB reserves is expected to remain positive. Neither of the two interdependent crucial implicit postulations is supported by analytical arguments. In sum, the central bank is basically assumed rather than demonstrated to maintain its monopoly position in the provision of the generally accepted medium of exchange and the unit of account at zero marginal costs. Consequently, there is no threat to the implementation of monetary policy by assumption.

Freedman (2000) distinguishes between stored-value cards (SVCs) and network money in his definition of electronic money. He emphasises that a number of means of payment are currently in use and that SVCs should simply be interpreted as an additional choice. Credit and debit cards have already reached a considerable market share in medium sized transactions. SVCs offer less protection from loss and theft than other means of payment, so that they will be used for low-value payments. Even in the unlikely event that they fully substitute for currency the entire payment system continues to be based on CB money, as final settlement takes place on the books of the central bank. The crucial issue of how the link between SVCs and CB money is institutionally designed is not elaborated any further. One can only assume that SVCs are denominated in the dominant unit of account and that redeemability in CB money is the rule. Consequently, CB money remains the generally accepted medium of exchange and the unit of account. The balance sheet of central bank shortens, but current monetary policy instruments (i.e. announced target level for the main operating target in combination with OMOs and standing facilities) ensure the efficacy of monetary policy implementation.

Freedman (2000) regards the settlement of interbank balances by either private clearinghouses or the transfer of low risk assets (i.e. treasury bills) as the more serious threat to the efficacy of monetary policy. But even in these cases, he regards CB money as superior medium of final settlement and expects the demand to remain positive. The major drawbacks of private clearinghouses are supposed to be (i) potential bankruptcy of the clearing-house,[25] (ii) an informational disadvantage of private clearinghouses vis-à-vis a central bank which combines prudential supervision with the operation of the large value interbank payment system, and (iii) the banks' reluctance to see a competitor gaining a competitive advantage by resuming the role as a clearinghouse. However, the disadvantages of private clearinghouses can be overcome in principle, as the informational disadvantages disappear, if the supervision of members and the operation of the wholesale payment system are combined.[26] Freedman does not demonstrate that the institutional structure and the accompanying governance mechanisms cannot be adapted to provide a level playing field for the participants and the operator of a private clearinghouse. The model indicates that an entity different from the privately operated clearinghouse seems to maintain a monopoly to issue the generally accepted medium of exchange. Hence, Freedman's model of private clearing and settlement systems presupposes the continuing role of CB money as the medium of final settlement and the unit of account. In this case the model collapses to one where even private clearinghouses would not at all endanger the position of the note-issuing authority, as the system remains firmly rooted on the generally accepted medium of exchange (CB money). However, participants of the payment system would economise on their holding costs of medium of final settlement by netting arrangements.[27]

But Freedman takes his thought experiment a step further – banks could transfer low risk assets to settle imbalances rather than reserves at the central bank or at private clearinghouses. He concludes that (i) the lack of a lender of last resort (LLR), (ii) holding costs of low risk assets, and (iii) declining volumes of outstanding government debt present the major drawbacks of this alternative system. It remains unclear whether there is a generally accepted medium of exchange, a unit of account and a medium of final settlement in his model at all. Finally, he rejects the hypothesis that the world will regress towards a pure barter economy, as the costs would be too large. Thus, the demand for CB money will remain positive since CB reserves will retain their function as medium of final settlement for interbank imbalances so that the central bank continues to be able to steer money market interest rates. CB money seems to remain the generally accepted medium of exchange and the unit of account.

Woodford (2000) argues that a sharp reduction of the demand for CB money makes the implementation of monetary policy by quantity-targeting techniques (e.g. targeting non-borrowed reserves) increasingly difficult. But as long as that demand remains positive, the central bank maintains the ability to control short-term interest rates. He discusses the 'channel'-approach as a feasible alternative institutional arrangement for the implementation of monetary policy. Under such a system the central bank can control the short-term interest rate without changing the size of its balance sheet substantially. The 'channel'-system is based on the provision of standing facilities, for instance, a deposit and a lending facility at which the banks can draw on reserves from the central bank without limits. Since there is a spread between the deposit and the lending rate – of about 50 basis points in the case of New Zealand – banks have an incentive to trade reserves in the money market to manage their overnight settlement balances. The target rate, that is, the equilibrium money market rate, usually is halfway between the deposit and the lending rate. In theory the banks' objective would involve zero overnight balances, so that due to the absence of reserve requirements the expected overnight reserves of the entire system would be zero on average. In practice, however, a small positive target for the aggregate level of overnight reserves turned out to be more effective in ensuring that the equilibrium money market rate is close to the target rate. Monetary policy is implemented by changing the rates on the standing facilities without adjusting the target level of overnight reserves. Quantity adjustments by intraday credit are limited to manage short-term liquidity shocks in order to avoid excessive volatility of the market rate.

The diffusion of electronic money does not pose a threat to the efficacy of monetary policy, in a 'channel'-system. According to Woodford, the demand for currency is not a prerequisite for the system to work. Its elimination would reduce exogenous shocks to the volume of settlement reserves and, hence, might reduce the scope of liquidity management operations. A reduction of the demand for settlement balances due to improved treasury management by the participants in the payments system would reduce the average, aggregate volume of overnight settlement balances. But as both theory and experience show, the size of these is of limited relevance, in principle. A reduction of the interest elasticity of the demand for settlement balances would lead to a higher volatility in the equilibrium money market rate within the channel. Narrowing the channel could reinforce the stability of the market rate. Finally, Woodford counters the argument that alternative settlement systems among commercial banks would render monetary policy ineffective by invoking the low costs of the 'channel'-system. In the worst case the channel would narrow further to decrease the expected opportunity costs of holding overnight settlement reserves so that banks would not switch to alternative settlement mechanisms.

Palley (2002) models the threat to CB money as arising from the emergence of e-settlement money that eventually replaces settlement balances in CB money. He argues that the spread of innovations in information technology would enable banks to value their assets to market in real time. Instead of settling mutual debts in CB money, banks would exchange assets – which are not further specified – directly (so called mutual fund e-settlement). Also non-bank agents would increasingly rely on the transfer of assets in settling debt. The relevant interest rates would be set in a 'loanable funds'-style asset market, so that mutual fund e-settlement dominates CB money in the rate of return. Palley fears that the system of mutual fund e-settlement would be unstable. Despite the prevalence of mutual fund e-settlement in normal times, agents would prefer CB money in times of crises. The reduced demand for e-settlement balances could lead to the return of 'old-fashioned bank runs' (Palley 2002, 223). The inherent uncertainty of mutual fund e-settlement leads to a positive demand for CB money, because it is subject to zero nominal price fluctuations.

In addition to the analysis of the demand for bank settlement balances, Palley studies the effect of eMoney on the demand for required reserves, on non-bank currency demand, on tax payment balances, and on international interbank settlement balances. With respect to required reserves he concludes that the ongoing decline in their importance is likely to continue. Several countries abolished reserve requirements. Their ability to implement monetary policy effectively rests on the positive demand for CB money for transactions and settlement balances. The current role of non-bank currency demand in monetary policy implementation is negligible, so that a further decline does not affect the efficacy of monetary policy implementation.

The demand for tax payment balances remains a source of demand for CB money. Governments must require taxes to be paid in CB money to ensure this source of demand to constitute an effective channel for monetary policy. The demand for CB money resulting from international interbank settlement balances results primarily from the choice of reserve media of other central banks. Palley conjectures that central banks are likely to hold their foreign reserves in assets denominated in CB money rather than in risky mutual funds, in order not to put public wealth at risk. He concludes that in the future the demand for CB money will be further reduced relatively to total assets and liabilities in the economy, but that it will remain positive due to a positive but highly volatile demand for settlement balances (due to the inherent uncertainty of mutual fund e-settlement) and due to governments requiring tax payments in CB money. The reliance of tax payments to implement monetary policy would lead to increased interest volatility, as tax payments are highly seasonal and often paid with delay.

DISCUSSION

Currency transactions routinely require face-to-face contact so that their advantage in terms of anonymity might partly vanish. But be that as it may. A positive demand for currency is not a sufficient condition for the efficacy of the traditional instruments of monetary policy. Goodhart's position is criticised by Friedman (2000) as the 'one drug dealer' argument. Discretionary changes in the supply of currency are usually not an instrument of monetary policy implementation. The fundamental issue is not addressed in the controversy. Instead of focusing on the choice of means of payment the choice of the generally accepted medium of exchange is critical for the analysis of the future efficacy of monetary policy. Whether economic agents transfer claims on the generally accepted medium of exchange via cheques, credit or debit cards, bank transfers, direct debit is of interest for fine-tuning the liquidity operations of the central bank and the sponsors of the relevant retail and wholesale payment systems, but not for the elementary position of the central bank as a monopoly provider of the generally accepted medium of exchange at negligible marginal costs.

The size of the underground economy using currency is of indirect relevance only. Unless demand for currency is large enough to maintain its unit of account function, currency will be comparable to contemporary alternatives to money, for instance, LETS (Local Exchange Trading Systems) or widely accepted coupon schemes.[28] Despite the positive demand for alternative currency units in LETS the expansion and contraction of their supply has no effect on macroeconomic activity either at the margin or on average. The currency units of various LETS possess neither the generally accepted medium of exchange function nor the uniform unit of account function of money. The coupon schemes are denominated in the unit of account of the relevant market and offer redeemability in goods and services by the issuer. Some of them are also accepted at par by establishments other than the issuer. Their supply and demand are determined by the equilibrium condition that the real marginal revenue (i.e. the real interest earned on the float at the margin) equals the real marginal costs of operation, and that the real marginal costs equal marginal utility (i.e. real opportunity costs of holding vis-à-vis expected discounts etc.). Equivalently, neither the growth rate nor the level of supply of coupons affects aggregate economic activity. Furthermore, the central bank could exert some control over the supply and demand of coupons via its ability to influence the real rate of interest and, thus, the equilibrium condition.

Woodford (2000) argues that low expected opportunity costs of holding overnight settlement reserves in the 'channel'-system and the creditworthiness of the central bank result in a comparative advantage of CB sponsored settlement relative to potential competitors. It would even suffice that the central bank provided infinitely elastic borrowing and lending facilities regardless of the actual volume of transactions on the central banks book. Instead the central bank maintains the ability to steer the interest paid on its own liabilities in terms of its own liabilities at zero marginal costs. However, the impact of changes of this rate of interest on the demand and supply of the generally accepted medium of exchange and on aggregate economic activity are questioned by Friedman.[30] Woodford (2000, 255) argues that the efficacy of the central bank's monetary policy depends on '… how many people still chose to contract in terms of the currencies the values of which [the central bank] continues to determine.' Hence, Woodford argues that the role of CB money as the generally accepted medium of exchange and unit of account are crucial for the efficacy of monetary policy.

Palley's (2002) model of mutual fund e-settlement assumes that mutual fund shares used in e-settlement are valued in real time. He does neither state what the assets are denominated in nor against what they are valued in real time. There are basically two options. First, the assets are traded against each other and not denominated in a unit of account, but rather claims to real wealth. That would imply that there are $[n_A(n_A-1)]/2$ relative asset prices in the economy for n_A assets. As Palley does not mention a generally accepted medium of exchange or a unit of account, there would be $[n_A n_G]$ goods prices for n_G goods in the economy. The economy would resemble a barter economy based on an electronic exchange mechanism, but still relying on a double coincidence of wants. The assets exchanged in mutual fund e-settlement would exchange at a spread, unless they were perfect substitutes. Consequently, the equilibrium is unstable as mutual funds that exchange at lower spreads would dominate others as means of settlement.[31]

The second interpretation of Palley's model is more likely, namely that it resembles the current tiered system of payments. Individuals employ bank balances to pay debts and to acquire goods. Rather than writing cheques on nominally fixed bank deposits, they draw them on mutual funds. The cheques continue to be denominated and settled in CB money, eventually. The means of payment will be subject to change, but CB money will remain the generally accepted medium of exchange. Mutual fund e-settlement would add another layer to the tiering structure of the interbank settlement system. In order to reduce their demand for CB reserves, banks defer settlement by extended netting arrangements, in which they employ mutual fund shares as collateral. According to Palley, the demand for CB money remains positive and it is the only asset that exhibits zero nominal price fluctuations. It is therefore the only asset that guarantees economic finality in settlement. This interpretation is more likely to reflect Palley's underlying model, as he argues that agents demand settlement in CB money in abnormal times and that the sharp increase in demand for CB money causes a liquidity shortage. That implies that liquidity refers to CB money.

Models based on a publicly sanctioned, uniform unit of account without a generally accepted medium of exchange

Privately issued fiat-type electronic monies

Costa Storti and De Grauwe (2003) analyse the efficacy of current monetary policy instruments (standing facilities and open market operations – OMOs) in a society without money. They assume that the unit of account remains tied to the nation state and continues to be 'provided' by the state. Banks and other institutions issue private fiat-type monies in the form of deposits or eMoney. These institutions are not subject to minimum reserve requirements nor do they hold settlement balances with the central bank. Instead, they are assumed to hold liquid assets such as shares or bonds as assets.

The nominal share price – and consequently the nominal value of reserves of banks holding shares as liquid asset – equals the discounted expected nominal dividend stream. Costa Storti and De Grauwe argue that the expected nominal dividends are a function of the expected money stock (presumably some aggregate of privately issued fiat-type eMonies), so that the price level is indeterminate as any expected growth rate of the nominal stock of money leads to a corresponding growth rate of future nominal dividends and, consequently, to an increase in the current nominal value of assets. The current value of the 'nominal money stock' increases as well. There is no inherent equilibrating mechanism to pin down the price level.

If banks' portfolios consist of bonds the dis-equilibrating forces arise in a more complex fashion. As the bond price eventually returns to its face value, destabilising effects are supposed to arise via the quantity of bonds on the bank's balance sheet. An increase in the stock of money has positive effects on economic activity so that firms issue more debt. At the same time the transactions demand for money increases and both sides of the bank balance sheet expand in parallel. Again there is no inherent constraint to the expansion of banks' balance sheets and, thus, money creation.

Furthermore, the expansion might also work via the value of collateral. The expansion of the money stock leads to an increase in the value of assets in general and to that of collateral in particular. The value of banks' assets increases as the money stock does. Costa Storti and De Grauwe conclude that the price level might be indeterminate and inflation might arise in their model.

As the demand and supply functions of all agents in the model are homogenous of degree zero in nominal prices the price level cannot be pinned down. But what about a central bank that does focus on nominal variables – can it steer nominal interest rates in the model and anchor the system?

An increasingly accepted view among monetary economists holds that the central bank does not have to conduct large-scale financial transactions in order to manipulate money market rates. Its monopoly power to create settlement balances at zero marginal costs suffices to ensure the credibility of its target announcements for the main operating target.[32] In Costa Storti and De Grauwe the central bank has lost its monopoly in providing the generally accepted medium of exchange. As the central bank has to borrow funds in order to lend funds via its standing facilities, arbitrage opportunities arise. Not only will it incur large losses, it will also fail to affect the available liquidity in the system and merely redistribute funds, according to Costa Storti and De Grauwe. A similar line of reasoning applies to OMOs: in this case, though, the central bank can buy treasury bills from commercial banks with its own liabilities, for instance, bank deposits similar to those issued by commercial banks. The commercial banks will present these for re-conversion into treasury bills afterwards and, thus, keep the amount of treasury bills circulating outside the central bank largely unaffected. Furthermore, the small size of the central bank balance sheet and the potentially large losses it incurs in attempts to steer money market rates result in a loss of control over short-term money market interest rates.

Can the central bank regain control over money market rates if granted unlimited access to funds by the treasury at zero marginal costs? Costa Storti and De Grauwe argue that this would only increase the opportunities for arbitrage without empowering the central bank to manipulate the total liquidity in money markets. If it had unlimited access to treasury bills, it could manipulate the outstanding quantity of these bills based on a given market demand schedule. 'Thus, in a sense in a cashless society, treasury securities become the ultimate means of payments' (Costa Storti and De Grauwe 2003, 254).

Costa Storti and De Grauwe suggest prudential regulation and supervision as alternative instruments for monetary policy. The central bank certifies eMoney institutions. By taking macroeconomic conditions into consideration it can employ the capital adequacy ratio as an instrument of monetary policy. Legal reserve requirements in 'high quality' private money are judged to be of less importance in practical policy implementation, as their impact is supposed to be large and their flexibility low, making their accurate implementation very hard.

DISCUSSION

In the following discussion I argue that the Costa Storti and De Grauwe model is theoretically inconsistent, its institutional set-up is incomplete and the main results are questionable; that is, there is no institutional arrangement that links the privately issued fiat-type monies to the unit of account, there is no generally accepted medium of exchange in the model, it remains unclear what 'liquidity' in the market for inter-issuer settlement balances (money market) exactly means and the price levels of privately issued fiat-type monies are not indeterminate but infinite. The electronic monies do not perform the generally accepted medium of exchange function of money, let alone the unit of account function.

The literature on the time inconsistency problem associated with the issue of private fiat-type money concludes that there is no effective constraint on individual issuers credibly preventing them from inflating infinitely.[33] Costa Storti and De Grauwe offer a number of explanations for the indeterminacy of the price level, that all involve the argument that there are multiple equilibria consistent with an infinite set of expectations concerning the nominal money supply and the resulting nominal value of assets (shares/bonds/collateral). In the case of redeemable privately issued commodity monies the argument is wrong, as the redeemability constraint can be binding for each individual bank at the margin, even if it were not binding in the case of a concerted expansion of banks' balance-sheets.[34] However, in the case of privately issued fiat-type monies their argument can be simplified. The most straightforward way for each individual bank to increase its note issue and its assets in unison is to purchase assets (stocks/bonds etc.) on financial markets at the prevailing market price. As the issuers of fiat-type electronic money face zero marginal costs of issuing additional money, they buy collateral until the expected marginal return is zero as well.[35] Consequently, the price levels are determined – they are infinite for each of the privately issued fiat-type monies. There is no generally accepted medium of exchange, no unit of account in the model and consequently no money. Therefore, it is not surprising that there is neither a meaningfully defined price level nor any monetary policy instruments available to the central bank for its stabilisation.

According to Costa Storti and De Grauwe the inability of the central bank to manipulate the liquidity in the system results from the fact that an expansionary OMO would be sterilised immediately as banks reconvert their CB deposits into financial assets, thus leaving the amount of outstanding deposits unchanged. In principle, the same argument holds true for any of the issuers in the model at the margin. It remains unclear why CB deposits are supposed to be inferior to other banks' deposits so that they are not held for transaction purposes. Furthermore, there are no arbitrage opportunities in the Costa Storti and De Grauwe model: the central bank's bid and ask prices for financial assets (stocks, bonds, treasury bills etc.) have to rise above the prevailing market bid and ask prices in terms of CB deposits, in order to change the opportunity costs of CB money. At the same time the central bank is expected to convert these deposits into financial assets at a predetermined conversion rate on demand. This conversion rate corresponds to the ask price and the market price in terms of CB money would increase to this conversion rate in terms of CB deposits. But that does not necessarily affect the market price in terms of any other bank's deposits so that the deposits of various banks – the various privately issued fiat-type monies – do not necessarily exchange at par. Costa Storti and De Grauwe mention 'high quality' electronic money in their argument concerning reserve requirements. If there are quality differences between electronic monies, they will not exchange at par, unless they are adjusted for by interest payments on electronic money, which does not seem to be the case in this model.

Consequently, the question arises what the unit of account in this model is. Costa Storti and De Grauwe (2003, 242) state that it is 'provided by the state' as one *US$* or one €. But that does not meaningfully define a unit of account. The continuous availability of market prices for all goods and for all electronic monies in terms of the unit of account is a necessary precondition for the availability of goods prices in terms of all electronic monies in the model, unless the electronic monies are denominated in the unit of account themselves.[36] In the absence of a mechanism that links all eMonies to the unit of account this denomination remains nominalistic and arbitrary. Such a mechanism would be a redeemabilty requirement into a good embodying the unit of account (such as CB money). However, in their model there is neither CB money nor any other good embodying the unit of account, for example, whose price in terms of the unit of account is irrevocably fixed. There is no exchange between any such good and all other goods in the economy, so that no goods prices in terms of the unit of account can be determined in exchange. As the goods and the electronic monies would fluctuate in terms of an abstract unit of account, market exchange between any good and any electronic money could only determine a relative price but not a nominal price in terms of an abstract unit of account. Only nominal prices in terms of various electronic monies could be observed, if they were not infinite due to the prevailing time inconsistency problem.

Furthermore, the model is inherently unstable, as for a high quality electronic money (EM_1) the price of a certain good in terms of the number of units of account (x *US$* in terms of EM_1) is lower than for a low quality electronic money (z *US$* in terms of EM_2; $z > x$). As the various electronic monies are not perfect substitutes, their exchange will involve spreads. In general, prices will be lowest for the electronic money that exchanges at the lowest spread, which will, as a consequence, drive the others out of the market.[37] There is neither a discussion of the mechanism of nominal price formation nor an analysis of the institutional set-up that links the publicly sanctioned unit of account to the eMonies in the model.

There is no medium of final settlement in the model as eMonies can only be reconverted into financial assets, which in turn pay dividends or interest rates in electronic monies or more stocks and bonds. The model suffers from circularity, so that no electronic money is linked to any good embodying the unit of account directly or indirectly.[38]

The model is incomplete as the authors do not model a money market (or a market for settlement balances between issuers of electronic monies). The authors state that CB money will no longer be used as medium of (final) settlement. They analyse a market for 'liquidity',[39] but fail to state what is supposed to be exchanged there, in what kind of (financial) asset(s) this liquidity is embodied. Due to the circularity of conversion there is no medium of final settlement and, therefore, no market in which such a good can be traded. The authors mention that treasury bills might assume the role of final settlement media in a world without money. They conclude that the central bank could control the total amount of liquidity in the economy in that case by varying the volume of treasury bills. Their conclusion holds, if the treasury ceases to issue treasury bills without consent of the central bank. Otherwise, the treasury would control the total amount of liquidity in the economy. The scenario implies that treasury bills would assume the role of the generally accepted medium of exchange and the incidental functions of money (i.e. the unit of account and store of value function). The liabilities of the treasury would substitute for the liabilities of the central bank as money. Again, the general acceptance of these liabilities in exchange would depend predominantly on the credibility of the treasury to provide a nominal anchor to the system.

In addition, the model is incomplete because there is no rationale for intermediation. The banks that issue electronic money do not offer any service – there is no risk, liquidity, maturity and volume transformation. The question arises why individuals should transfer electronic money that is convertible into stocks and bonds rather than the stocks and bonds themselves. Presumably the transaction costs involved in the transfer of assets are larger than those involved in the transfer of eMonies, but the authors do not make that assumption explicit nor do they discuss its bearing on the consistency of their model.

Final settlement by the transfer of wealth

King (1999) offers a similar but more radical proposal as he eliminates intermediation from the payments system and attempts to develop an indirect exchange economy with a unit of account. Transactions are settled in real time by the transfer of wealth, so that there is demand neither for CB money nor for a generally accepted medium of exchange. The buyer obtains funds by a real time sale of a financial asset, transfers these to the seller, who immediately reinvests in financial assets. In order to reduce transaction costs, all financial markets transactions are completed automatically based on pre-agreed algorithms. Financial assets qualify for inclusion in the barter system, if they are traded on markets administered by the system, which would match demand and supply, ensure efficient price formation and settlement continuously. All prices are supposed to be quoted in a publicly announced, uniform unit of account. King concludes that there is no role for central bank money. Hence, central banks cannot implement monetary policy.

DISCUSSION

King's model presumes that market prices for electronically traded financial assets, goods and services exchanged exist, and that all these prices are quoted in the uniform unit of account. In fact, the model does not describe an indirect exchange economy. Financial assets are sold instantaneously and 'funds' are transferred which are reinvested upon receipt. However, it remains unclear what these 'funds' are. If they are risky financial assets that are as liquid as the initial portfolio held by the buyer, then there is no point in exchanging them for 'funds' in the first place. If they are more liquid than other financial assets, then these 'funds' are a means of payment and possibly a generally accepted medium of exchange and the economy is not an indirect exchange economy. Similarly, in Costa Storti and De Grauwe's (2003) term 'liquidity', the term 'funds' is not clearly defined.

Furthermore, it remains unclear how these funds – and indeed the financial assets in general – are linked to the unit of account. In a Walrasian economy all goods are equally liquid and any one of them can be chosen as the numeraire. As this is traded on markets continuously against all other goods, there are always well-defined relative prices available for all goods vis-à-vis the numeraire. Via the going market price of any good in terms of the numeraire all nominal prices are determined at all times. In King's model there is no good or service that is the numeraire. Instead the unit of account is subject to regulation and supervision such as weights and measures. In principle, the weight or the length of an arbitrary good can be defined as the unit of measurement. The weight and length of any other good is derived from a comparison with the standard good that entirely relies on objective criteria. But how does this logic apply to goods and financial assets? An arbitrary good, an abstract unit called, for example, *US$*, is defined as the unit of account and the value of any other good is derived from the standard by a direct comparison of value. Unfortunately, the comparison involves subjective values and cannot be undertaken objectively, compared to the inspection of weights and measures. Consequently, any such comparison necessarily presupposes the existence of markets in which goods are exchanged – directly or indirectly – for the standard. The exchange of goods for the good embodying the standard (e.g. the generally accepted medium of exchange) constitutes the intersubjective comparison. The analysis of separability of the generally accepted medium of exchange and the unit of account usually lacks an analysis of the formation of nominal prices.[40] The standard can be linked to a financial asset by fixing its price through redeemability in the generally accepted medium of exchange. If that is what King has in mind, then the 'funds' in his model serve as the generally accepted medium of exchange and the unit of account. Final settlement would take place in the generally accepted medium of exchange and various forms of financial assets could serve as means of payment (e.g. deposit transfers, cheques etc.). Without any such medium of final settlement the model is characterised by circularity, as financial assets are claims to financial assets. If, however, some financial assets are claims to goods and services (e.g. one ounce of gold) at a fixed ratio, the system will be nominally anchored. In that case it would resemble a traditional commodity standard. Whether or not the central bank has the power to manipulate the nominal and/or the real short-term interest rate of the generally accepted medium of exchange depends on the institutional set-up, that is, control over the production of the commodity, large stocks of the commodity, regulation of international flows of the commodity and so on.

King's model can be interpreted in two ways: (i) the first interpretation resembles a Walrasian economy with all goods and services being equally liquid. There is no money and no central bank. One of the goods is arbitrarily chosen as the numeraire but it has to be either a good or a service. It would be as liquid as any other good and continuously traded vis-à-vis all other goods and services. An illiquid abstract unit of account would not do the job. But as information is not costly in this economy there is no need for a numeraire in the first place. No transaction would be intermediated by 'funds'; every transaction would be settled by direct or indirect barter, which are equivalent in terms of transaction costs as these are all zero. Monetary policy is impossible and indeed would only be harmful as all markets clear instantaneously and the resulting allocations would be Pareto-efficient; (ii) The second interpretation reveals that the model is basically a traditional commodity standard with an advanced electronic retail payment system with very liquid financial assets (e.g. mutual money market funds). The underlying commodity would serve as the generally accepted medium of exchange and resume the unit of account function and financial assets could be increasingly employed as means of payment. The challenges to monetary policy implementation would largely result from the nature of the system as a commodity standard and not from the technology of the means of payment. Although a more sophisticated system could increase the costs of supervision of any underlying regulation (e.g. regulation of international flows of the underlying commodity). If the 'commodity' ('funds') is CB money, the central bank will retain the monopoly of issuing the generally accepted medium of exchange and the unit of account at zero marginal costs. Hence, the efficacy of monetary policy would not be affected, in principle.

Further models proposing final settlement by the transfer of wealth

Browne/Cronin (1995) propose a model similar to King's that is based on the transfer of shares of mutual funds and a unit of account without a generally accepted medium of exchange. New technology in retail and wholesale payment systems eliminates the demand for CB money. The unit of account function of money would be preserved by numismatists collecting CB coins and banknotes. Another option would be a commodity-based unit of account. Similar criticism applies to their concept as to King's (1999). However, they provide a few counter-arguments to White's (1984) criticism of the separation of the unit of account and generally accepted medium of exchange, in particular the reduction of (operational) transaction costs by advances in technology (i.e. optic fibre and smart cards) and the low share of currency in the total transaction media already observable, to mention but two. To argue that a reduction in operational costs could eliminate the spread between bid and ask prices, which according to White constitutes a central element of transaction costs of settlement by the transfer of wealth relative to monetary exchange, reveals an unduly narrow concept of the determinants of the spread (see first section). That currency constitutes only 1 per cent of the transaction media is irrelevant for the argument, because CB reserves constitute CB money as well. But, more importantly, the argument confuses the different concepts of 'medium of exchange' and 'means of payment'. Even if most payments are conducted by credit, debit cards, bank transfers, cheques and other non-cash means of payment, CB money remains the underlying, generally accepted medium of exchange and the non-cash transactions constitute claims to CB money. Contrary to their claim, a transaction initiated by non-cash means of payment does not constitute a separation of the generally accepted medium of exchange from the unit of account.

Kroszner (2001) envisages a future of the parallel use of multiple units of account rather than a single abstract one, but the various units would all be based on mutual funds. In addition to confusing currency competition and the parallel use of multiple units of account, he also treats competition of means of payment as equivalent to competition in the generally accepted medium of exchange. Neither Kroszner nor Browne and Cronin model the mechanisms of price formation within their institutional settings.

Similar to King (1999), Centi and Bougi (2003) base their 'New Monetary Order' on a world in which transaction media are backed by equity claims. They also reach the conclusion that CB money (i.e. outside money in general) and monetary policy would vanish. Contrary to King, they do not mention a unit of account explicitly. It remains unclear what the generally accepted medium of exchange, the unit of account and the medium of final settlement are in the model. The institutional structure of electronic money schemes is sketched rudimentarily. Competition of issuers of fiat money backed by real assets is conceptualised in a way similar to Klein (1974). Issuers invest in brand name capital in order to generate trust among customers. However, as shown by White (1999), the potential loss of brand name capital does not provide sufficient incentives to prevent overissue and hyperinflation. He concludes that competition of privately issued fiat monies is infeasible. Centi/Bougi briefly discuss dynamics in the market, according to which 'good' money would drive out competitors. They seem to insinuate that more than one competing money would prevail in equilibrium, but fail to derive the conditions under which such an equilibrium can exist and be stable.[41]

Conclusion

Friedman (1999, 2000) argues that the proliferation of alternative media of exchange and units of account will render monetary policy irrelevant. He rests his case on the observation that privately operated retail and wholesale payment systems economise on CB money. The reduction of the ratio of CB money to measures of aggregate economic activity (e.g. GDP) will eventually lead to its irrelevance, particularly in the limit when CB money is eliminated. He does not present evidence that this ongoing process has already reduced the efficacy of monetary policy. Furthermore, the relatively small volume of OMOs compared to daily turnover is irrelevant, as price formation works at the margin and the central bank is in the unique position to manipulate the supply at the margin at zero marginal cost. Comparing the small size of OMOs and the liquidity deficit to turnover in interbank markets is therefore misleading, as it relates the continuous reallocation of aggregate reserves among market participants to discretionary and exogenous changes in aggregate reserves. Friedman assumes that reaching the limit has no structural effects on the economy. The institutional structure of the monetary system in the limit is not discussed. He fails to demonstrate why market participants should change their perception of CB power as long as it retains the monopoly to supply the generally accepted medium of exchange and the unit of account at zero marginal costs – that is, before the limit is reached. He does not highlight the conditions under which the central bank loses this monopoly before the limit is reached, nor, if a new generally accepted medium of exchange emerges, and if so, under which circumstances and what the process of transition would look like once the limit is reached. In response to his critics, he argues that financial markets will eventually discontinue acting upon the interest rate announcements of the central bank. If the demand for central bank money remains positive in some parts of the economy, monetary policy would still affect economic activity in this part of the economy. He doubts that central banks would be able to influence the general price level, nominal output and asset prices in the entire economy, at the margin. If the demand for CB money remains positive in some parts of the economy, the question arises, which generally accepted medium of exchange(s) and unit(s) of account prevail in the other parts of the economy and how they are related to CB money.

In response to Friedman (1999, 2000), a number of papers argued that the demand for CB money will not vanish and that the limit will not be reached. Some of the models focus on the public's demand for currency, others on the banks' demand for CB reserves. The motifs for the positive demand for CB money vary (e.g. anonymity, legal tender provisions, first mover advantage, transaction costs of electronic barter, precautionary reserves). Models that highlight the residual demand for currency focus on the demand for CB money as means of payment. That does not necessarily imply that it is also the generally accepted medium of exchange and the unit of account. They implicitly assume what is to be shown; namely that CB money maintains its role as generally accepted medium of exchange and unit of account. They do not discuss how the residual demand for CB money as means of payment relates to its function as generally accepted medium of exchange and unit of account. Arguments that stress the comparative advantage of central banks to provide final settlement usually rest on the critical presumption that they maintain their monopoly to supply the generally accepted medium of exchange and the unit of account at zero marginal costs. The argument is circular in as far as it assumes the crucial role of central banks (as provider of the generally accepted medium of exchange and the unit of account) to demonstrate their comparative advantage to provide final settlement, so that the demand for CB reserves remains positive and CB money remains the generally accepted medium of exchange and the unit of account. This class of models implicitly builds on an institutional framework that resembles the one currently in place: CB money remains the generally accepted medium of exchange and the unit of account but the degree of tiering in the payments system increases further. All means of payments are denominated in the uniform unit of account and claims to CB money, the means of final settlement.

Models that are based on a publicly sanctioned, uniform unit of account, either envisage privately issued fiat-type electronic money or final settlement by the transfer of wealth. Presenting a model of the first variant of a society without money, Costa Storti and De Grauwe (2003) argue that the price level would be indeterminate and monetary policy based on traditional instruments (OMOs) impossible. Their model is incomplete and inconsistent as there is no institutional arrangement that links the privately issued fiat-type eMonies to the uniform unit of account. As there is no good embodying the unit of account, there is no exchange between this good and any other good in the economy. Consequently, nominal prices in the unit of account cannot be established through exchange and there is no uniform unit of account in the economy. The mechanisms of nominal price formation are not discussed. There is no medium of final settlement in the model, so that there is no meaningfully defined money market and the model is characterised by circularity. As eMonies do not exchange at par, their exchange will involve different spreads. The model is unstable, as the eMoney with the lowest spread will, in principle, drive its competitors out of the market. The price levels in the various eMonies are infinite rather than indeterminate. A further problem arises, as financial intermediaries do not seem to offer any intermediation services – it remains unclear why individuals should exchange eMonies backed by assets rather than the assets themselves.

Models that are based on a publicly sanctioned, uniform unit of account and the transfer of wealth face similar difficulties: there is no generally accepted medium of exchange, no well-defined price level and no unit of account, as the models fail to establish a link between the publicly sanctioned, uniform unit of account and the means of payment. They also lack an analysis of the formation of nominal prices and simply assume market prices in terms of the unit of account as given. Wealth is exchanged in an indirect manner via 'funds' but the term is not clearly defined. I suggest two interpretations that resemble either a Walrasian economy without any transaction costs or a commodity standard. While monetary policy is indeed ineffective, its feasibility depends on the choice of the underlying good in the 'commodity' standard. If eMonies or assets are redeemable in CB money, it resumes the function as the generally accepted medium of exchange and the unit of account and the central bank remains in control of the short-term interest rate.

Many of the models discussed assume an institutional structure of the monetary system that involves the separation of the unit of account from the generally accepted medium of exchange. The analysis demonstrates that these models lack an analysis of the mechanisms of price formation and that nominal prices in the unit of account presuppose the direct or indirect exchange of goods for the generally accepted medium of exchange which embodies the unit of account in competitive markets.

Table 5.1 summarises the common features of many models discussed in the previous sections albeit few of them combine all the features.

Table 5.1 Common features of models on eMoney and monetary policy

Neglect of transition process from existing monetary system based on GAME & uniform unit of account to monetary systems envisaged for the future
Monetary systems envisaged for the future usually neglect the question whether GAME & uniform unit of account exist
Neglect of literature on time inconsistency and privately issued fiat-type monies
Concepts of 'means of payment' & 'medium of exchange' often confused
Neglect of analysis of price formation mechanisms under envisaged monetary systems
No link between publicly sanctioned unit of account & means of payment
'Liquid funds' traded in money market not well defined
On closer inspection: Models collapse to Walrasian economy or commodity standard or current monetary systems

If ICT is supposed to overcome all frictions, all goods are equally liquid and there is no need for a generally accepted medium of exchange and a uniform unit of account. All demand and supply schedules are homogenous of degree zero in nominal prices and neither the price level nor the rate of inflation is defined unambiguously. Any good or service can serve as numeraire. But relative prices remain to be determined. As there are no transaction costs and there are relative market prices for all goods at all times, their prices in terms of the numeraire are available permanently at no cost. All markets clear and as there is no need for monetary policy, there is no need to nominally anchor the economy.

Until the world economy resembles the Arrow-Debreu model, transaction costs will remain positive and a generally accepted medium of exchange – that also fulfils the function of the uniform unit of account – will further reduce transaction costs relative to an economy without a generally accepted medium of exchange. The institutional structure is likely to involve redeemability of eMonies in the generally accepted medium of exchange and the respective uniform unit of account will prevail in the economy. The dominant medium of exchange in the respective market has a comparative advantage with respect to alternative units of account at current moderate levels of inflation. The diffusion of eMoney might reduce the threshold for currency substitution in high inflation regimes slightly. But the central bank is likely to maintain its monopoly in the provision of the generally accepted medium of exchange and the unit of account at zero marginal costs. Current EU-regulation (Directive 2000/46/EC of the European Parliament and of the Council of 18 September 2000 on the taking up, pursuit of and prudential supervision of the business of electronic money institutions) reinforces that prediction (i.e. article 3 on redeemability of eMoney). In principle, monetary policy will remain effective. In the unlikely case that the monetary system discontinues to be rooted in CB money, another generally accepted medium of exchange and unit of account emerges (e.g. commodity standard). In that case the efficacy of monetary policy depends on the concrete institutional arrangements. Nevertheless, the ongoing institutional change in the payments system – at the retail and the wholesale level – will necessitate adaptations of monetary statistics and of the instruments and the implementation of monetary policy. A challenge central banks have proven to cope with quite successfully so far.

References

Arnone, M. and Bandiera, L. (2004) 'Monetary Policy, Monetary Areas, and Financial Development with Electronic Money', IMF Working Paper WP/04/122, Washington, D. C.: IMF.

Berentsen, A. (1998) 'Monetary Policy Implications of Digital Money', *Kyklos,* 51: 89–117.

Borio, C. E. V. (1997) 'The Implementation of Monetary Policy in Industrialized Countries: A Survey', *Economic Paper No. 187*, Basel: Bank for International Settlement.

Browne, F. X. and Cronin, D. (1995) 'Payment Technologies, Financial Innovation, and Laissez-Faire Banking', *Cato Journal 15* http://www.cato.org/pubs/journal/cj15n1-6.html (accessed 26 August 2004).

Browne, F. X. and Cronin, D. (1996) 'Payment Technologies, Financial Innovation, and Laissez-Faire Banking: A Further Discussion of the Issues', in J. A. Dorn (ed.), *The Future of Money in the Information Age*, Washington, D. C.: Cato Institute http://www.cato.org/pubs/books/money/money18.htm (accessed 26 August 2004).

Capie, F. H. and Wood, G. E. (2001) 'E-Money, Lender of Last Resort, and the Role of the Central Bank', paper presented at the SUERF Meeting, 25–27 October, Brussels.

Centi, J. P. and Bougi, G. (2003) 'The Possible Economic Consequences of Electronic Money', in J. Birner and P. Garrouste (eds), *Austrian Perspectives on the New Economy*, London: Routledge, 259–81.

Cesarano, F. (1995) 'The New Monetary Economics and the Theory of Money', *Journal of Economic Behaviour and Organization,* 26: 445–55.

Chaum, D. (1996) 'Privacy and Social Protection in Electronic Payment Systems', in J. A. Dorn (ed.) (1996), *The Future of Money in the Information Age*, Washington, D. C.: Cato Institute http://www.cato.org/pubs/books/money/money12.htm (accessed 26 August 2004).

Cohen, B. J. (2002) 'Monetary Instability: Are National Currencies Becoming Obsolete?' in J. Busumtwi-Sam, M. Griffin Cohen, L. Dobuzinskis and S. McBride (eds), *Turbulance and New Directions in Global Political Economy*, London: Palgrave MacMillan, 125–40.

Costa Storti C. and De Grauwe, P. (2003) 'Monetary Policy in a Cashless Society', in M. Balling, F. Lierman, and A. Mullineux (eds), *Technology and Finance, Challenges for Financial Markets, Business Strategies and Policy Makers*, London: Routledge, 241–60.

Cowen, T., and Kroszner, R. (1992) 'German-Language Precursors of the New Monetary Economics', *Journal for Institutional and Theoretical Economics,* 148: 387–410.

Cowen, T., and Kroszner, R. (1994) *Explorations in the New Monetary Economics*, Oxford: Blackwell Publishers.

Crede, A. (1995) 'Electronic Commerce and the Banking Industry: The Requirement and Opportunities for New Payment Systems Using the Internet', *Journal of Computer*

Mediated Communication 1. http://www.ascusc.org/jcmc/vol1/issue3/vol1no3.html (accessed 26 August 2004).

Eichenbaum, M. S. and Wallace, N. (1985) 'A Shred of Evidence on Public Acceptance of Privately Issued Currency', *Quarterly Review Federal Reserve Bank of Minneapolis* 9. http://minneapolisfed.org/research/qr/qr911.pdf

England, C. (1996) 'The Future of Currency Competition', in J. A. Dorn (ed.), *The Future of Money in the Information Age*, Cato Institute, Washington, D. C. http://www.cato.org/pubs/books/money/money18.htm (accessed 26 August 2004).

Freedman, C. (2000) 'Monetary Policy Implementation: Past, Present, and Future – Will the Advent of Electronic Money Lead to the Demise of Central Banking?' *International Finance,* 3: 211–27.

Freixas, X., Holthausen, C., Terol I. and Thygessen, C. (2001) 'Settlement in Commercial Bank Money versus Central Bank Money', paper presented at the SUERF Meeting, 25–27 October, Brussels.

Friedman, B. (1999) 'The Future of Monetary Policy: The Central Bank as an Army with Only a Signaling Corps?' *International Finance,* 2: 321–38.

Friedman, B. (2000) 'Decoupling at the Margin: The Threat to Monetary Policy from the Electronic Revolution in Banking', *International Finance,* 3: 261–72.

Good, B. A. (1998) 'Private Money: Everything Old is New Again', *Economic Commentary Federal Reserve Bank of Cleveland* (April) http://www.clevelandfed.org/Research/com98/0401.pdf

Goodhart, C. A. E. (1989) *Money, Information, and Uncertainty*, London: Macmillan.

Goodhart, C. A. E. (2000) 'Can Central Banking Survive the IT Revolution', *International Finance*, 3: 189–209.

Greenfield, R. L. and Yeager, L. B. (1983) 'A Laissez Faire Approach to Monetary Stability', *Journal of Money, Credit and Banking,* 15: 302–15.

Guthrie, G. and Wright, J. (2000) 'Open Mouth Operations', *Journal of Monetary Economics,* 46: 489–516.

Henckel, T., Ize, A. and Kovanen, A. (1999) 'Central Banking Without Central Bank Money', IMF Working Paper WP/99/92, Washington, D. C.: IMF.

King, M. (1999) 'Challenges for Monetary Policy: Old and New', paper prepared for the Symposium on "New Challenges for Monetary Policy", 27 August, sponsored by the Federal Reserve Bank of Kansas City at Jackson Hole, Wyoming.

Klein, B. (1974) "The competitive supply of money", *Journal of Money, Credit and Banking*, 6: 423–53.

Kobrin, S. J. (1997) "Electronic Cash and the End of National Markets", *Foreign Policy*, 107: 65–77.

Kroszner, R. S. (2001) 'Currency Competition in the Digital Age', paper prepared for 'The Origins and Evolution of Central Banking', 21–22 May, Federal Reserve Bank Cleveland.

Krüger, M. (1999) 'Towards a Moneyless World?' University of Durham, Department of Economics & Finance, Working Paper No. 9916, Durham.

Matonis, J. W. (1995) "Digital Cash and Monetary Freedom", paper prepared for INET 95, 26–30 June, Honolulu, Hawaii.

McCallum, B. T. (2000) 'The Present and the Future of Monetary Policy Rules', *International Finance,* 3: 273–86.

Menger, C. (1909) 'Money' translated from 'Geld', Handwörterbuch der Staatswissenschaften 3rd edition, Jena, in M. Latzer and S. W Schmitz (2002) (eds), *Carl Menger and the Evolution of Payments Systems: From Barter to Electronic Money*, Cheltenham: Edward Elgar, 26–108.

O'Hara, M. (1997) *Market Microstructure Theory*, Oxford: Blackwell Publishers.

Palley, T. I. (2002) 'The E-Money Revolution: Challenges and Implications for Monetary Policy', *Journal of Post Keynesian Economics,* 24: 217–33.

Rich, G. (2000) 'Monetary Policy without Central Bank Money: A Swiss Perspective', *International Finance,* 3: 439–69.

Schmitz, S. W (2002a) 'Carl Menger's "Money" and the Current Neoclassical Models of Money', in M. Latzer and S. W Schmitz (eds), *Carl Menger and the Evolution of Payments Systems: From Barter to Electronic Money*, Cheltenham: Edward Elgar, 111–32.

Schmitz, S. W (2002b) 'The Institutional Character of Electronic Money Schemes', in M. Latzer and S. W Schmitz (eds), *Carl Menger and the Evolution of Payments Systems: From Barter to Electronic Money*, Cheltenham: Edward Elgar, 159–83.

Sellon, G. H. and Weiner, S. E. (1997) 'Monetary Policy without Reserve Requirements: Case Studies and Options for the United States', *Federal Reserve Bank of Kansas City Economic Review* (Second Quarter): 6–30.

Selgin, G. A. (1994) 'Free Banking and Monetary Control', *Economic Journal,* 104: 1449–59.

Selgin, G. A. (1996) 'E-Money: Friend or Foe of Monetarism?' in J. A. Dorn (ed.) (1996), *The Future of Money in the Information Age*, Washington, D. C.: Cato Institute http://www.cato.org/pubs/books/money/money13.htm (accessed 26 August 2004).

Selgin, G. A. and White, L. H. (1987) 'The Evolution of a Free Banking System', *Economic Inquiry,* 25: 439–57.

Selgin, G. A. and White, L. H. (2002) 'Mengerian Perspectives on the Future of Money' in M. Latzer, S. W. Schmitz (eds), *Carl Menger and the Evolution of Payments Systems: From Barter to Electronic Money*, Cheltenham: Edward Elgar, 133–58.

Stix, H. (2002) 'Die Auswirkungen von elektronischem Geld auf die Geldpolitik', *Wirtschaftspolitische Blätter,* 49: 110–19.

Streissler, E. W. (2002) 'Carl Menger's Article "Money" in the History of Economic Thought', in M. Latzer and S. W. Schmitz (eds), *Carl Menger and the Evolution of Payments Systems: From Barter to Electronic Money*, Cheltenham: Edward Elgar, 11–24.

Taub, B. (1985) 'Private Fiat Money with Many Suppliers', *Journal Monetary Economics,* 16: 195–208.

Thornton, D. L. (2000) 'The Relationship Between the Federal Funds Rate and the Fed's Federal Funds Rate Target: Is it Open Market or Open Mouth Operations?' Federal Reserve Bank of St. Louis Working Paper, St. Louis.

White, L. H. (1984) 'Competitive Payments Systems and the Unit of Account', *American Economic Review,* 74: 699–712.

White, L. H. (1999) *The Theory of Monetary Institutions,* Oxford: Blackwell Publishers.

Woodford, M. (1998) 'Doing Without Money: Controlling Inflation in a Post-Monetary World', *Review of Economic Dynamics,* 1: 173–219.

Woodford, M. (2000) 'Monetary Policy in a World without Money', *International Finance,* 3: 229–60.

Woodford, M. (2002) 'Financial Markets Efficiency and the Effectiveness of Monetary Policy', *Federal Reserve Bank of New York Economic Policy Review*, 8: 85–94.

Notes

1 I am grateful to my discussant Cornelia Holthausen and the participants of the project workshop at the Austrian Academy of Sciences for suggestions and comments.

2 See the introduction to this volume.

3 See Menger 1909, Krüger 1999, Schmitz 2002b, Selgin and White 2002 and Streissler 2002.
4 Another potential direction of research would address the following question: Will the institutional change in the payments system reduce the marginal costs of coordination to reduce the marginal costs of a socially concerted adoption of a new generally accepted medium of exchange and a new unit of account? This question is, however, beyond the scope of this paper.
5 Inter alia King (1999, 26) illustrates the focus on technology in reasoning about institutional change in the payments system: 'The key to such developments [final settlement by the transfer of real wealth] is the ability of computers to communicate in real time to permit instantaneous verification of the credit worthiness of counterparties, thereby enabling private sector real time gross settlement to occur with finality. Any securities for which electronic markets exist could be used as part of the settlement process'. See also Friedman (1999, 329) and Kroszner (2001, 8).
6 In the literature on New Monetary Economics and its predecessors the transition is not conceptualised uniformly. Some models argue that a new unit of account emerges in an evolutionary manner with the potential for the parallel use of multiple units of account, others assume that a new unit of account can only be introduced by government regulation (see Cowen and Kroszner 1992, 1994, Krüger 1999).
7 Crede (1995), Matonis (1995), England (1996), Kobrin (1997), Cohen (2002) and Kroszner (2001) suggest the parallel use of multiple units of accounts is desirable and indeed likely due to the diffusion of eMoney.
8 Models of the parallel use of multiple units of account often confuse this concept with currency competition (e.g. Cohen 2002, Kroszner 2001).
9 Individuals joining a new electronic payments system invest in the new technology in various ways (including software, acquiring the necessary technology competence and buy an initial balance of electronic funds).
10 Similar arguments with respect to the role of network effects are also advanced in Krüger 1999.
11 The spread is determined by the degree of risk and uncertainty, the risk and uncertainty preferences of individuals, resource costs of holding inventory positions in different risky assets (i.e. not nominally fixed with respect to the generally accepted medium of exchange) and the related risk and uncertainty, the market structure, potential asymmetries of information amongst traders, and transaction as well as information costs (see O'Hara 1997, Goodhart 1989). It is the price for the service provided by market makers – the service of immediacy. The generally accepted medium of exchange is the most liquid good in the economy, the good with the highest marketability and, thus, involves the lowest spread (Menger 1909). It is unlikely that the spread is completely eliminated by technological innovation unless transaction costs are completely eradicated (see Krüger 1999 and Schmitz 2002b).
12 For a more detailed discussion of monetary policy implementation see chapter 7.
13 Selgin 1996 and Selgin and White 2002 argue that monetary policy becomes even more effective as the elimination of currency would reduce the variability of the money multiplier and, thus, increase the predictability of the relationship between central bank (CB) money and nominal spending. Furthermore, the ratio of CB money to broad money is so reduced that each unit change becomes more effective at the margin.
14 See Freedman 2000.
15 See Sellon and Weiner 1997 and Woodford 2002.
16 Many proposals discussed in this section display similarities to the BFH approach to monetary economics pioneered by Black, Fama, Hall, developed by Greenfield and Yeager (1983) and summarised in Cowen and Kroszner (1994) as New Monetary Economics. Krüger (1999) critically discusses the BFH approach to eMoney and the structure of the financial/monetary system.

17 E.g. Crede 1995, Matonis 1995, England 1996, Selgin 1996 and Kobrin 1997.
18 See chapter 7 for an exposition of monetary policy implementation.
19 See e.g. the papers presented at the FRBNY Conference on Financial Innovation and Monetary Transmission, 5–6 April 2001, New York <http://www.ny.frb.org/pihome/news/speeches/finmon/finmon.html>.
20 See Freixas *et al.* 2001 for wholesale payment systems. For alternative media of exchange and the parallel use of multiple units of account see Crede (1995), Matonis (1995), England (1996), Selgin (1996) and Kobrin (1997), Cohen (2002), and Kroszner (2001) and for criticism of their positions see Schmitz 2002b and Selgin and White 2002.
21 A similar approach is adopted in Woodford (1998) and discussed in McCallum (2000) and Selgin and White (2002).
22 See the introduction to this volume.
23 E.g. Chaum 1996. But he also argues that – while technologically possible – complete anonymity might not be desirable in electronic payment systems.
24 Credibility and enforceability of the respective legislation as well as the appropriate organisational structure of the operator of the payment system and its effective supervision might be added.
25 The major reasons for the stability attributed to central banks are (i) its rather narrow field of activities, (ii) its large reserves and seigniorage and (iii) the backing by government, and, most importantly, (iv) its comfortable monopoly to issue liabilities which the government forces other banks (reserve requirements) and individuals to accept. As these are a legal tender, the bank's debtors cannot refuse to accept it – central banks can always restore its own solvency and liquidity at negligible marginal costs.
26 Selgin and White 1987.
27 Selgin and White 2002.
28 Eichenbaum and Wallace 1985 and Good 1998.
29 Note removed.
30 That is the economic rational behind Friedman's critique of Woodford's argument: 'With nothing to back up the CB's expression of intent [of changes in the equilibrium rate of interest on the money market], I suspect that the market would cease to do the CB's work for it' (Friedman 2000, 16).
31 For a more detailed discussion of the final settlement by the transfer of wealth see further.
32 E.g. Borio 1997, Guthrie and Wright 2000 and Thornton 2000.
33 See inter alia White (1999) and Schmitz (2002b) for a discussion and the related literature.
34 Selgin 1994.
35 Taub 1985.
36 This price formation mechanism constitutes an example of price matching; market prices for all goods are available in the unit of account and converted into electronic money units at the prevailing market price for electronic monies in terms of the unit of account. A price discovery strategy, on the other hand, would entail price setting mechanisms for each electronic money constrained only by no-arbitrage conditions across goods markets denominated in different electronic monies (Schmitz 200b).
37 Schmitz 2000b.
38 White 1984.
39 See in particular Costa Storti and De Grauwe (2003, Figure 13.2).
40 E.g. Cowen and Kroszner 1994.
41 For a detailed demonstration of the inefficiency of the parallel use of multiple units of account see Schmitz (2002b).

6 What drives demand for and supply of electronic money? Theoretical background and lessons from history

Cornelia Holthausen

Introduction

A wide range of models on electronic money have been published over the last years. Some assume that electronic money will exist side-by-side with central bank money, some conjecture that demand for central bank money will be driven to zero and that only the new forms of payment will circulate among economic agents. There are also papers assuming that all payments will be made directly via transfer of wealth.

Models of all these different types are reviewed in Schmitz' paper. In his critical assessment, however, he argues that some important issues are left aside in most papers. Some essential features of the new monetary regime are often conjectured instead of being discussed or derived. In particular, it is usually simply assumed whether or not the widespread use of electronic money will indeed imply that the demand for central bank money will vanish completely. Similarly, there is no thorough analysis on whether a reduction of demand for central bank money really reduces the efficacy of monetary policy or whether central banks will maintain the ability to conduct efficient monetary policy. Furthermore, most papers remain silent on how an economy without central bank money will look and how this equilibrium is reached. Schmitz pays particular attention to whether there will be one or perhaps several units of account; whether central bank money will remain the unit of account; and to how the medium of exchange will be chosen among different currencies.

In my view, to answer some of these questions, a more careful modelling of demand is needed. It is not possible to conjecture a certain payment behaviour by economic agents if it is unclear what drives their usage of money. Similarly, and connected to this, the ability and incentives for potential money issuers to provide a stable currency should be analysed.

In the following section, I will cite some of the existing literature on private money that has tackled this issue in more detail, even if not in the context of electronic money. The third section addresses issues of currency competition, both on a national and an international level, which can be applied to the case of electronic money. In the fourth section, some historical experiences with private monies will be reviewed. An evaluation of these 'free-banking' episodes can be useful when hypothesising how a world with widespread usage of electronic money will look like. Finally, the fifth section concludes.

Modelling money demand

Even though analytical tools for analysing situations with privately issued currencies have existed for some time, most of the papers reviewed by Schmitz develop their own scenario instead of drawing upon the results of the existing literature. Indeed, the coexistence of public and private monies as media of exchange has received quite a lot of attention in the literature in the past, even if not linked to the possibility of electronic devices.

As a starting point, it is necessary to analyse why agents hold and use money at all. As is well known, money serves a purpose of transferring wealth when there is no *double coincidence of wants*, that is, when the seller of a good has no interest in consuming the good that the buyer has to offer. In this case, it is beneficial to use other commodities as a means of payment. In particular, as modelled by Kiyotaki and Wright (1989), a seller would prefer to accept a good in exchange for another that is most likely to be accepted by others as a medium of exchange. Only if the resale value is large enough will a good (private money) be accepted as means of payment.

Still, even if there is no double coincidence of wants, money may not be necessary to conduct trades. One can conceive of situations in which agents buy and sell on credit, or take part in a (circular) chain of trading relationship. However, such mechanisms tend not to work because there are other frictions that make money useful: *asymmetry of information* and the *lack of commitment* or a lack of enforcement. When agents are not fully informed for example about the quality or amount of the other agents' good on offer, they would prefer receiving some commonly accepted money instead of some other agent's good. Similarly, when agents are not able to enforce a certain contract, they will refrain from using complex contracting arrangements and rather accept money. Thus, in the presence of these frictions, money is important and beneficial, because better allocations of goods can be reached.

However, as argued by Kocherlakota (1998a,b), it is precisely those frictions leading to the essentiality of money that make the acceptance of private money problematic. Let me analyse each of them separately.

Enforcement is limited whenever agents can default on their obligations without being punished, that is, at no or little cost. An inefficient legal framework can, for instance, be the reason behind this. Limited enforcement poses a problem for the circulation of private money: private money is more easily accepted when it is clear that the promised claim will be fully redeemed by the issuer (or, rather, that there is a common belief that this will be the case).[1]

In a world where contracts cannot be enforced by an authority, contracts have to be self-enforcing. That means they have to be constructed in such a way that honouring the contract is incentive-compatible. Such contracts can be constructed in models in which agents meet again at some point in the future. Here, feedback effects (e.g. through punishment) are possible, even if the future connection goes via third parties. For instance, an agent pays by issuing a claim (on the generally accepted medium of exchange or another good), the seller then purchases another good using this claim and so on. If this claim circulates among agents, it is called private money. In Kiyotaki and Moore (2000), agents cannot commit to their promises except for the one agent that issued the claim. In this scenario, inside money circulates. However, they do not shed light on the question why some agents should be more able to commit themselves than others. Many recent models analysing private money simply assume that enforcement is possible.

Asymmetry of information may also create problems for the acceptance of a certain type of money. Agents wanting to use this money are not able to fully control the prudent behaviour of the issuer, who has incentives to misbehave (see e.g. Schreft, 1997). Issuers of private money can have incentives either to reduce the backing of the currency, or to hold assets that are of a lower quality than promised.

If information about money issuers is scarce, reputation can be a way to overcome this problem. Indeed, as already argued by Bagehot (1873), an important element in the acceptance of money is trust. This is one of the crucial differences between private and public money: Governments whose money has circulated for a long time have been able to establish some kind of reputation. Issuers of private money, on the other hand, still need to build up some degree of trust.

Cavalcanti and Wallace (1999) examine a model in which an agent can build up reputation. They assume that some agents have access to a type of technology, which Cavalcanti and Wallace assume to be banks, which keeps record of all past actions taken. If they can make access to this information freely available to the public, these banks can then produce private claims. Because complete information about these banks is available, economic agents can punish a misbehaving bank, for example by not accepting its money. Therefore, it provides incentives for the banks to behave prudently and leads to acceptance of their money. The authors show that such an economy with private money is able to support more outcomes than one with only outside (government) money, so it ex-ante improves the allocation. One might complain that the result hinges upon only banks having access to the record-keeping technology, because it is not clear why other agents should not be able to use it. One possibility is that it is related to the agent's size – the larger the institution, the better known, and the more likely consumers will build up trust in the institution.

One arrangement that can help to build up and maintain trust in issuers is a clearinghouse. As argued by Gorton and Mullineaux (1987), clearinghouses indeed were often used to deal with asymmetric information (this issue will be addressed in more detail in the fourth section).

Currency competition

In an economy with electronic money in circulation, several private issuers will most likely offer competing monies as means of payment. Will competition be beneficial, providing incentives to issue the best, that is most stable money? Or can it be harmful in the sense that issuers have incentives to 'cheat' and provide backing of lower quality in order to stay competitive?

This dilemma has been at the heart of the early debate on private money. Both Hayek (1976) and Klein (1974) argued that the government monopoly of note issue created a situation in which there was no discipline for the monetary authorities to maintain a stable value of their currencies. Both authors proposed to solve this incentive problem by allowing competition for the provision of outside money. With several competing currencies circulating, the public would quickly replace any unstable currencies. Knowing this, monetary authorities would refrain from the over-issuance of notes.

By contrast, Friedman (1960) argued that free currency competition would lead to an infinite price level. These diverse predictions are the result of different underlying assumptions: Friedman assumed that notes by different issuers would be indistinguishable, hence, issuers would have incentives to back their notes as little as possible, and this would lead to a downward spiral in terms of the value of notes (this effect is similar to Gresham's law). Klein and Hayek, on the other hand, argued under the assumption that notes were distinguishable by issuer. Under this scenario, an inflationary bank could only keep its notes in circulation if it paid higher interest rates on its liabilities, so that consumers were indifferent between the different types of monies.[2]

The area of international currency competition can be used to take a closer look at the Hayek-Klein scenario, as here, indeed several distinguishable currencies are competing. A few papers study the competition between national currencies in an international context. Matsuyama, Kiyotaki and Matsui (1993) extend the Kiyotaki-Wright setup to a model with two currencies and show that, in equilibrium, three types of regimes can occur: in the first, each country uses its own currency, in the second, one currency emerges as the only means of payment in both countries, and in a third, both currencies are perfect substitutes to each other. Thus, their theory predicts that it is indeed possible to have a situation in which more than one currency is actually being used by agents. Other papers rationalising the usage of several currencies are Zhou (1997) and Rey (2001).

The results of these papers could be very illuminating for predictions on the future use of electronic money. One important feature of all the above models is that there is generally *equilibrium indeterminacy*, that is, in many cases both types of equilibria (with one and with several currencies in circulation) exist, and it is impossible to say which one will be chosen by economic agents. Multiple equilibria are a typical feature that arise in the presence of *network externalities*. A good exhibits network externalities if the usefulness of consuming a certain good increases in the number of other agents consuming the same good. A typical example is a telephone network, where it is beneficial to join a network that already has many other members. Money is another example, because clearly, the more agents accept a certain type of money, the more useful it is to hold this type instead of another. The models by Jones (1976) and Kiyotaki and Wright (1989) also draw upon this feature. In these models, agents accept the good they believe will be accepted my most other agents.

Network externalities are clearly a feature exhibited by electronic money, and can explain why its usage around the world has generally been much lower than anticipated by many. Essentially, there are two types of these externalities, both on the demand and the supply side: for consumers, it is only worth holding a certain type of e-money if they believe they are able to use it for purchases. At the same time, merchants will only invest in the technology needed to process electronic money if sufficiently many consumers want to pay with it. Even though the usage of electronic money may be more efficient than the one of, say, cash, the economy can be 'stuck' in the old equilibrium without much usage of electronic money, because of the equilibrium indeterminacy. Moreover, it is difficult to predict what would encourage economic agents sufficiently to switch to an equilibrium with more usage of electronic money.

Given these difficulties to reach an equilibrium with electronic money, it seems even more far-fetched to believe that several electronic monies could be in circulation as media of exchange. Again, network externalities may hinder the wide acceptance of more than one e-purse. At the same time, it may be the case that it is not worthwhile for issuers to enter the market, because money may be most efficiently supplied by a single supplier. In other words, is money a natural monopoly? Both network externalities and a natural monopoly industry are likely to lead to a very concentrated environment. In order to maintain competition, some regulation would be appropriate in order to ensure competition, or at least, to make the market contestable.

Looking at the historical evidence, at first glance one is tempted to conclude that money is indeed a natural monopoly. However, as pointed out by Vaubel (1990), money was usually issued by a single supplier because competition was restricted, and not necessarily because it was more efficient to do so. Still, there were a few times in history when competition between money issuers was possible, namely the so-called free-banking episodes. We will turn to these in the next section.

Can we learn from history?

While electronic money is naturally a relatively new phenomenon, the coexistence of several currencies within a country – be they private and/or public – is not. Therefore, it is useful to analyse past experiences of local currency competition. Private and public money (or different private monies) have been in circulation together during several periods in the past. Generally, these episodes took place before the establishment of central banks with a monopoly of money issuance. Commercial banks were allowed to issue and circulate notes themselves, independently of publicly issued notes. Still, the unit of account usually remained the public currency or gold.

The term 'free banking' is often used to describe these episodes. It originally refers to the period from 1837 to the founding of the Federal Reserve Bank in 1913 in the US, even though this period was not free of banking regulation, as the term might seem to suggest. According to Laidler (1992), free banking is now most commonly used to describe periods of largely unregulated banking activity without a central bank.

Study of these episodes can be very helpful in conjecturing features of a monetary system in which a public currency circulates together with electronic money. Moreover, historical experience can give answers to several important questions. A central question is whether the circulation of private money is sufficiently stable. Also, if private money circulates, can the financial system regulate itself or is there reason for a public authority to regulate its issuance? In particular, is it necessary to require redeemability at par to ensure a stable supply of private money?

One early example of private money is the Scottish Free Banking system, described in White (1995). When the monopoly on note issue of the Bank of Scotland was not extended in the beginning of the seventeenth century, two more banks, the Royal Bank of Scotland and the British Linen Bank, entered the note-issuing business. The notes of these three banks circulated in parallel. Banks made profits from note issue because they invested in interest bearing assets while their notes were in circulation. Naturally, the longer the notes were circulating, the higher were bank profits, and this gave rise to some attempts to maximise the circulation of notes: some banks agreed not to seek redemption of each other's notes. Still, the system was quite stable and relatively developed, as can be seen from its relatively wide branching network.

The Scottish banks set up branching systems, which also helped to increase the circulation of notes. From the fact that many banks had branching networks across the country, White concludes that there was no evidence of a natural monopoly in the production of currency. The experience with free banking in Scotland thus supports the notion that there can be several competing currencies in use in single country.

In the US, two prominent free-banking episodes can serve as examples of private co-operations between banks that facilitated the circulation and acceptance of a multitude of private monies. Under the Suffolk Banking system (1825–58), notes from many different banks circulated in the Boston area. Under the leadership of the Boston-based Suffolk Bank, a system of net clearing of notes was established. All members of the system had to make a significant non-interest bearing deposit with the Suffolk Bank, providing a certain degree of backing to the Suffolk Bank.

This system brought a number of advantages to the financial system. First, because in its function as a clearing institution the Suffolk Bank accepted notes from other banks, it had incentives to monitor both their portfolio management and their note-issuing behaviour. This in turn gave incentives for banks to behave prudently and led to a higher degree of stability of the banking sector than that obtained in other regions of the country at the same time. Second, the system was very successful in achieving a uniform currency throughout New England. All notes were traded at par, with no discount reflecting the geographic distance to the issuer. Hence, the experience suggests that it is not always necessary to require redeemability at par by regulation.

However, one criticism of the system refers to the Suffolk Bank's dominant position in the market and asks whether it was able to obtain monopoly rents. Indeed, the original aim of the system was to eliminate the circulation of banks notes that had been issued by banks located outside Boston. The literature is divided on this issue. Using balance sheet data, Rolnick, Smith and Weber (1998) find that the Suffolk Bank was able to achieve unusually high profits and conclude that the note clearing business was a monopoly. Calomiris and Kahn (1996), on the other hand, argue that the system was the result of a joint agreement between many banks in the Boston area, and thus constitutes an example of co-operative behaviour leading to a superior outcome.

As a final historic example of private money, I would like to mention the New York Clearing House Association (NYCHA). The NYCHA was mainly a clearinghouse for interbank large value payments. However, it was special because at several points during its existence it provided liquidity in times of crisis, and thus took on a function that is usually seen as typical for a central bank.

The liquidity was issued in the form of Clearing House Loan Certificates (CHLC). This was a temporary loan made from the banks of the association to other member banks in need of liquidity. Typically, a situation in which CHLCs were issued was one where a bank faced massive deposit withdrawals which would have resulted in its inability to settle its interbank claims in the clearinghouse. To avoid a chain reaction (leading to the possible failure of even more system members), the NYCHA decided to issue the CHLCs to help overcome temporary liquidity problems. This system was acceptable to members because any member defaulting on interest payments resulting from the loan would be evicted from the system, which was a strong incentive for repayment and helped to maintain trust for the other members.

As Cannon (1901) writes, these notes should not be regarded as real currency because they could only circulate among the members of the clearinghouse. Still, I believe that they constitute an interesting example of privately organised co-operative activities in the absence of a central bank, which increased financial, and ultimately also price, stability.

The above-mentioned examples provide evidence that the private system, to some extent, is able to maintain a stable currency system even in the absence of strong government regulation or central bank involvement. However, there are also a few drawbacks of free-banking episodes.

First, the monetary system in those episodes was generally less stable than those with central bank money. The number of bank failures was significant, and this made the issued currencies worthless to their holders (see Carr and Mathewson (1988) reporting failures in Scotland, and Dwyer (1996) or Hammond (1957) for the US). Often, the reason for failure was simple portfolio mismanagement. Seemingly, many of the failed banks had too illiquid portfolios which made them very vulnerable to bank runs (see Economopoulous, 1990). Some form of government regulation might have alleviated those problems.

Another problem concerns the significant costs of monitoring a multitude of issuers. Gorton (1999) states that, during the free banking era, several hundred banks were issuing notes. A profession of the time was the one of note broker. These devoted significant resources to gathering information. One source of information was the so-called note reporters, that is, newspapers containing information on issuers.

Would a system with electronic money face the same problems of information dissemination? The need to obtain information on issuers would clearly be there. However, modern computer facilities would lead to more detailed and faster information flow, facilitating the process immensely. Moreover, a more thorough governmental regulation as mentioned earlier could to some extent reduce the need for decentralised information gathering.

Do we need a new form of monetary policy?

In the discussion on the future of central bank money, a core theme is the ability of the central bank to continue to conduct monetary policy. In particular, it is argued that the emergence of electronic money will remove the link between supply of central bank money and the price level. The possibly extreme consequent reduction of demand for central bank money is often seen as being problematic.

However, the emergence of electronic money per se does not constitute a problem for the conduct of monetary policy. At present, it is usually the case that e-money purses are loaded either with cash, or are using bank account balances, while the receiver then discharges the amount to his current account. Therefore, even if the demand for central bank money may be reduced as a consequence, a direct link between e-money and central bank money continues to exist. Monetary policy can be conducted as before, albeit with new estimates for the velocity of money.

As soon as electronic money can be used independently of central bank money, however, this link may be destroyed. This might be the case if the receiver of electronic money does not deposit the received amounts on his current account but instead uses it to make further payments to third parties. In other words, if a certain type of electronic money is used for payments repeatedly, say in a network of merchants, the central bank will no longer be able to control the money supply. This is the reason why for instance the European Central Bank has issued a regulation which restricts issuers of electronic money (see ECB 1998, 1999).

Relatively little is said about possible alternatives to monetary policy as we know it today. Perhaps policy methods need to change in line with developments on the supply side? The main goal of monetary policy is to maintain a stable price level. Given that there is only one currency in circulation, this stability refers to the one currency only. How would this goal be defined if several monies circulated in the economy? Instead of thinking about a price level, one would possibly need to take into account a multitude of prices. This would apply both to a circulation of private paper money as well as a replacement of paper money by electronic devices.

One way of controlling the price level would be to try to control exchange rates between the different monies in circulation and central bank money (if the latter still exists). Here, the role of monetary policy would need to be replaced by other policy instruments such as regulation and supervision of issuers. The goal of the applied measures would be to avoid problems such as over-issuance, imprudent backing of notes or fraud. The policy framework would thus need to make use of tools currently employed by supervisors of financial institutions.

Conclusion

There are many open issues regarding the future evolvement of electronic money. The literature on e-money so far has only picked up a few of these issues.

In order to have a full-fledged theory on electronic money, it is first of all necessary to model what drives demand for money, be it supplied by a governmental agency or by a private bank. Second, one needs to model the competition between different issuers of money (again, private and/or public) in order to determine the future supply of different monies. These analyses would serve as a useful background to conjecture to what extent electronic money is going to have a significant role in the future, whether central bank money will still be in demand, and how monetary policy may need to adjust.

Furthermore, it is useful to take a look at historic experiences with currency competition, by examining, for example, the free banking episodes. Here, useful insights can be drawn on the ability of the private sector to provide a stable monetary environment. From past experiences, it seems that private agents are indeed to a large extent able to fulfil this aim. Arrangements such as clearinghouses, for instance, proved to be important in reducing problems of asymmetric information and incentives. Still, if there is private money in circulation, replacing central bank money fully or to some extent, issuers should be closely supervised. One would like to avoid imprudent portfolio management by issuers. Instead, one should think about adequate regulation of issuing institutions, perhaps similar to banking regulation. Finally, given that electronic money exhibits network externalities and its production resembles a natural monopoly, regulation would be useful in order to maintain a competitive environment.

References

Bagehot, W. (1873) *Lombard Street; A Description of the Money Market*, London: H.S. King.

Calomiris, C. and Kahn, C. (1996) 'The Efficiency of Self-Regulated Payments Systems: Learning from the Suffolk System', *Journal of Money, Credit and Banking*, 28: 766–97.

Cannon, J. (1901) *Clearing Houses: Their History, Methods and Administration*, London: Smith Elder and Co.

Carr, J. and Mathewson, F. (1988) 'Unlimited Liability as a Barrier to Entry', *Journal of Political Economy*, 96: 766–84.

Cavalcanti R. and Wallace, N. (1999) 'Model of Private Bank-Note Issue', *Review of Economic Dynamics*, 2(1): 104–36.

Dwyer, G. P. Jr. (1996) 'Wildcat Banking, Banking Panics, and Free Banking in the United States', *Federal Reserve Bank of Atlanta Economic Review*, 81: 3–6.

Economopolous, A. (1990) 'Free Banking Failures in New York and Wisconsin: A Portfolio Analysis', *Explorations in Economic History* 27: 421–41.

European Central Bank (1998) *Report on Electronic Money*, Frankfurt/Main: ECB.

European Central Bank (1999), *Opinion of the European Central Bank on Electronic Money and on Credit Institutions*, Frankfurt/Main: ECB.

Friedman, M. (1960) *A Program for Monetary Stability*, New York: Fordham University Press.

Gorton, G. (1999) 'Pricing Free Bank Notes', *Journal of Monetary Economics*, 44: 33–64.

Gorton, G. and Mullineaux, P. (1987) 'The Joint Production of Confidence: Endogenous Regulation and Nineteenth Century Commercial-Bank Clearing Houses', *Journal of Money, Credit, and Banking*, 19: 457–84.

Hammond, B. (1957) *Banks and Politics in America from the Revolution to the Civil War,* Princeton: Princeton University Press.

von Hayek, F. A. (1976) *Denationalisation of Money – The Argument Refined*, Hobart Paper Special 70, London: Institute of Economic Affairs.

Jones, R. (1976) 'The Origin and Development of Media of Exchange', *Journal of Political Economy*, 84: 757–75.

Kiyotaki, N. and Moore, J. (2000) 'Inside Money and Liquidity', mimeo London School of Economics.

Kiyotaki, N. and Wright, R. (1989) 'On Money as a Medium of Exchange', *Journal of Political Economy*, 97: 927–54.

Klein, B. (1974) 'The Competitive Supply of Money', *Journal of Money, Credit and Banking*, 6: 423–53.

Kocherlakota, N. (1998) 'Money is Memory', *Journal of Economic Theory*, 81: 232–51.

Kocherlakota, N. (1998b) 'The Technological role of fiat money', *Federal Reserve Bank of Minneapolis Quarterly Review*, Summer 1998: 2–10.

Laidler, D. (1992) 'Free Banking: Theory', J. Eatwell, M. Milgate and P. Newman (eds) *The New Palgrave Dictionary of Money and Finance*, London: Palgrave, 196–97.

Matsuyama, K., Kiyotaki, N. and Matsui, A. (1993) 'Toward a Theory of International Currency', *Review of Economic Studies*, 60: 283–307.

Rey, H. (2001) 'International Trade and Currency Exchange', *Review of Economic Studies,* 68: 443–64.

Rolnick, A., Smith, B. and Weber, W. (1998) Lessons From a Laissez-Faire Payments System: The Suffolk Banking System (1825–58). *Federal Reserve Bank of Minneapolis Quarterly Review*. Vol. 22, No. 3: 11–21.

Schmitz, S. (2002) 'The Institutional Character of New Electronic Payments Systems: Redeemability and the Unit of Account', in M. Latzer and S. Schmitz, *Carl Menger and the Evolution of Payment Systems – from Barter to Electronic Money*, Cheltenham: Edward Elgar, 159–83.

Schreft, S. (1997) 'Looking Forward: The Role for Government in Regulating Electronic Cash', *Federal Reserve Bank of Kansas City Economic Review* (Fourth Quarter): 59–84.

Vaubel, R. (1990) 'Currency Competition: Free Entry Versus Governmental Legal Monopoly', in K. Groenveld, J. Maks, J. Muysken, (eds), Economic policy and the Market Process, pp 23–38.

White, L. (1995) *Free Banking in Britain. Theory, Experience and Debate, 1800–1845* (second edition), London: Institute of Economic Affairs.

White, L. (1999) *The Theory of Monetary Institutions*, Oxford: Basil Blackwell.

Williamson, S. (1999) 'Private Money', *Journal of Money, Credit, and Banking*, 31: 469–91.

Zhou, R. (1997) 'Currency Exchange in a Random Search Model', *Review of Economic Studies*, 64: 289–310.

Notes

1 Schmitz (2002) provides a discussion on whether privately issued money always needs to be fully redeemable in order to be accepted. See also White (1999).

2 For a different view of the feasibility of competition of privately issued 'fiat-type' monies see White (1999) and Schmitz (2002).

7 Monetary policy in a world without central bank money

Stefan W. Schmitz[1]

A number of papers in the current debate on the impact of innovation in payment systems on monetary policy address the issue in an economic set-up without money. I demonstrate that these models fail to elaborate the institutional structure of the payment system they attempt to model; and they neglect issues regarding the existence of a generally accepted medium of exchange and of a medium of final settlement in the underlying payment systems.

Schmitz (2002b) concludes that the most likely institutional structure of the payment system will maintain the pivotal role of central bank (CB) money. Nevertheless, it is important for central banks to understand the potential implications for monetary policy implementation of a hypothetical world without CB money, even if it is considered unlikely at the moment.[2]

The role of CB money as a generally accepted medium of exchange is a precondition for the implementation of monetary policy in the current institutional set-up. In the paper I show that conferring certain regulatory powers to central banks enables them to implement an equivalent to monetary policy in a world without CB money. The analysis is based on the conceptualisation of a payments system that does not settle in CB money; a system in which the demand for CB money is actually zero. It explicitly provides a role for a generally accepted medium of exchange and a medium of final settlement. The relevant instruments available to central banks are the imposition of minimum reserve requirements in the generally accepted medium of exchange and the competence to grant or charge interest on reserves held as deposit balances at the central bank. The ability to apply these instruments is independent of the monopoly position of central banks to provide the generally accepted medium of exchange at zero marginal costs. It is a consequence of their role as public institutions endowed with certain regulatory competencies. Thus, central banks would be able to manipulate the opportunity costs of holding minimum reserves without manipulating the market price of the medium of final settlement. As shown by an analysis of the legal foundations of the operations of the ECB and the Fed, central banks do in fact already possess the necessary regulatory powers. Politico-economic objections to granting central banks the necessary regulatory powers would also apply to the institutional frameworks currently in place in the Euro area and the US.

In the first section, I review the current proposals for monetary policy in 'moneyless' worlds. The second section discusses monetary policy implementation in a world without CB money that explicitly provides a role for a generally accepted medium of exchange, a unit of account and a medium of final settlement. In the second section, I first conceptualise the sequence of instruments of monetary policy implementation in a world with CB money. Second, I discuss their potential application by a central bank that does not issue the generally accepted medium of exchange[3] to conduct a functional equivalent to monetary policy. Third, I analyse politico-economic issues of the proposed alternative instruments of monetary policy implementation. The third section summarises and concludes the paper.

Proposals for the conduct of monetary policy in a world without central bank money

For the purpose of his analysis of monetary policy without money Goodhart (2000) assumes that all payments are based on the transfer of eMonies denominated in various distinguishable units. The various electronic means of payments (eMonies) float against each other. There is no generally accepted medium of exchange and, hence, no uniform unit of account. The central bank also offers an eMoney and quotes a bid price (deposit rate) and an ask price (loan rate) just like all other financial institutions operating in the market for liquid funds. The spread between the bid and the ask price of liquidity is determined by real factors such as uncertainty, uncertainty preferences, resource costs of holding inventory positions in various financial assets and the related uncertainty, potential asymmetries of information among market participants, operating costs as well as transaction and information costs.[4]

As the central bank is a not-for-profit organisation and the government's bank, it can afford to offer a lower spread and incur potentially large losses, because the government offers unlimited financial backing. Assuming credibility of the government's commitment, the central bank's bid and ask price move the market rate for liquid funds even if it is not the monopoly supplier of liquidity.[5] Apart from the fact that the government might eventually face a budget constraint[6] as well, the proposal seems incomplete and inconsistent. As there is no uniform unit of account, there is no uniform price level the central bank can attempt to stabilise.[7] The market for liquid funds seems to consist of short-term financial assets but there is no tradable, most liquid asset that exchanges at the lowest spread relative to all other assets. The market for liquid funds seems to consist of funds that are less liquid than electronic means of payment (eMonies), that's why there is demand for eMonies despite the spread involved in acquiring them in exchange for liquid financial assets. As there is no medium of final settlement the model is faced with problems of circularity. If issuers offer bid and ask spreads (interest payments) solely in their own electronic money unit, the exact form of the budget constraint is not clear, unless the units are redeemable in some asset that is costly to acquire or produce for each issuer (outside money). It is unclear to what extent monetary policy provides a nominal anchor for the real economy in the proposal, as neither the concept of nominal prices nor the mechanisms of nominal price formation are defined in this model.

Furthermore, the effects of monetary policy on macroeconomic activity appear to be limited in the model. A contraction of monetary conditions in the eMoney issued by the central bank directly affects the price level measured in the respective eMoney unit and, hence, directly influences macroeconomic activity only in the share of the economy dealing in this particular electronic money unit. The system seems to be unstable. What are the indirect effects of the central bank's policy on eMonies issued by competing institutions? Expansionary monetary policy implies that the central bank decreases its spread on the market for liquid financial assets so that it potentially attracts more agents willing to sell and, correspondingly, issues a larger volume of its own electronic means of payment. At the margin a monetary expansion has the following effects: The CB eMoney unit depreciates relative to its competitors and the price level in the CB unit increases. However, the price levels in all other units remain unchanged. Covered interest rate parity ensures the isolation of all other nominal spheres from that of the central bank.[8] This argument assumes that the exchange rates between eMonies are more flexible than goods prices quoted in the other eMonies. As the entire debate rests on the assumption that information and communication technology overcomes frictions in the economy, exchange rates between eMonies are indeed likely to be less sticky than goods market prices. Assuming that competitors follow, they incur losses and, eventually, bankruptcy would be the consequence, as they face a strict budget constraint. The central bank eventually emerges as the sole issuer of eMoney and it can resume the role of the monopoly issuer of the generally accepted medium of exchange and uniform unit of account. Alternatively, its competitors leave their spread unchanged. The central bank attracts all trades and drives its competitors out of the market, unless the respective price level in the CB eMoney unit increases and its exchange rates vis-à-vis its competitors depreciate accordingly. Again, nominal prices in other eMonies would remain unchanged by the expansionary monetary policy of the central bank.

Goodhart further assumes that electronic money issued by the central bank is '... always acceptable (since it is the government's bank), so it can always force out unto the system as much [of its own electronic money] as it wants ...' (Goodhart 2000, 28). This insinuates that it is the generally accepted medium of exchange and, hence, the unit of account. In that case the model collapses to the current institutional arrangement for the conduct of monetary policy with a large number of competing electronic means of payments, but a single generally accepted medium of exchange and a uniform unit of account.

Freedman (2000) also offers a thought experiment on the implementation of monetary policy in a world of alternative settlement mechanisms off the central bank's books. He provides two proposals: (i) the central bank could sell treasury bills and restrict acceptable means of payment to its own liabilities. Unless it is the sole source of treasury bills, it remains unclear why other banks cannot buy treasury bills at the going market rate from other market participants or the Treasury. Regulation ensures the acceptance of CB money as means of payment for treasury bills, but not necessarily as generally accepted medium of exchange and medium of final settlement in other transactions. It remains unclear what the unit of account is in the model, what the treasury bills are denominated in, and how final settlement is supposed to take place when treasury bills mature.

(ii) The central bank continues to provide liquidity to the market via standing facilities even when settlement takes place off its books. It would finance these standing facilities by its own liabilities, which apparently continue to be accepted by market participants. Furthermore, CB money seems to remain the generally accepted medium of exchange, the unit of account and the medium of final settlement. But the details of the institutional structure of the payment system are not explicated in the model and can only be inferred from the general description of the model. Consequently, the model does not offer much of an alternative to current systems. Private settlement systems reduce the demand for CB money further, but in principle it remains positive and the entire system continues to be firmly rooted on CB money. Essentially, the model fails to describe a world without CB money.

Henckel/Ize/Kovanen (1999) discuss the conduct of monetary policy without base money in the following model. Automatic end-of-day settlement takes place on the books of private clearing and settlement institutions (CSI). Net debtors and net creditors would pay and receive, respectively, the rate of interest for their end-of-day net positions. Treasury bills would collateralise these credit transactions. The exchange of treasury bills would provide finality without settlement on the books of the central bank. Collateralised overnight positions would extend the netting process infinitely. Although there is no money in the model, the central bank retains the power to set the overnight rate, by changing the borrowing and the lending rates on end-of-day net credit and net debit balances in the private clearing and settlement system. These must be demanded through the central bank due to regulation. This enables the central bank to determine both the borrowing and the lending rates, independently of whether its own liabilities serve as medium of final settlement, in principle. It sets the rate solely for the net positions in the overnight market and not for the stock of reserves. In the model the stock of reserves consists of treasury bills and the opportunity costs of holdings; these define the costs of liquidity rather than the rates on end-of-day net positions, which are largely a residual of the payments process.

The ability of the central bank to set the overnight interest rate – for the automatic end-of-day settlement – lends support to the interpretation that CB money remains the medium of final settlement, the generally accepted medium of exchange, and the unit of account. Hence, the demand for CB money must be positive. The authors argue that the central bank can impose its target rate on the market for overnight settlement by changing the borrowing and the lending rates on its overnight facilities sufficiently. But the credible ability to provide funds and accept funds from the market without limits or regulation are less is a prerequisite for the efficacy of such a policy instrument, as Friedman (1999, 2000) and Woodford (2000) point out.

Despite the continuing monopoly position of the central bank the authors attempt to provide a solution to the problem of price level determination with purely endogenous money. They derive a Taylor-type rule from a small macro-model to show that the announcement of the target inflation rate is sufficient to anchor the system and determine the price level in this economy.

The model explicitly mentions neither a generally accepted medium of exchange nor a unit of account. But, it seems that CB money remains the generally accepted medium of exchange and the unit of account in the model. Consequently, the transfer of Treasury bills does not provide settlement finality in an economic sense, as these constitute claims to CB money. As the authors admit themselves, the transfer of treasury bills rather extends the netting process. Instead of a model without CB money the authors discuss a model with aggregate overnight settlement balances in the interbank market close to zero. Nevertheless, CB money remains the medium of final settlement, while treasury bills are means of settlement for end-of-day net positions without settlement finality.[9] Otherwise the model would imply circularity.

In order for a Taylor-type rule to be sufficient to determine the price level in this economy, the price level must be defined. If the demand for CB money is zero, the price level in CB money is defined; it is infinite. Again the set-up of the model is inconsistent, unless the demand for CB money – also the generally accepted medium of exchange in the model – remains positive and the money supply is not purely endogenous as the authors claim. Consequently, their model reduces to an exposition of extended net settlement and Taylor-type rules in a model with positive demand for CB money but aggregate overnight settlement balances close to zero. In principle, the individual overnight reserves can remain different from zero for at least some nights due to uncertainty. As such the institutional arrangement of the model is quite similar to the monetary framework in New Zealand.[10]

Lahdenperä (2001) offers a conceptualisation of the future state of the monetary system. The model assumes two competing settlement systems, both of which are assumed to provide final settlement in eMoney. One is operated by the central bank, the other one by a private clearing and settlement institution. Participants are free to choose, but switching between systems involves transaction costs. Both settlement agents provide standing facilities at the respective rates. Alternatively, participants can obtain funds in the money market. CB and privately issued eMoney trade are at par and a single money market rate prevails. In order to cope with liquidity shocks in both settlement systems, participants hold reserves in both eMonies. Can the central bank steer the money market rate? It is determined by the weighted average of the respective lending rates of the competing settlement agents. Lahdenperä concludes that the central bank maintains the power to manipulate the lending rate in its own settlement system and, hence, the money market rate. Its influence on the money market rate is only partial, as it is no longer the monopoly supplier of the medium of final settlement and of reserves in the system. The alternative provider of final settlement commands similar influence on the overnight rate. The relative impact of the policy decisions of the two settlement agents depends on the weights of their respective lending rates in an 'aggregate lending rate'. The weights correspond to the market shares of the competing settlement systems and their respective probabilities of a reserve deficiency or excess.

The model assumes that the competing eMonies trade at par, but does not discuss how parity is supposed to be maintained. The institutional arrangement supporting the assumed structure of the model is not discussed at all. It remains unclear whether the privately issued eMoney is backed by commodities, financial assets or fiat-type money. If CB money remained fiat money and the competing eMoney were backed by commodities or financial assets, parity would be maintained if and only if the respective portfolio values were expected to remain perfectly stable in nominal terms at all times. Unless privately issued eMoney is backed by CB money that condition is unlikely to be met. The eMonies differ only with regard to the respective lending rates. If eMonies are perfect substitutes in the money market, the differences of the lending rates can only be a temporary and transitory phenomenon caused by transaction costs of switching between systems. Over time the differences are expected to average out, unless other characteristics of the settlement systems (e.g. settlement and operational risk, supervisory functions, etc.) exactly balance the interest rate differential. Otherwise, the system with the lower lending rate would gain market share and eventually a monopoly position.

Furthermore, Lahdenperä does not clarify whether any of the competing eMonies fulfil the role of the generally accepted medium of exchange and the medium of final settlement. In a different section (p. 29, fn 18), however, he subscribes to King's (1999) position that a uniform unit of account '[...] could be provided mechanically by regulation as other weights and measures today'. As argued in Schmitz (chapter 5 in this volume) the analogy between the regulation of weights and measures and the unit of account is based on a misconception of the subjective nature of exchange in economics.[12]

If the model is taken seriously, the following implicit institutional arrangement supports its main features, for example, perfect substitutability, a single money market rate but different lending rates: CB money remains the generally accepted medium of exchange and the medium of final settlement. The alternative privately issued eMoney is denominated and redeemable in CB money. The alternative settlement system economises on CB reserves through netting arrangements. By incurring a higher settlement risk compared to real-time gross-settlement in CB money through netting and pooling of reserves the settlement agent can invest the resulting excess reserves in low risk government debt and the system can be profitable.

How does monetary policy work under this institutional arrangement? The central bank maintains the monopoly provider of the generally accepted medium of exchange at zero marginal costs. The demand for settlement balances to meet the redeemability requirement constitutes a constraint for the alternative eMoney issuer that consequently faces positive marginal costs in the provision of eMoney. The alternative eMoney serves as a means of payment – neither as the generally accepted medium of exchange nor as the medium of final settlement. Such arrangements are already widespread (e.g. CHIPS) and have posed no serious threat to the efficacy of monetary policy implementation, in principle.

Monetary policy in a world without money

In the first part of this section, I present a conceptualisation of the instruments employed by central banks to implement monetary policy in a world with CB money. Subsequently I discuss the choice of the medium of final settlement in a world without CB money. Then I assess whether and to what extent the instruments available to central banks are sufficient to conduct and implement an equivalent to monetary policy in a world without CB money. In the final part, I briefly consider the ensuing politico-economic implications of the proposed instruments of monetary policy implementation in a world without CB money.

The money market and monetary policy in a world with CB money

Bindseil (2004) presents a historical account of monetary policy implementation at the Bank of England, the Deutsche Bundesbank (formerly Deutsche Reichsbank), and the US Federal Reserve System. Throughout most of their histories the Bank of England and the Deutsche Bundesbank focused on the money market rate as their main operating target rather than quantity variables. The Fed on the other hand favoured targeting quantity variables until the 1990s. In recent years the ECB, the Fed, and the Bank of England all rely on interbank money market interest rates as operating targets in monetary policy implementation.[13] Also Borio (2001) shows that central banks in industrial countries implement monetary policy by manipulating interbank money market interest rates and through open market operations (OMOs).[14] They implement monetary policy by manipulating the relative price, the opportunity costs of holding the medium of final settlement, that is, the spread between the rate of interest on CB money held on accounts with them and the rate on the optimal alternative investment.

I will restrict the analysis to five instruments of monetary policy implementation, namely (1) the communication strategy of central banks – the announcement of a specific level for the operating target (the main policy variable), (2) minimum reserve requirements, (3) open market operations, (4) intraday credit[15] and (5) standing facilities.

Although payment system participants are not necessarily legally required to settle in CB money, they generally do so. The role of CB money in wholesale payment systems is the nexus between the central bank, the economy wide payment system, and nominal GDP as well as the price level. Its role as medium of final settlement is an incidental function of its role as generally accepted medium of exchange. In principle, the reliance on CB money at the level of wholesale payment systems eliminates credit and liquidity risks after settlement, for example, vis-à-vis the clearing and settlement institution.[16] Settlement in CB money ensures finality in an economic sense (as opposed to finality in a legal sense as unconditional and irrevocable payment), since CB money is neither an explicit claim to real resources nor to nominal payments. Reserve requirements are usually averaged over a fulfilment period and the same account at the central bank can usually be employed to administer settlement balances, to fund and defund in the interbank settlement process, and to fulfil reserve requirements. In interbank payment systems CB reserves are the medium of final settlement. This guarantees a positive demand for CB money, irrespective of the means of payment employed in retail payment systems, as long as these are denominated in the CB money and, thus, linked to the interbank market.[17]

Settlement on the books of central banks has additional advantages. As public institutions they are required to provide access to their accounts and to intraday credit on fair, equal, and non-discriminatory conditions. Freedman (2000) argues that settling on the books of a competitor could lead to a competitive advantage for the private clearing and settlement institution, that their liabilities carry some credit risk, and that they cannot increase liquidity at zero marginal cost as can central banks and credibly act as lender of last resort (LLR).

The starting point of the analysis is the *announcement of a level for the main operating target* directly (e.g. Federal funds rate) or indirectly (e.g. via the rate at which OMOs are conducted such as the minimum bid rate). The credibility of the announcement and its impact on the interbank money market rate are a consequence of the capacity of central banks to increase aggregate reserves at zero marginal costs. Despite the relatively small size of their OMOs, they can manipulate the main policy rate very well. It was frequently argued that they can largely rely on the impact of their communicated target values for the operating target rates ('open mouth operations').[18] This simplification of monetary policy implementation is not justified, despite the relatively small size of OMOs. Central banks do in fact employ a number of additional instruments, in order to actually implement the intended market rate and to contain the volatility of the operating target around its announced level.

At the intended level of the main policy variable (i.e. the overnight interest rate – r^{pol} in Figure 7.1) a structural liquidity deficit in the payment system prevails. It is defined as the difference between demand $D(r^{pol})$ and supply $S(r^{pol})$ of overnight reserves at the intended level of the main policy rate.[19] The structural liquidity deficit implies that money market participants demand more CB reserves on aggregate than are available on the market. In principle, the variation of *minimum reserves requirements* would be an additional instrument for central banks to manipulate aggregate demand for CB reserves D and its volatility throughout the maintenance period. Minimum reserves requirements change very infrequently and their role in containing the volatility of D rests largely on averaging arrangements during the fulfilment period.

Central banks estimate the (expected) level of the structural liquidity deficit and set the volume of refinancing operations ΔR^S, in a way that the aggregate supply of reserves $S(r^{pol}) + \Delta R^S$ equals their (expected) aggregate demand $D(r^{pol})$ at the intended overnight rate r^{pol}, in other words they determine the volume of OMOs according to $\Delta R^S = D(r^{pol}) - S(r^{pol})$. The manipulation of aggregate supply by OMOs is the instrument to actually implement the intended market rate on the market. The equilibrium will only prevail temporarily, as central banks conduct refinancing operations which are reversed after a prespecified period (repos), such that the structural liquidity deficit is covered only temporarily.[20] The structural liquidity deficit ensures that at least some market participants have to bid for additional aggregate reserves, if their outstanding debt with the central bank matures. Comparing the small size of OMOs and the liquidity deficit to turnover in interbank markets is therefore misleading, as it relates the continuous reallocation of aggregate reserves among market participants to discretionary and exogenous changes in aggregate reserves.

The aggregate volume of overnight reserves consists of the sum of the overnight reserves of individual banks. The level of aggregate overnight reserves is manipulated by *OMOs*. The slope and position of the demand curve D are not

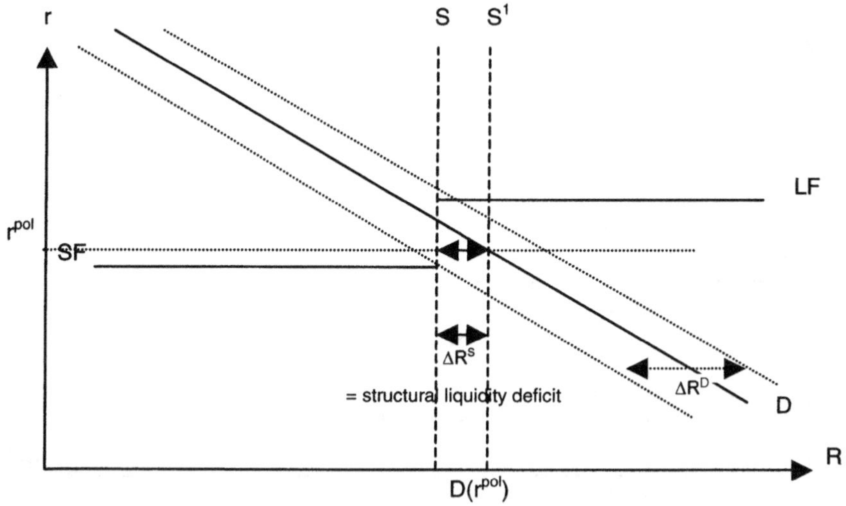

Figure 7.1 Aggregate overnight reserves and the structural liquidity deficit in the overnight market

known to central banks with certainty, neither is the size of the structural liquidity deficit. The precise demand for CB reserves varies within the band indicated by ΔR^D. The demand for CB reserves at OMOs depends primarily on the level of minimum reserve requirements, the expected working balances over the maintenance period, the averaging arrangements in place and the expected future overnight interest rates. In equilibrium, the expected discounted marginal costs of borrowing in the overnight market until the next refinancing operation must equal the expected marginal costs of borrowing from the central bank via OMOs at the current refinancing operation. The relatively small size of OMOs compared to daily volume is irrelevant, as price formation works at the margin and the central bank is in the unique position to manipulate the supply at the margin at zero marginal cost. Unless the liquidity situation between OMOs deviates substantially from expectations, market participants have no incentive to borrow or lend at rates substantially over and under the intended level of the main operating target.

Central banks can address this uncertainty by auctioning off additional aggregate liquidity ΔR^S, in order to allow some degree of flexibility. Figure 7.2 illustrates that ΔR^S is endogenised between the bounds $[0, \Delta R^{Smax}]$, which are determined by central banks, as is the minimum bid rate r^{OMOmin}. If the aggregate demand for refinancing D_2^{OMO} is below the maximum volume of a specific refinancing operation, all bids will be satisfied at the respective bid rates[21] and the volume will equal the sum of the bids $\Delta R_2^S < \Delta R^{Smax}$. If the sum of the bids D_1^{OMO} exceeds ΔR^{Smax}, not all bids will be satisfied and the allotment of additional funds and the marginal allotment rate will depend on the allotment mechanism in place.

The overnight rate remains close to the target level also between OMOs, as central banks determine the maximum operational volume of OMOs precisely

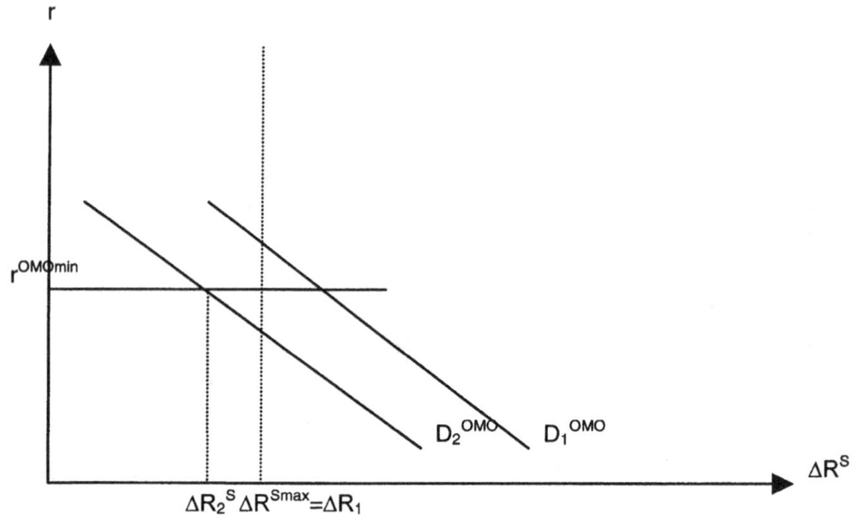

Figure 7.2 The maximum volume of OMOs, demand for additional CB reserves, and the realised increase in aggregate CB reserves

with the intention to cover the estimated structural liquidity deficit in the money market at the announced level of the operating target. The implementation process is designed in a way to ensure that aggregate supply and aggregate demand intersect at the announced level of the operating target, unless central banks' estimates of the structural deficit are wrong and/or conditions in the money market change unexpectedly. In equilibrium, commercial banks bidding for overnight reserves have no incentive to pay overnight rates substantially above the target level, as they arrange their bidding behaviour at OMOs accordingly. In addition, the effects of temporary liquidity shocks on aggregate demand for overnight reserves are (partly) absorbed by averaging arrangements for reserve requirements over the fulfilment period. The longer the remaining fulfilment period, the more of a temporary shock can be absorbed by intertemporal substitution.[22] Given that the frequency of OMOs is relatively high with respect to the fulfilment period market participants can to some extent intertemporally substitute bidding at OMOs for overnight credit.

After refinancing operations are concluded, the supply of aggregate reserves is determined and it is beyond the discretion of the participants of the interbank market and the payment system. They are active on the intraday and the overnight money market and supply and demand on both markets are interdependent. In order to address larger liquidity shocks or those occurring towards the end of the fulfilment period, central banks have additional instruments at their discretion that enable them to stabilise the operating target in the period between OMOs: intraday credit and standing facilities.

Individual banks' demand and supply of intraday liquidity on the intraday market are determined by their initial CB reserves at the beginning of the trading day, the

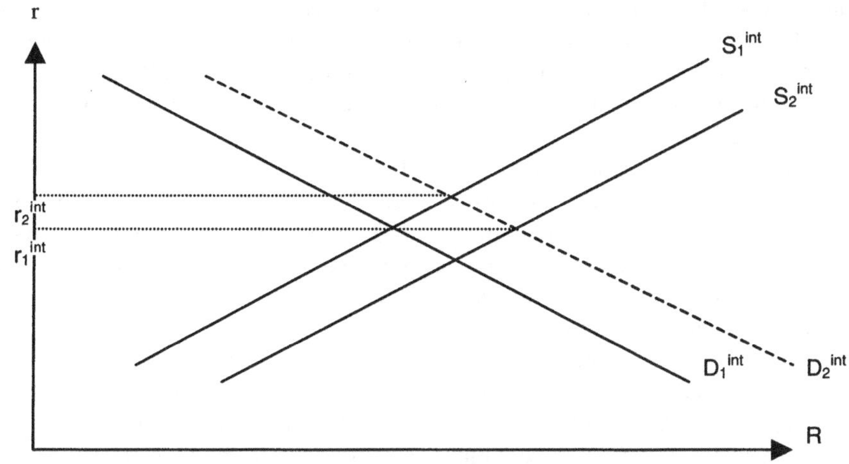

Figure 7.3 The intraday money market and the availability of intraday credit from central banks in RTGS

processes of payments credited and debited, their degree of synchronicity and the target level of overnight CB reserves as well as the institutional structure of the payment system. Intraday reserves yield a decreasing marginal liquidity service yield and the demand schedule D^{int} is downward sloping (Figure 7.3). The sequence of incoming and outgoing payments is largely a stochastic process and beyond the discretion of individual banks in the very short run.[23] Hence, individual banks' demand and supply on the intraday market are subject to uncertainty and so are their aggregates. In a net settlement system these short run liquidity shocks are likely to average out during the day as participants grant each other implicit credit.

Most interbank payment systems in industrialised countries are RTGS (real time gross settlement systems) with *intraday credit* provided by central banks.[24] In RTGS the dynamics can lead to a liquidity gridlock and an increase of aggregate demand for intraday liquidity from D_1^{int} to D_2^{int} and to an increase in the intraday market rate from r_1^{int} to r_2^{int}. In order to contain the volatility in the intraday market, which would imply welfare costs due to the costs of hedging against the implied uncertainty and obscure market signals on the liquidity situation, central banks can provide intraday credit, which absorbs very short term temporary liquidity shocks, to market participants and shift the supply curve from S_1^{int} to S_2^{int}. Intraday credit also increases the stability of the interbank payment system vis-à-vis net settlement systems by making payment obligations more visible and enhancing risk management. Hence, the supply of aggregate intraday liquidity is endogenised to some extent. In addition, intraday credit reduces the liquidity costs in RTGS. It is usually collateralised to decrease the credit risk of central banks and has to be retired at the end of the day, in order to prevent spill over into the overnight market, where it would exert downward pressure on the main operating target.[25]

As intraday credit has to be repaid at the end of the trading day, the aggregate supply of overnight reserves is independent of intraday liquidity management by central banks. The demand for overnight CB balances is primarily determined by a number of related factors: end-of-day balance of banks' settlement accounts, minimum reserve requirements, the remaining duration of the fulfilment period and the expectations concerning future overnight interest rates until the end of the fulfilment period.[26]

Given the remaining duration of the fulfilment period, banks' expectations concerning the future overnight interest rates until the end of the maintenance period, and their expectations concerning the overnight interest rate at the end of the day, the banks formulate their targets for overnight reserves. Given these targets banks try to utilise their (limited) room for manoeuvre during the day to reach end-of-day balances equal to the targets. After realisation of end-of-day balances banks lend excess reserves or borrow to cover deficiencies in the overnight market. Their lending and borrowing decisions are not mechanically determined by end-of-day balances relative to the overnight reserve target, but also reflect deviations of the overnight rate from expectations. Given banks' expectations concerning future overnight rates, increases in current overnight rates provide an incentive for banks to decrease their overnight reserve target and to increase lending or decrease borrowing in the market. The elasticity of supply and demand with respect to overnight rates depends on banks' risk preferences.[27] Due to the decreasing marginal liquidity service yield CB overnight reserves provide, their aggregate demand is a decreasing function of the overnight rate. Their aggregate supply is determined exogenously.

Changes in expectations of future overnight rates over the maintenance period shift the demand and supply curves in the current overnight money market. Increases in expected future rates shift the current demand schedule upwards as current reserves can be substituted for future reserves over the averaging period. Correspondingly, decreasing expected future rates shift the demand schedule downwards.

In addition to OMOs and intraday credit, central banks usually grant access to (some sort of) *standing facilities* to park (deposit facility) or to raise liquidity (lending facility) at a premium relative to market rates. The rates charged on these (r^{DF} and r^{LF} in Figure 7.4) set a floor and a ceiling for the overnight money market rate. The zero marginal cost of providing CB reserves and the function of CB money as generally accepted medium of exchange are preconditions for the ability of central banks to define floors and ceilings for money market rates. They do not face budget constraints with respect to r^{DF} and r^{LF} at the margin. In Figure 7.4 the deposit facility *DF* and the lending facility *LF* ensure that the main operating target remains within the bounds $[r^{DF}, r^{LF}]$ despite shifts in the demand from D to D_1 or to D_2.

As r^{DF} and r^{LF} constitute penalty rates deviating from the interbank money market rate, participants have an incentive to borrow and deposit funds on the overnight market before turning to standing facilities. A more liquid market is an additional intermediate policy objective for central banks, as it constitutes an important feature of an environment conducive to smooth monetary policy implementation and financial market stability. Standing facilities are not employed to steer market liquidity at large, but to reduce the volatility of the overnight rate in

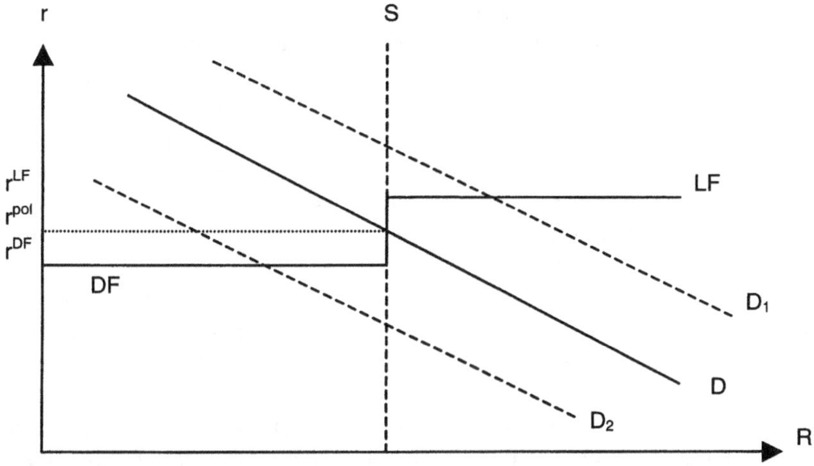

Figure 7.4 The overnight market for CB reserves and standing facilities (between OMOs)

cases of temporary liquidity shocks exceeding the absorptive capacity of minimum reserve requirements.[28]

The money market and monetary policy in a world without central bank money

Friedman (1999) and Woodford (1998) extrapolate trends of decreasing ratios of CB money to aggregate spending to the mathematical limit. The amount of CB money necessary to operate wholesale and retail payment systems finally reaches zero. They implicitly assume that the behaviour of the monetary system while approaching the limit, and once it has reached the limit exhibits structural continuity, in principle. Even though CB money is expected to become irrelevant in the limit, the monetary system does not exhibit any signs of instability or structural changes.[29]

Contrary to their approach, I discuss the institutional arrangements of the interbank payment system once the limit is reached and the implications for monetary policy in a world without CB money. The questions that have to be addressed are: (1) what is the medium of final settlement in the interbank payment system and how does it relate to the generally accepted medium of exchange (if one exists)? (2) What are the instruments available to central banks to manipulate price and/or quantity on the money market? (3) What are the politico-economic consequences of alternative instruments of monetary policy implementation?

The choice of the medium of final settlement

In a world with CB money the generally accepted medium of exchange (CB money) also functions as the medium of final settlement in the interbank payment system. Schmitz (2002b) argues that, for efficiency reasons, a single generally accepted medium of exchange and a unified unit of account in the relevant market prevail in a world without CB money. All means of payment are claims to the medium of final settlement. In order to reduce the spread between bid and ask interest rates in the interbank market by eliminating credit, liquidity and market risk, the generally accepted medium of exchange will also serve as the medium of final settlement in the interbank market. It is the only medium that is not a direct or indirect claim on future resources and that ensures settlement finality in the interbank payment system.[30]

A number of papers that present models of worlds without money argue that debt instruments or real wealth would serve as media of final settlement.[31] What would the implications for the efficiency of the settlement process be?

(1) If there were no generally accepted medium of exchange and settlement took place in claims on real wealth, settlement would imply credit, liquidity and market risk of the debt instrument. Upon maturity of the debt instruments the underlying real resources would have to be exchanged (bartered) for the goods actually demanded at additional transaction costs. The eligible instruments would only exchange at par if they were perfect substitutes and equally liquid. Otherwise, the most liquid settlement instrument would exchange at the lowest bid-ask spread and drive out other debt instruments in the settlement process. The price level would be defined in terms of the underlying real resource. Its stability would depend on the institutional arrangements constraining the issue of the debt instruments and the production function of the underlying real resource.

(2) The existence of a generally accepted medium of exchange would increase efficiency, as claims on real wealth would be dominated by financial assets denominated in a generally accepted medium of exchange but indexed to the prices of the underlying real resources.[32] If there were a generally accepted medium of exchange and interbank payments were finally settled in debt denominated in the generally accepted medium of exchange, the transaction costs are higher compared to settlement in the generally accepted medium of exchange due to credit, liquidity and market risk. Each settlement in debt instruments would require negotiations concerning the instruments accepted in settlement and the relevant relative price. The eligible instruments would be perfect substitutes at the relevant market price if the bid-ask spread were zero and all eligible assets would be equally liquid. However, final settlement in the generally accepted medium of exchange also involves transactions costs and opportunity costs of holding reserves in the generally accepted medium of exchange. Market participants economise on reserves in various payment systems by extended netting, queuing mechanisms and intraday credit in payment systems. Nevertheless, all settlement media remain claims to the generally accepted medium of exchange and settlement finality in an economic sense is only provided by the generally accepted medium of exchange.

(3) If debt instruments (and interest thereon) are settled in further debt instruments in the future, the process will be subject to circularity and no effective

constraint of the issue of debt is in place for an individual issuer at the margin, unless debts are eventually settled in real resources. If debt instruments are eventually redeemed in outside money, the system will resemble a form of extended netting.

In a world without CB money, the generally accepted medium of exchange will be outside money that will be available to issuers of electronic means of payment at non-zero marginal costs only. In the case of commodity money, its aggregate supply is determined by its marginal costs to the market participants.[33] If individual transaction balances vanish in the face of innovation in the retail payment system (e.g. credit, debit, and cash cards as well as ubiquitous electronic access to deposits), the demand for the medium of final settlement (and the generally accepted medium of exchange) would be determined only by the demand for settlement balances in the interbank payment system.

The instruments available to CBs in a world without CB money

The market on which central banks would implement monetary policy in a world without CB money is the market for the respective medium of final settlement, that is, the generally accepted medium of exchange (interbank or money market). Central banks lose their monopoly in the provision of the generally accepted medium of exchange at zero costs at the margin. They face the same demand and supply schedules as other market participants. How does that affect the efficacy of the instruments of monetary policy implementation? The (1) communication strategy of central banks – the announcement of a specific level for the operating target rate – and the following instruments will be considered: (2) open market operations, (3) minimum reserve requirements, (4) intraday credit and (5) standing facilities.

The *announcement of a specific level of the relative price of the medium of final settlement* by central banks would be insufficient to steer market rates effectively in a world, in which central banks have lost their monopoly in the provision of the medium of final settlement at zero marginal cost. They are no longer in a position to impose a structural liquidity deficit on the money market by shifting the supply curve of the medium of final settlement at zero marginal costs. In principle, they can withdraw quantities of the medium of final settlement from the market by OMOs (i.e. open market purchases) as can all other market participants, as Goodhart (2000) argues correctly. Like them central banks would have to bear the resulting costs. The volume of open market purchases necessary to effectively steer market rates and the resulting losses are ultimately empirical questions, as is the sustainability of political support for covering the resulting costs by public funds. Central bank interventions in foreign exchange markets can serve as analogy. Currency crises teach that both the funds available to central banks and the political will of societies to cover costs related to large scale foreign exchange interventions are not unlimited. Evidence shows that central banks failed to defend fixed exchange rates in foreign exchange markets, despite their previous explicit commitment and strong incentives in terms of often substantial welfare losses in the aftermath of currency devaluation. The monopoly provision of the generally accepted medium of exchange is a precondition for effectively steering money market rates by imposing a structural liquidity deficit on the money market and by announcing specific levels for the operating target.

Central banks can impose *minimum reserve requirements in terms of the medium of final settlement* as a ratio of market participants' liabilities as instrument of monetary policy implementation. In principle, they could impose minimum reserve requirements in terms of CB reserves on market participants by statutory regulation.[34] Hence, they could force a positive demand for CB money upon market participants. As this paper focuses on the analysis of monetary policy in a world without CB money, I will not consider this option further. In addition, minimum reserve requirements in terms of CB money are not necessarily sufficient to ensure the role of CB money as generally accepted medium of exchange. In order to ensure the efficacy of monetary policy implementation, minimum reserve requirements must be imposed in the generally accepted medium of exchange. Minimum reserve requirements in any asset enable policy makers to manipulate the marginal costs of financial intermediation, just like policy induced changes of other input prices.[35] Unlike changes of the opportunity costs of the generally accepted medium of exchange, changes in input prices do not change the relative price of the medium of final settlement (the generally accepted medium of exchange) vis-à-vis all other assets and goods in the economy. A change in the relative price of the generally accepted medium of exchange can only be reflected in a change in the nominal prices of all other goods in the economy, as the nominal price of the generally accepted medium of exchange in terms of the unit of account is fixed. Changes in input prices only affect the relative price of intermediation services to all other assets and goods in the economy. For the relative price increase of intermediation services to have a similar effect on the aggregate price level as an increase in the opportunity costs of holding the generally accepted medium of exchange, the nominal price of intermediation services would have to remain constant and the nominal prices of all goods in the economy would have to adjust. There is no mechanism that fixes the nominal price of intermediation services and the nominal price of financial intermediation is likely to adjust faster than the nominal prices of all other goods in the economy. That is not to say that an increase in the nominal price of bank credit might not eventually affect aggregate demand and the nominal price level at all, but the transmission mechanism is essentially different from the monetary policy transmission mechanism based on manipulation of the marginal opportunity costs of holding the generally accepted medium of exchange.

The proposed prominent role of minimum reserve requirements in the generally accepted medium of exchange in monetary policy stems from the prominent role of the banking system and bank liabilities in the payment system and from the role of the bank credit channel in the transmission of monetary policy. Monetary policy is implemented via the money market precisely because it is a peculiar input market, not because it is just one of the input markets of financial intermediation. In a tiered payment system all payments are eventually settled in the generally accepted medium of exchange, so that changes in the marginal opportunity costs of the generally accepted medium of exchange affect the marginal costs of all payments in the economy. The implementation of monetary policy in the market for the generally accepted medium of exchange captures other transmission mechanisms as well, such as transmission along the yield curve and the interest rate channel, as long term debts are denominated in the generally accepted medium of exchange.

Averaging arrangements over the fulfilment period would have the advantage of absorbing short term liquidity shocks and smoothing demand for the medium of final settlement. In order to be effective at the margin, minimum reserve requirements would have to be binding, that is, exceed settlement balances. The ability to impose minimum reserve requirements is a consequence of the character of central banks as public institutions endowed with regulatory competencies and is independent of the monopoly to issue the generally accepted medium of exchange at zero marginal costs.

The instrument of providing *intraday credit* below money market rates in RTGS is available to central banks only at positive marginal costs. These consist of the opportunity costs associated with holding reserves in the medium of final settlement and the costs of lending below market rates. Lending below market rates would provide an opportunity for arbitrage for market participants, who borrow funds from central banks and lend them at higher rates in the money market. The monopoly provision of the generally accepted medium of exchange is a precondition for the costless provision of intraday credit in RTGS.

Standing facilities provided at penalty rates deviating from the market rate, on the other hand, constitute a potential source of income for central banks. However, as long as market rates are within the floor and the ceiling defined by the penalty rates, market participants have no incentive to deposit with or lend from central banks. If market rate fluctuations exceed the bound, standing facilities can only be offered at costs for central banks and provide arbitrage opportunities for market participants. The monopoly provision of the generally accepted medium of exchange is a precondition for standing facilities to effectively define of a floor and a ceiling for money market rates.

Monetary policy in a world without CB money is feasible by a combination of minimum reserve requirements in the medium of final settlement and interest paid or charged on these. These competencies are a consequence of the central banks' role as public institutions with certain regulatory authorities transferred to them by the respective legislature.[36] They are independent of the loss of central banks' monopoly to issue the generally accepted medium of exchange at zero marginal costs. They can entail the transfer of authority to impose obligations on third parties such as the authority to impose minimum reserve requirements in the medium of final settlement as well as to specify an *interest rate paid or charged* on these for the purpose of monetary policy implementation.

The opportunity costs of holding additional reserves in the medium of final settlement are determined by the marginal costs of obtaining it on the market minus the (positive or negative) remuneration of minimum reserve requirements at the margin. Irrespective of the loss of the monopoly provision of the medium of final settlement central banks can manipulate the opportunity costs of holding reserves at the margin. Rather than assuming the money market rate to be the main policy target, central banks can treat the market rate of the medium of final settlement as exogenous and steer liquidity conditions (i.e. the opportunity costs of holding reserves at the margin) by manipulating the interest rate paid or charged on minimum reserves held by market participants directly. Comparable to the implicit taxation of financial intermediation by imposing minimum reserve requirements in a world with CB money, remuneration paid or fees charged on minimum reserve requirements in a world without CB money correspond to a subsidy or to a tax, respectively, on the liabilities of market participants.

An increase (decrease) of the interest charged on minimum reserves shifts the stock of reserves held on average over the maintenance period and, hence, the aggregate demand for the medium of final settlement downwards (upwards), respectively, at a given market rate. The supply schedule of the aggregate stock of the medium of final settlement is unaffected by changes of opportunity costs of holding reserves, as it is determined by marginal costs of supply of the medium of final settlement (e.g. marginal costs of production in the case of a commodity standard). The equilibrium price in the market for the medium of final settlement decreases (increases). Under the precondition that the supply of the medium of final settlement is not infinitely inelastic, the equilibrium price decreases (or increases) less than the interest rate on minimum reserves; thus, the opportunity costs of the stock of minimum reserves increase (or decrease) at the margin. This tightens (or eases) liquidity conditions for market participants.

In addition to the aggregate stock of the medium of final settlement banks supply end-of-day excess reserves on the overnight market. How will the supply of excess reserves influence the marginal costs of the aggregate supply? The demand and the supply of excess reserves is an unplanned residual of the payments processed during the operation hours of the payment system. After realisation of end-of-day balances banks lend excess reserves, which are not remunerated, or borrow to cover deficiencies in the overnight market. As interest is neither paid nor charged on excess reserves, their supply and demand are independent of the opportunity costs of holding the stock of minimum reserves. If the time it takes to adjust the aggregate stock of the medium of final settlement is below the maintenance period, arbitrage opportunities ensure that market participants have no incentive to borrow from each other at costs above the marginal costs of the medium of final settlement. In analogy to the determination of the opportunity costs of holding reserves in a world with CB money, the opportunity costs of the stock of aggregate minimum reserves held are determined by the marginal costs of the aggregate stock supplied and not by the rate on the flow of the medium of final settlement, due to demand and supply of excess reserves and to the interest charged on minimum reserves.

In principle, central banks can manipulate the opportunity costs of holding reserves at the margin but with less accuracy, as the discontinuation of standing facilities and intraday credit deprives them of additional instruments to absorb liquidity shocks and to stabilise money market rates. They lose control of the supply of the medium of final settlement, such that supply shocks add to the uncertainty they face in monetary policy implementation in a world without CB money.

Politico-economic consequences of alternative instruments of monetary policy implementation

The transfer of authority to pay or charge interest on minimum reserves, that is, to levy a tax or to grant subsidies on the liabilities of credit institutions, for central banks raises *politico-economic* questions concerning the legitimacy of the transfer of such powers from the respective legislature to an independent institution.

Central banks are public institutions endowed with regulatory powers (e.g. in areas such as monetary policy implementation and payment system oversight). As public institutions the rule of law requires their competencies to be based on explicit legal foundations like central banking acts and statutes, such as the Protocol on the Statute of the European System of Central Banks and the European Central Bank (1992) and the Federal Reserve Act (1913). These constitute the legal foundations for actions of the ECB and the Fed including decisions which impose obligations on third parties. In general, legislatures grant central banks the discretion necessary to execute the respective acts independently and effectively, while retaining legislative authority.

Article 110 (1) of the Treaty establishing the European Union and Article 34.1 of the ECB Statutes confer regulatory power to the ECB to the extent necessary, inter alia, to define and implement monetary policy and to promote the smooth operation of the payment system. Article 110 (3) of the Treaty and Article 34.3 of the ECB Statutes grant the ECB the right to impose sanctions in cases of non-compliance with its regulations and decisions within the limits and under the conditions adopted by the EC Council. The acts and omissions of the ECB are subject to judicial control by the Court of Justice according to Article 35 of the ECB Statutes. The EC Council is required to adopt the necessary complementary legislation after consultation with the Commission, the European Parliament, and the ECB (Article 42 of the ECB Statutes and Article 107(6) of the Treaty establishing the European Union).

In particular Article 19.1 of the ECB Statutes authorises the ECB to require credit institutions established in the member states to hold minimum reserves on accounts with the ECB, levy penalty interest and to impose other sanctions in cases of non-compliance. The regulations concerning the calculation and determination of the required minimum reserves may be established by the Governing Council. The application of minimum reserve requirements is restricted to the pursuance of the ECB's monetary policy objectives. However, Article 19.2 ensures that the EC Council (in accordance with the procedure laid down in Article 106 (6) of the Treaty establishing the European Union) maintains the legislative authority over the definition of the basis for minimum reserves, the maximum permissible minimum reserve ratios, as well as the appropriate sanctions in cases of non-compliance, which are defined in Council Regulation (EC) No 2531/98 and No 2532/98 of 23 November 1998. ECB Regulation (EC) No 2157/1999 further specifies the details of infringement procedures.

In accordance with Article 110 (1) of the Treaty, Article 5 of Council Regulation (EC) No 2531/98 and Article 6 of Council Regulation (EC) No 2532/98 explicitly grant regulatory power to the ECB for the purpose of non-discriminatory exemptions from minimum reserve requirements and for the purpose of more detailed specifications than provided in Article 3 of the respective regulation of the basis for minimum reserve requirements, for the specification of the reserve ratios as well as for more detailed specifications of sanctions. Article 4 (1) of Council Regulation (EC) 2531/98 specifies that the ratios may not exceed 10 per cent of any relevant liabilities forming part of the basis for minimum reserve requirements but may be 0 per cent. The ECB may impose sanctions in cases of non-compliance – in accordance with Article 110 (3) of the Treaty establishing the European Union and specified in Article 7 (a) and (b) of Council Regulation (EC) 2531/98 – of up to 5 percentage points above the ECB's marginal lending rate or twice the ECB's marginal lending rate of the reserve shortage, or may require the relevant institution to hold a non-interest-bearing deposit with the ECB up to three times the amount of the shortage. Consideration (5) of Council Regulation (EC) 2531/98 explicitly states that the ECB must have the flexibility to react to new payment technologies such as the development of electronic money. Consideration (6) of Council Regulation (EC) 2531/98 restricts the ECB's flexibility in the implementation of the regulation to act in the pursuance of the objectives of the ESCB as laid down in Article 2 of its statutes and in the principle of not inducing significant undesirable delocation or disintermediation in the financial system. Similarly, consideration (5) of Council Regulation (EC) 2532/98 emphasises that, in order to provide an effective regime for the administration of sanctions, the ECB must have some discretion within the limits and conditions of the respective regulation.

Based on the regulatory discretion conferred upon it the ECB specifies the details of the application of minimum reserve requirements in Regulation (EC) No 1745/2003 of the European Central Bank. Article 2 defines the institutions subject to minimum reserve requirements as credit institutions and branches according to the relevant directive (2000/12/EC); Article 3 specifies the reserve base as consisting of deposits and debt securities issued, unless they are owed to any other institution subject to reserve requirements or to the ECB or an NCB. The reserve ratios applicable are defined in Article 4 as 0 per cent for all deposits and debt instruments with a maturity over two years, repos, and deposits redeemable at notice over two years, and 2 per cent for all other liabilities included in the reserve base. Article 6 states that institutions shall hold their minimum reserve on accounts of the NCBs and that the reserves shall be denominated in euro. Article 8 defines the remuneration of reserves.

Similar institutional frameworks are in place in the US. Congress transfers substantial regulatory authority to the Federal Reserve System in a number of areas, including the conduct and implementation of monetary policy but also supervisory and regulatory authority over a wide range of financial institutions. The Fed issues Federal Reserve Regulations from Regulation A (Extension of Credit by Federal Reserve Banks) to Regulation EE (Netting Eligibility for Financial Institutions). The US Constitution gives the right to coin money and set its value to the US Congress, which delegates the right to the Federal Reserve System in the Federal Reserve Act of 1913. Accordingly, the Fed is subject to oversight by Congress.

Section 19 paragraph (2) sub-paragraphs (A) and (B) of the act impose minimum reserve requirements on depository institutions, that is, on their transaction accounts and their non-personal time deposits. The act authorises the Board of Governors to define the terms used in the section, to prescribe regulations it deems necessary to effectuate the purpose of Section 19, and to determine the exact reserve ratio by regulation within broad bounds defined in the act. Paragraph (2)(A)(i) determines the ratio at 3 per cent for that proportion of each depository institution's transaction accounts of $25,000,000 or less.[37] In paragraph (2)(A)(ii) the act grants the board some discretion with respect to the ratio applicable to that proportion a depository institution's transaction accounts exceeding the dollar amount in sub-paragraph (i). The board may prescribe a ratio not greater than 14 per cent and not less than 8 per cent. Sub-paragraph (B) authorises the board to impose minimum reserve requirements on non-personal time deposits. The applicable ratio has to be between zero and 9 per cent. The regulatory authority, in imposing minimum reserve requirements on transaction accounts and on non-personal time deposits, is restricted to the purpose of implementing monetary policy.[38]

Paragraph (4) enables the board to impose a supplemental reserve requirement on depository institutions of not more than 4 per cent, if that increases reserves to a level essential for the conduct of monetary policy. Supplemental reserves have to be maintained in Earnings Participation Accounts and are remunerated. The board is entitled to remunerate supplemental reserves at a rate not more than the rate earned on the securities portfolio of the Federal Reserve System during the previous quarter. Subsection (c)(1) contains the promulgation of rules and regulations regarding the maintenance of balances but does not stipulate that the reserves are to be denominated in US dollar. Sub-paragraph (l)(9) entitles the board to prescribe regulations establishing procedures as may be necessary to impose civil money penalties on depository institutions violating any provision of Section 19.

The detailed provisions concerning reserve requirements are contained in the Code of Federal Regulations Chapter II (Federal Reserve System) Part 204 (Reserve Requirements of Depository Institutions – Federal Reserve Regulation D). Paragraph 204.1 (c) defines the depository institutions which are required to hold minimum reserves. Paragraph 204.7 (a) authorises the Fed to assess charges for deficiencies in required reserves at a rate of 1 percentage point per year above the primary credit rate. The precise ratios applicable to the different categories of liabilities of credit institutions are defined in paragraph 204.9. For net transaction accounts over $6.6 million and up to $45.4 million the ratio is 3 per cent and for net transaction over $45.4 million the ratio is 10 per cent of the amount over $45.4 million plus $1,164,000. For all other categories it is zero. The Fed may impose emergency reserve requirements under extraordinary circumstances for up to 180 days, after which affirmative action of at least five members of the board is required for each extension (paragraph 204.5), and supplemental reserve requirements to increase the amount of reserves maintained to a level essential for the conduct of monetary policy for up to one year, after which the board shall review and determine the need for continuation (paragraph 204.6). In both cases reports to Congress shall be transmitted promptly stating the reasons for imposing additional reserve requirements. Currently, no reserve requirements are imposed under either paragraph. Reserve requirements are not remunerated, but the Fed pays interest on service-related balances.

The analysis of the current institutional framework concerning the ECB demonstrates that the EC Council and the European Parliament have already conferred substantial regulatory power to the ECB, but these powers are both subject to judicial control by the Court of Justice and subject to the legislative authority of the EC Council and the European Parliament. In particular, the ECB has the competence to impose minimum reserve requirements and to remunerate them. The framework provides the ECB with substantial operational flexibility and discretion. Politico-economic objections to granting central banks the power to impose minimum reserve requirements on market participants, or to pay or charge interest thereon in a world without CB money, apply to the current framework as well.

Indeed, the current legal framework hardly needs to be adapted to govern monetary policy implementation in a world without CB money. The obligation to hold minimum reserves denominated in the euro is at the discretion of the ECB. It is laid down only in the relevant ECB Regulation but not in the relevant Council Regulations or the ECB Statutes. The framework would have to be adapted marginally with respect to the right to charge interest rates on minimum reserves in addition to the right to remunerate them. The adaptation is not one in substance as the current framework already allows imposing financial obligations on institutions subject to minimum reserve requirements in the form of opportunity costs associated with holding reserve requirements.

Similarly, the Federal Reserve Act transfers regulatory authority to the Board of Governors. Despite the fact that the Act provides more details with respect to the imposition of minimum reserve requirements than the statutes of ECB, the Fed enjoys substantial discretion in imposing and administering minimum reserve requirements. The Federal Reserve Act does not require minimum reserve requirements to be denominated in US dollar, nor does Regulation D.

Conclusions

Many papers presenting proposals for monetary policy without CB money turn out to assume that the central bank maintains a monopoly in the provision of the generally accepted medium of exchange and the medium of final settlement on closer inspection of the implicit institutional structure of the monetary system presented. Unfortunately, they do not make the institutional structure explicit, for example, the money market, the existence of a generally accepted medium of exchange and a medium of final settlement are rarely discussed in detail. The models are, thus, incomplete and inconsistent. The efficacy of monetary policy is discussed mostly from the perspective of the demand for CB money. Rarely the role of the generally accepted medium of exchange, the unit of account, and the medium of final settlement as well as their monopoly provision by central banks at zero marginal costs are taken into proper account. The regulatory authority of central banks is mostly neglected.

In contrast, this paper provides a conceptualisation of monetary policy in a world without CB money based on a generally accepted medium of exchange that also serves as medium of final settlement. Central banks can implement monetary policy by imposing reserve requirements in terms of the medium of final settlement and by paying or charging interest thereon. These instruments are independent of their monopoly providing the generally accepted medium of exchange at zero costs at the margin. The smaller set of instruments and particularly the loss of control over the aggregate supply of the medium of final settlement impair the power of central banks to contain the volatility of the target rate. Politico-economic objections to this institutional framework also apply to the current practice of transferring regulatory powers and substantial discretion to central banks. Indeed, the current legal frameworks of the ECB and the Fed hardly need to be adapted. They already confer the necessary regulatory authority to central banks to conduct monetary policy based on the proposed instruments of implementation in a world without CB money.

References

Allen, W. A. (2002) 'Bank of England Open Market Operations: The Introduction of a Deposit Facility for Counterparties', BIS Papers No. 12, Basel: Bank for International Settlement.

Arnone, M. and Bandiera, L. (2004) 'Monetary Policy, Monetary Areas, and Financial Development with Electronic Money', IMF Working Paper, WP/04/122, Washington, DC.

Bartolini, L. and Prati, A. (2003) 'The Execution of Monetary Policy: A Tale of Two Central Banks', Federal Reserve Bank of New York Staff Report No. 165, New York.

Berentsen, A. (1998) 'Monetary Policy Implications of Digital Money', *Kyklos,* 51: 89–117.

Bierut, B. K. (2002) 'On the Optimal Frequency of the Central Bank's Operations in the Reserve Market', Tinbergen Institute Working Paper, Rotterdam.

Bindseil, U. (2000) 'Towards a Theory of Central Bank Liquidity Management', *Kredit und Kapital,* 3: 346–76.

Bindseil, U. (2004) *Monetary Policy Implementation: Theory, Past, Present*, Oxford: Oxford University Press.

Bindseil, U., Camba-Mendez, G., Hirsch, A. and Weller, B. (2003) 'Excess Reserves and the ECB's Implementation Of Monetary Policy', mimeo ECB, Frankfurt/Main.

Bordo, M. D., Jonung, L. and Siklos, P. L. (1997) 'Institutional Change and the Velocity Of Money: A Century Of Evidence', *Economic Inquiry,* 35: 710–25.

Borio, C. E. V. (1997) 'The Implementation of Monetary Policy in Industrialized Countries: A Survey', Economic Paper No 187, Basel: Bank for International Settlement.

Borio, C. E. V. (2001) 'Comparing Monetary Policy Operating Procedures Across the United States, Japan and the Euro Area', BIS Papers No 9, Basel: Bank for International Settlement.

Buiter, W. H. (2004) 'A Small Corner of Intertemporal Public Finance – New Developments in Monetary Economics: Two Ghosts, Two Eccentricities, a Fallacy, a Mirage and a Mythos', NBER Working Paper 10524, Cambridge.

Centi, J. P. and Bougi, G. (2003) 'The Possible Economic Consequences of Electronic Money', in J. Birner and P. Garrouste (eds) *Austrian Perspectives on the New Economy*, London: Routledge, 259–81.

CPSS – Committee on Payment and Settlement Systems (2003) *The Role of Central Bank Money in Payment Systems*, Basel: Bank for International Settlements.

Costa Storti C. and De Grauwe, P. (2003) 'Monetary Policy in a Cashless Society', in M. Balling, F. Lierman, and A. Mullineux (eds) *Technology and Finance, Challenges for Financial Markets, Business Strategies and Policy Makers*, London: Routledge, 241–60.

ECB (2004) *The Implementation of Monetary Policy in the Euro Area*, Frankfurt/Main: European Central Bank.

European Union (1992) 'Treaty Establishing the European Union', Official Journal of the European Communities C 191, Brussels.

European Union (1992) *Protocol on the Statute of the European System of Central Banks and the European Central Bank* (annexed to the Treaty establishing the European Union), Official Journal of the European Communities C 191, Brussels.

Edwards, C. L. (1997) 'Open Market Operations in the 1990s', *Federal Reserve Bulletin*, 859–74.

Ewerhart, C. (2002) 'A Model of the Eurosystem's Operational Framework for Monetary Policy Implementation', European Central Bank Working Paper no. 84, Frankfurt/Main.

Ewerhart, C., Cassola, N., Ejerskov, S. and Valla, N. (2003), 'The Euro Money Market: Stylized Facts and Open Questions', mimeo European Central Bank, Frankfurt/Main.

Freedman, C. (2000) 'Monetary Policy Implementation: Past, Present, and Future – Will the Advent of Electronic Money Lead to the Demise of Central Banking?' *International Finance,* 3: 211–27.

Freixas, X., Holthausen, C., Terol, I. and Thygessen, C. (2001) 'Settlement in Commercial Bank Money versus Central Bank Money', paper presented at the SUERF Meeting, 25–27 October, Brussels.

Friedman, B. (1999) 'The Future of Monetary Policy: The Central Bank as an Army with Only a Signaling Corps?' *International Finance,* 2: 321–38.

Friedman, B. (2000) 'Decoupling at the Margin: The Threat to Monetary Policy from the Electronic Revolution in Banking', *International Finance,* 3: 261–72.

Goodfriend, M. (2002) 'Interest on Reserves and Monetary Policy', *Federal Reserve Bank of New York Economic Policy Review,* 8: 1–8.

Goodhart, C. A. E. (1989) *Money, Information, and Uncertainty*, London: Macmillan.

Goodhart, C. A. E. (2000) 'Can Central Banking Survive the IT Revolution', *International Finance,* 3: 189–209.

Guthrie, G. and Wright, J. (2000) 'Open Mouth Operations', *Journal of Monetary Economics,* 46: 489–516.

Heller, D. and Lengwiler, Y. (2003) 'Payment Obligations, Reserve Requirements, and the Demand for Central Bank Balances', *Journal of Monetary Economics,* 50: 419–32.

Henckel, T., Ize, A. and Kovanen, A. (1999) 'Central Banking Without Central Bank Money', IMF Working Paper WP/99/92, Washington, D. C.

Ho, T. and Saunders, A. (1985) 'A Micro Model of the Federal Funds Market', *Journal of Finance,* 40: 977–90.

King, M. (1999) 'Challenges for Monetary Policy: Old and New', paper prepared for the Symposium on 'New Challenges for Monetary Policy', 27 August, sponsored by the Federal Reserve Bank of Kansas City at Jackson Hole, Wyoming.

Kobrin, S. J. (1997) 'Electronic Cash and the End of National Markets', *Foreign Policy,* 107: 65–77.

Kroszner, R. S. (2001) 'Currency Competition in the Digital Age', paper prepared for 'The Origins and Evolution of Central Banking', 21–22 May, Federal Reserve Bank, Cleveland.

Krüger, M. (1999) 'Towards a Moneyless World?' University of Durham, Department of Economics & Finance Working Paper No. 9916, Durham.

Lahdenperä, H. (2001) 'Payment and Financial Innovation, Reserve Demand and Implementation of Monetary Policy', Bank of Finland Discussion Paper 26/2001, Helsinki.

Matonis, J. W. (1995) 'Digital Cash and Monetary Freedom', paper presented at INET 95, 26–30 June, Honolulu, Hawaii.

Palley, T. I. (2002) 'The E-Money Revolution: Challenges and Implications for Monetary Policy', *Journal of Post Keynesian Economics,* 24: 217–33.

Rich, G. (2000) 'Monetary Policy without Central Bank Money: A Swiss Perspective', *International Finance,* 3: 439–69.

Schmitz, S. W. (2002a) 'Carl Menger's "Money" and the Current Neoclassical Models of Money', in M. Latzer and S. W. Schmitz (eds) *Carl Menger and the Evolution of Payments Systems: From Barter to Electronic Money,* Cheltenham: Edward Elgar, 111–32.

Schmitz, S. W. (2002b) 'The Institutional Character of Electronic Money Schemes', in M. Latzer and S. W. Schmitz (eds) *Carl Menger and the Evolution of Payments Systems: From Barter to Electronic Money,* Cheltenham: Edward Elgar, 159–83.

Sellon, G. H. and Weiner, S. E. (1997) 'Monetary Policy without Reserve Requirements: Case Studies and Options for the United States', *Federal Reserve Bank of Kansas City Economic Review* (Second Quarter): 6–30.

Selgin, G. A. and White, L. H. (1987) 'The Evolution of a Free Banking System', *Economic Inquiry,* 25: 439–57.

Selgin, G. A. and White, L. H. (2002) 'Mengerian Perspectives on the Future of Money' in M. Latzer and S. W Schmitz (eds) *Carl Menger and the Evolution of Payments Systems: From Barter to Electronic Money,* Cheltenham: Edward Elgar, 133–58.

Stix, H. (2002) Die Auswirkungen von elektronischem Geld auf die Geldpolitik, *Wirtschaftspolitische Blätter,* 49: 110–19.

Taub, B. (1985) 'Private Fiat Money with Many Suppliers', *Journal Monetary Economics,* 16: 195–208.

Thornton, D. L. (2000) 'The Relationship Between the Federal Funds Rate and the Fed's Federal Funds Rate Target: Is it Open Market or Open Mouth Operations?' Federal Reserve Bank of St. Louis Working Paper, St. Louis.

Wetherilt, A. V. (2002) 'Money market operations and volatility in UK money market rates', *Bank of England Quarterly Bulletin (Winter)*: 420–29.

White, L. H. (1984) 'Competitive Payments Systems and the Unit of Account', *American Economic Review,* 74: 699–712.

White, L. H. (1999) *The Theory of Monetary Institutions,* Oxford: Blackwell Publishers.

Whitesell, W. (2003) 'Tunnels and Reserves in Monetary Policy Implementation', mimeo Board of Governors Federal Reserve System, Washington, D. C.

Woodford, M. (1998) 'Doing Without Money: Controlling inflation in a poor-monetary world', Review of Economic Dynamics, 1: 173–219.

Woodford, M. (2000) 'Monetary Policy in a World without Money', *International Finance,* 3: 229–60.

Woodford, M. (2001) 'Monetary Policy in the Information Economy', paper prepared for the symposium on 'Economic Policy for the Information Economy', August 30–September 1, Federal Reserve Bank of Kansas City, Jackson Hole, Wyoming.

Woodford, M. (2002) 'Financial Markets Efficiency and the Effectiveness of Monetary Policy', *Federal Reserve Bank of New York Economic Policy Review,* 85–94.

Notes

1 I am grateful to the discussant of the paper, Angelo Baglioni, and the participants of the project workshop at the Austrian Academy of Sciences for suggestions and comments.
2 CPSS 2003, 7.
3 E.g. a central bank under a gold standard.
4 Inter alia O'Hara 1997.
5 The Austrian central bank (OeNB) monopolised market making in the ATS/DEM foreign exchange market in the 1970s in basically the same way. It offered lower bid and ask prices and drove commercial banks out of the market.
6 The parallels to forex market intervention and potential currency crisis are apparent.
7 If demand for central bank money were positive, it could attempt to stabilise the price level in its own currency.
8 Covered interest rate parity assumes the existence of some form of option or futures markets for eMonies.
9 Freedman (2000) discusses the advantages of extended netting arrangements.
10 Sellon and Weiner 1997 and Woodford 2000.
11 Note removed.
12 See also Schmitz 2002b for an analysis of the unit of account function of the generally accepted medium of exchange and price formation.
13 For the role of excess reserves in the implementation of monetary policy in the Euro area see Bindseil *et al.* (2003), for the framework for monetary policy implementation in the Euro area, the UK, and the US see ECB (2004), Wetherilt (2002), and Edwards (1997), respectively.
14 For details concerning OMOs of the ECB, the Fed and the Bank of England see also ECB (2004), Bartolini and Prati (2003), and Allen (2002).
15 In fact, intraday credit is not an instrument of monetary policy implementation. I have included it in the current discussion as it forms an important feature of the wider implementation framework.
16 Freedman 2000.
17 Schmitz (2002b) demonstrates that the denomination of means of payment in retail payment systems in the generally accepted medium of exchange is strategically superior for issuers and customers than denomination in alternative units of account.
18 Friedman 1999 and Thornton 2000.
19 Minimum reserve requirements do play an important role in determining the size of the deficit, but they are not a necessary precondition for one to exist, as is demonstrated inter alia by the New Zealand framework of monetary policy implementation. For a description of the relevant features of the institutional framework operational in New Zealand see Woodford (2001), Sellon and Weiner (1997). Whitesell (2003) argues that, even though the implementation of monetary policy also works without reserve requirements, the systems would benefit from adding reserve requirements.
20 The maturity of the main refinancing operations in the Euro area is one week and in the UK it is two weeks.
21 If the participating banks anticipate that demand will be below ΔR^{Smax}, the respective bid rates will be r^{OMOmin}.
22 Ewerhart *et al.* (2003) present evidence that both the level and the volatility of the money market rate in the Euro area increase towards the end of the maintenance period (for the US see Woodford 2001, 30).
23 While the institutional structure is exogenous to the decisions problems of payment systems participants, the degree of synchronicity of payment flows can be increased at increasing marginal costs to the payment system participants to some extent in the medium term, e.g. by clustering credits and debits at pre-arranged points of time. But even under such arrangements exogenous factors – payments initiated by banks' customers – play a crucial role in determining the liquidity positions of participants.

24 Borio 2001.
25 In the Euro area intraday credits not repaid at the end of the day are treated as credit from the lending facility.
26 For a survey of the literature on models of banks' reserve management see Ewerhart *et al.* (2003).
27 Ho and Saunders 1985.
28 Standing facilities are the main instrument of monetary policy implementation under the 'channel'-approach. The spread between r^{DF} and r^{LF} is substantially smaller.
29 See also Selgin and White 2002.
30 Notwithstanding that in extended netting systems private CSI allow for the extension of settlement and the exchange of debt instruments (often highly liquid government bonds) as collateral in net payment systems to economise on CB reserves, final settlement takes place in the generally accepted medium of exchange eventually.
31 Inter alia Centi and Bougi 2003, Costa Storti and De Grauwe 2003, and King 1999. For a discussion see chapter 5 in this volume.
32 White 1984.
33 White (1999) demonstrates why the private issue of fiat-type money is infeasible. Examples of an eligible generally accepted medium of exchange are various types of commodity monies.
34 See e.g. Henckel, Ize and Kovanen 1999, Costa Storti and De Grauwe 2003, Palley 2002, Arnone and Bandiera 2004. Similar proposals were put forward in the discussion of this chapter by Angelo Baglioni and Dimitrios Tsomocos.
35 Examples of policy induced changes to input prices in financial intermediation include changes of capital adequacy requirements and credit contract fees (in place in Austria).
36 Buiter (2004) recognises that the central bank trades on the unique monopoly of the state to legitimately use force (or coercion), to tax and to regulate. He conjectures that the demand for CB money will never vanish completely as the state will always be more creditworthy than private agents.
37 The Board of Governors has to increase (or decrease) the dollar amount stipulated in paragraph 2 (A) (i) each year in line with the growth rate of the total transaction accounts of all depository institutions. The Federal Reserve Act defines the method of calculation of the increase in total transaction accounts and of the increase of the dollar amount applicable in paragraph 2 (A) (i).
38 In addition to the implicit taxation of bank liabilities the act also contained a section on the explicit taxation of bank liabilities until 1914. Section 27 of the act prescribed a tax on that proportion of circulating bank notes of national banks, which was not secured by bonds of the US. For the first three months the tax rate amounted to 3 per cent per annum upon the average amount of their notes in circulation, an additional one-half of 1 per cent per annum per month until a tax of 6 per cent per annum is reached.

8 The organisation of interbank settlement systems: current trends and implications for central banking

Angelo Baglioni[1]

Interbank settlement systems manage every day an impressive amount of money: for example, the two major US systems – Fedwire and CHIPS – handle together a *daily* flow of transfers equivalent to nearly 28 per cent of the *annual* US GDP: see Table 8.1, showing the relevant data for Europe as well.[2] The fast growth of volumes flowing through payment systems (in particular through systems dealing with large value payments, originated by financial transactions) raises some relevant economic issues. As a starting point, such issues may be captured by the trade-off between *settlement risk* and *liquidity cost*. The illiquidity (or insolvency) of a bank may have spill-over effects, affecting other institutions through the network of interbank claims, possibly generating a systemic crisis. Central banks have been active in promoting safe settlement systems, in order to minimize the systemic risk. On the other hand, such initiatives have often increased the cost of liquidity management, leading to a higher cost of financial intermediation.

The organisation of settlement systems is currently undergoing some major changes, leading to the so-called hybrid systems. The latter combine some features of both the traditional 'netting' systems (where a bank has to pay only the end-of-day balance between its outgoing and incoming payments) and 'gross'

Table 8.1 Interbank settlement systems: daily volumes and values

	Volumes (a) (number of payments)	*Values (b) (dollar billions)*	*Values/GDP as % of annual nominal GDP**	*Unit value: (b)/(a) (dollar millions)*
TARGET	253,016	1,467.6	17.0	5.8
BI-REL	37,696	93.2	7.9	2.5
RTGS^{plus}	125,070	462.8	23.3	3.7
TBF	14,958	336.9	23.5	22.5
EURO1	134,905	177.8	2.1	1.3
PNS	29,686	73.8	5.1	2.5
Fedwire	458,084	1,616.6	15.6	3.5
CHIPS	252,183	1,257.8	12.1	5.0

Note: Average data for 2002 (sources: ECB, Fed, CHIPS^{CO}, OECD). *TARGET and Euro1: GDP of EU15; for other systems: national GDP.

systems (where payments are settled one-by-one in real time). This evolution seems quite promising, as it might alter the above-mentioned trade-off between risk and liquidity cost. It also challenges the theoretical framework used by economists to analyse payment systems, which still relies on such a trade-off:[3] this traditional view basically assumes that any gain in liquidity saving has a cost in terms of settlement risk (and vice versa); to the contrary, I argue that the most recent technical innovations show that it is possible to gain liquidity saving without adding risk (and vice versa).

The settlement of payments raises another issue, that of *intraday* liquidity management. Banks have to optimise their liquidity management within the operating day, with regard to *when* and *where* to channel their payment orders; in particular, the *timing* of orders originates an interesting problem of strategic interaction among banks. Economic theory has begun only very recently to pay attention to such an issue.[4]

The intraday liquidity management is strictly linked to the management of liquidity on a daily basis. Therefore, the demand for bank reserves is significantly affected by the volume and volatility of payment flows, as well as by the organisation of payment systems. These factors might alter the equilibrium of the money market (in particular, of the overnight segment). Consequently, the settlement of payments becomes an issue relevant for the implementation of monetary policy: in managing the money supply, central banks have to take into account – and possibly forecast – any shock occurring to payment systems, in order to steer short term interest rates at their target level.

This paper is organised as follows. The next section briefly describes the convergence between gross and netting systems during the 1990s. The third section analyses the intraday management of liquidity as a coordination problem among banks, highlighting the role played by the central bank. The fourth section shows how the recent trend towards hybrid systems paves the way towards a greater efficiency in managing payments. The fifth section draws some implications for the implementation of monetary policy, starting by analysing how the demand for central bank money might be affected by the evolution of settlement systems. Finally, the sixth section summarises the main points made in this work.

The risk-liquidity trade-off: the evolution through the 1990s

In principle, there is a clear trade-off associated with the choice between real time gross settlement (RTGS) and multilateral net settlement (MNS) systems: the former are safer but more costly in terms of liquidity (see Figure 8.1). The basic features of each of these systems are well known. In an MNS system, banks typically settle only the balance of their payments, accumulated during a pre-specified time period (normally one day): at the end of a business day, each bank has to pay (or receive) the amount resulting from the net position of all its incoming/outgoing payments accumulated during that day vis-à-vis all other banks. To the contrary, in a RTGS system each payment is settled separately in real time.

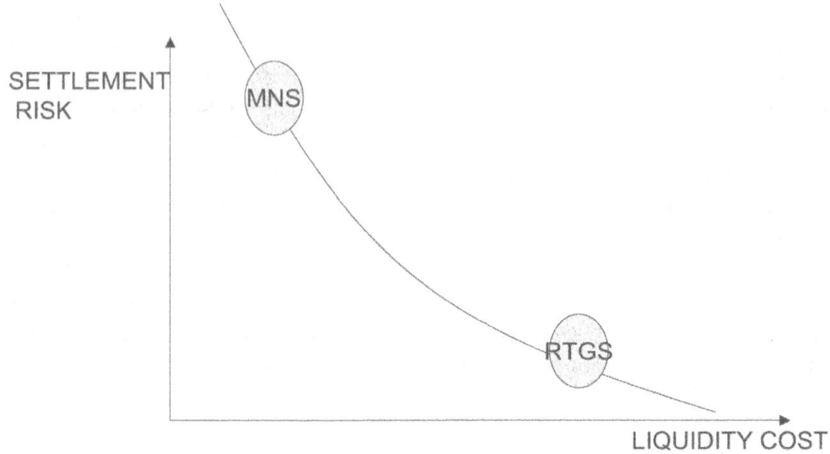

Figure 8.1 The risk-liquidity trade-off

During the 1990s, however, substantial changes occurred in the actual organisation of payment systems. Under the impulse of the Committee on Payment and Settlement Systems,[5] the safety of MNS systems has been considerably improved, for example through collateral requirements and debit caps. These changes have generally increased the liquidity cost of MNS: collateral requirements impose banks to deposit cash balances at the clearing house; debit caps set a limit to the netting mechanism (a bank constrained by a debit cap has to wait for incoming payments, before sending outgoing ones). On the other hand, central banks have tried to reduce the liquidity cost of RTGS systems in several ways, for example through intraday credit and queuing mechanisms. Thus, the evolution of settlement systems has shown a convergence between MNS and RTGS systems, along the risk-liquidity trade-off.

Empirical evidence shows that, following the above evolution, other factors – different from risk-liquidity considerations – may become important in the choice of banks among the available settlement systems. For example, Baglioni and Hamaui (2003) find that the cost structures of TARGET and Euro1 influence the choice of banks between the two systems; another relevant factor is the nature of payments (commercial versus financial payments). More specifically, Euro1 seems to be preferred by large banks, sending a huge number of commercial payments, due to its cost structure with high fixed cost and low marginal cost; on the other hand, TARGET – where the variable cost component prevails – is more popular within small banks.

Intraday liquidity: Central bank policy and coordination among banks

The settlement of payments requires an intraday management of liquidity. In principle, it is also possible to think of an intraday market for liquidity, enabling banks to exchange funds for shorter maturities than overnight. However, the emergence of such a market is unlikely, due to the central bank policy of providing intraday credit at a very low cost and in large quantity. Such a policy has a clear rationale: inducing banks to channel large value payments through RTGS systems, due to their safety features. As it is well known, in the euro area the intraday overdraft provided by the ESCB is free and unlimited, although collateralized.[6] To the contrary, in the US the Fed applies quantitative limits (caps) and explicit (although low)[7] fees for making use of the intraday facility, while it does not require any collateral.

The cost of intraday liquidity may be further reduced through the synchronisation of payment orders. Suppose a bank sends a payment through an RTGS system and, at the same time, it receives another one: only the difference between the two payments has to be debited (or credited) on its settlement account at the central bank; in other words, the incoming payment has been used to fund the outgoing one. When many banks are able to coordinate and send their payment messages in short time intervals, each of them benefits from synchronisation, reducing its use of intraday credit from the central bank. This mechanism may reduce the cost of intraday liquidity considerably, and it is already in place in many countries. For example, in Fedwire the bulk of payment orders are concentrated at the end of day, enabling banks to fund 40 per cent of outgoing payments through incoming ones.[8] In Italy, the bulk of payments are concentrated early in the morning, enabling banks to fund a large share of outgoing payments through incoming ones.

The timing of payment orders is relevant also for the information available to banks. At each moment in time, the current overall position in payment systems is valuable information for a bank treasury department, in order to estimate its end-of-day balance on the central bank settlement account. Now, if payment orders are concentrated in the early operating hours, the information available to each bank improves, as it is able to observe – at a given time – a large share of its daily payment flows; the opposite holds true if payments are delayed until the end of day. Thus, banks have a clear *collective* interest in *synchronising* payment orders at the *beginning* of the day.

Unfortunately, banks have also an *individual* interest in *delaying* payments. If a bank sends a payment order immediately, absent synchronisation, it bears the full liquidity cost. If, to the contrary, it waits for an incoming payment to fund the outgoing one, it is able to shift the burden of liquidity onto another bank. This introduces a coordination problem among banks, which resembles the classic 'prisoner's dilemma' game. The outcome may be quite inefficient, with banks delaying payments and suffering from a reduction of information.

A simple example may help in clarifying this point. Let's consider two banks (i,j): each of them has to send a payment to the other one through an RTGS system; for simplicity, assume that the two payments are of equal amount. We are at time t_1: each bank has to decide whether to send its outgoing payment immediately or to delay that until a later time (t_2). If the two payment messages are synchronised, the implied liquidity cost is zero for both banks. On the other hand, without synchronisation only that bank sending first its payment message, bears

Table 8.2 The intraday liquidity game

		Bank j	
		t_1	t_2
Bank i	t_1	I, I	$-C, I$
	t_2	$I, -C$	$0, 0$

a liquidity cost (say C). Moreover, if one bank sends its message in t_1, the other one gets a benefit (say I) in terms of information about its incoming payments: this allows a better estimate of its own overall position in the payments system. Table 8.2 shows the payoffs for the two banks ($payoff_i$, $payoff_j$), as a result of the strategy chosen by each of them – strategies are denoted by t_1 ('not delay') and t_2('delay').

It is quite obvious that strategy t_2 is dominant, so the unique Nash equilibrium – in dominant strategies – is (t_2, t_2). This is clearly inefficient, as it is Pareto dominated by another equilibrium (t_1,t_1): if the two banks were able to synchronize their payments in t_1, they would both gain the information benefit I; unfortunately, this is not the natural outcome in a non-cooperative framework.

At this point the coordinating role of the central banks becomes relevant: by designing the systems rules, they have the means for inducing banks to synchronise their payment messages early in the day. In UK, CHAPS rules require banks to send half of their payments (in value) no later than noon and 75 per cent no later than 2.30 p.m. In Switzerland, the SIC system applies penalising fees for delayed payments. I am not aware of any other major settlement system (e.g. Fedwire, CHIPS, TARGET) currently applying such a kind of rule; therefore, there may be some scope for future developments in this area.

The current trend: hybrid systems

As we have seen in the second section, MNS and RTGS systems have been converging during the 1990s, moving along the risk-liquidity trade-off. Current trends show a further convergence between the two kinds of systems, thanks to the creation of the so-called hybrid systems: these try to combine the features of gross and net settlement. The mechanism at work may be defined as 'real time net settlement' (RTNS): payments are queued and settled, as soon as possible, by offsetting payment orders of opposite sign; the manager of the system checks queues, so as to implement this netting process very frequently during the day.

Despite the technical complexity of the algorithms used to implement the RTNS method, in principle the idea is simple: maximise the *synchronisation* among payment orders. In such a way, two goals may be achieved. First, liquidity saving: as we have seen in the preceding section, synchronisation of payment messages allows banks to settle only the balance among payments. Second, reduction of risk: as netting takes place very frequently – instead of being deferred until the end of day like in traditional MNS – the settlement lag is reduced to a minimum and banks benefit from an immediate finality of incoming

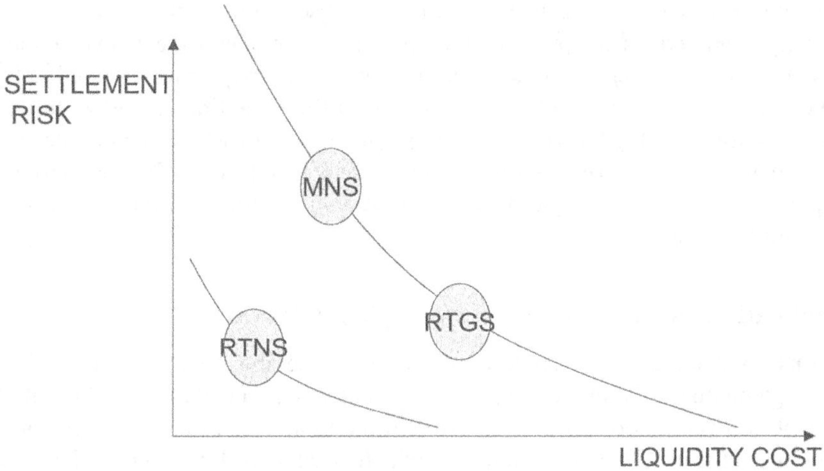

Figure 8.2 The current trend: hybrid systems

payments. Therefore, RTNS seems able to improve the risk-liquidity trade-off (see Figure 8.2).

Examples of hybrid systems are the following:

- *CHIPS:* At the beginning of the operating day, each participant deposits an amount ('prefunding') on its CHIPS account: payments are settled by debiting/crediting this account (its balance is set to zero at the end of the day). The system manages queues through a continuous netting process, both on bilateral and multilateral basis.
- *PNS:* The queuing management process is similar to that employed by CHIPS (prefunding and continuous netting, both bilateral and multilateral).
- *RTGS-plus:* Banks may set limits to the liquidity employed in real time settlement: once a limit has been reached, payments are queued and cleared only on a 'payment versus payment' (PVP) basis (by synchronising and netting payment orders of opposite sign). Each bank retains the option of sending 'express' payments, for which the immediate use of all the available liquidity is authorised. This mechanism allows banks to keep under control the liquidity absorbed by the settlement process, thus saving liquidity relative to a traditional RTGS system.
- *New BI-Rel:* Like in RTGS-plus, banks may set priorities: a specific amount of liquidity (which may be changed during the day) is devoted to the settlement of express payments. Queued payment orders are synchronised and settled on a bilateral basis.

In addition, one could mention CLS (Continuous Linked Settlement). Despite some relevant differences with the above-mentioned systems, the synchronisation principle is at work here as well. CLS is specialised in the settlement of foreign exchange transactions, adopting the PVP principle. Consider, for example, a dollar/euro exchange: one leg of the transaction (say the euro payment) is settled only if the other leg (dollar payment) may be settled at the same time, thereby eliminating the settlement lag between the two payments (from which the counterparty risk – named 'Herstatt risk' – arises). Participants benefit from the compensation of payments of opposite sign in each currency: this netting mechanism provides a liquidity saving device.[9]

Implications for monetary policy implementation

At this point we can draw some implications of the above-mentioned trends for the implementation of monetary policy. The latter is assumed to work through the control of a very short term interest rate of the money market, say the overnight rate: this is the usual operational target, which is achieved by an appropriate management of the supply of central bank money. We also – momentarily – assume that there is no minimum reserve requirement (MRR).

The demand for bank reserves is defined as the desired level of the end-of-day balance on the settlement accounts held by banks with the central bank. Banks have a positive target on their end-of-day balance: this is due to the fact that the variability of payments generates a risk of ending the day with a negative balance, incurring in a penalty – such as borrowing from the central bank at a higher rate than the market level. Let us call $\bar{R}$ a prudential level of bank reserves. The demand for bank reserves (R^D) is determined by trading-off such a precautionary need with the opportunity cost of holding idle balances with the central bank, namely the (overnight) interbank interest rate (i). Formally, the representative bank will minimise the following loss function (L_1):

$$\min_{R^D} L_1 = \frac{1}{2}(R^D - \bar{R})^2 + \alpha R^D i$$

where the first item is a (quadratic) function of the deviation of the reserve level from its target and the second one is the opportunity cost of reserves; α is the (relative[10]) weight attributed to the second objective. First order condition leads to the following demand equation:

$$R^D = \bar{R} - \alpha \cdot i$$

By estimating the aggregate daily demand for bank reserves, and by controlling its supply (R^S), the central bank is able to set the money market rate at the desired level, say i^* (see Figure 8.3).

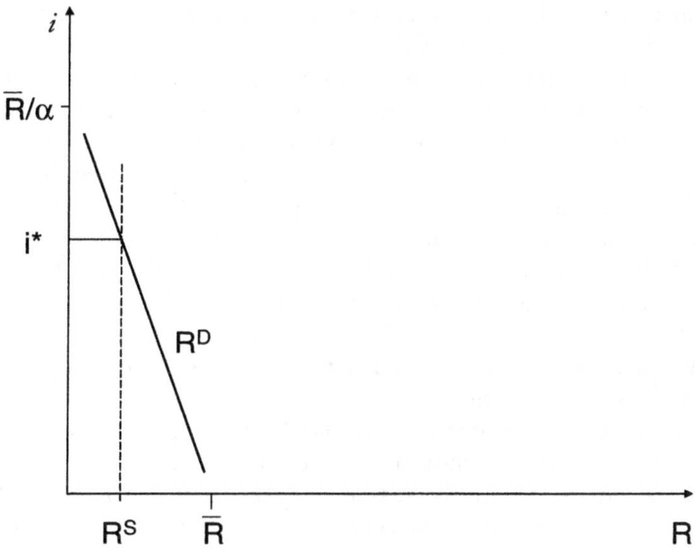

Figure 8.3 Money market equilibrium with positive demand for central bank money

How does the evolution of settlement systems impact on the demand for bank reserves? We may understand that by observing that the end-of-day desired level of the settlement account balance for each bank – say bank i – is:

$$R_i^D = MB_i + INT_i$$

where MB_i is its end-of-day multilateral balance on settlement systems (the sum of all incoming payments less the sum of all outgoing ones) and INT_i is its daily demand for funds – net borrowing – in the interbank (overnight) market.

By summing up the above equations across the whole banking system (say for all i from 1 to N, the latter being the total number of banks), we get the aggregate demand for bank reserves as follows:

$$R^D = \sum_{i=1}^{N} R_i^D = \sum_{i=1}^{N} INT_i$$

because by definition $\sum_{i=1}^{N} MB_i = 0$. Then, a positive R^D is equivalent to an aggregate net demand for funds in the interbank market. This net borrowing position of the banking system as a whole has to be met by a positive supply of central bank money: this is another way to see how the central bank is able to steer the money market interest rate.

As we said before, the fundamental reason why a bank has a positive target for the end-of-day balance on its settlement account with the central bank ($R_i^D > 0$) – equivalently a positive demand for central bank money – is the uncertainty relative to the flows of in-out payments, originating the risk of ending the day with a negative balance. Eliminating this uncertainty would lead to a zero target on the settlement account balance: a bank would be able to exactly offset its multilateral position in the payment system with its position in the interbank market: $INT_i = -MB_i$. At the aggregate level: $R^D = \sum_{i=1}^{N} INT_i = 0$. Then, the daily demand for bank reserves would vanish, as well as the aggregate net demand for funds in the interbank market, preventing the central bank from being able to steer the money market interest rate.

The above scenario is of course a limit case, but some factors – mentioned in the previous sections – are currently moving the institutional framework into that direction. The introduction of hybrid systems have greatly enhanced the efficiency of the intraday management of payments, also by exploiting the synchronization principle:[11] by reducing the cost of (intraday) liquidity, such systems should also reduce the incentive to delay payments; this in turn should contribute to improve the information available to a bank about its own position in the payments system, thus reducing the uncertainty relative to its end-of-day overall position. Some further efforts by banks to synchronize their payment orders – possibly thanks to the coordinating role of the central bank – might also contribute to limit the random in-out flows of payments to be settled at the end of the operating day. These factors, together with the provision of intraday liquidity by the central banks, reduce the need for an end-of-day positive demand for central bank money. The increasing efficiency of the interbank market points to the same direction, as it enables banks to easily offset 'last minute' payments by trading in the market.

Let us try to imagine what would happen if the end-of-day demand for central bank money – for settlement purposes – were driven to zero, while only an intraday demand would survive. Would the central bank retain its ability to steer the money market interest rate?

An answer to that question relies on the power of central banks to set a minimum reserve requirement (MRR) on banks: this is a way to 'impose' a positive demand for central bank money. This tool is currently employed in many countries, like US and the euro area – although not everywhere (for example, there is no MRR in the UK[12]). In those countries, MRR is implemented together with the 'averaging' facility: only the average of daily balances with the central bank – computed throughout a 'maintenance period' – has to be (at least) equal to a minimum, as a ratio to deposits in the previous period.[13]

To illustrate how monetary policy works in such a framework, let us suppose that the end-of-day need of central bank money for settlement purposes is zero ($\bar{R} = 0$); on the other hand, banks are required by regulation to keep a balance equal to MRR with the central bank, as an average throughout a maintenance period which (for simplicity) we set equal to two days. The optimisation problem for the representative bank is now the following:

$$\min_{R_1^D} L_2 = \tfrac{1}{2}\left(R_1^D - MRR\right)^2 + \alpha[R_1^D i_1 + R_2^D E_1(i_2)]$$

$$\text{subject to } \tfrac{1}{2}(R_1^D + R_2^D) = MRR$$

where R_i^D is the demand for bank reserves in day $i = 1{,}2$, i_1 is the current overnight rate and $E_1(i_2)$ is today's expectation of tomorrow's interest rate. In L_2 (as in L_1) the first item is a (quadratic) function of the deviation of the reserve level from its target[14] and the second one is the opportunity cost of reserves; again, α is the (relative) weight attributed to the second objective. The first order condition yields:

$$R_1^D = MRR + \alpha[E_1(i_2) - i_1]$$

while R_2^D is determined by the constraint. The above demand for bank reserves is shown in Figure 8.4; its elasticity depends on the propensity (α) of banks to engage in the so-called intertemporal arbitrage: the averaging facility allows banks to substitute today's reserve for tomorrow's, responding to expected fluctuations in the overnight interest rate.[15] For example, if $E_1(i_2) > i_1$, a bank may profit by borrowing today in the interbank market – thus increasing R_1^D – and doing the opposite tomorrow. By controlling the supply of bank reserves (R^S), the central bank is still able to set the money market rate at the desired level (i_1^*).

The MRR is a classic tool of monetary control, so it provides an answer to the earlier question (how to implement monetary policy, absent an end-of-day demand for central bank money) in line with the tradition of central banking. A completely new perspective relies on the possibility of steering an interest rate on a shorter maturity than overnight (say one hour, or one minute?). In such a way, monetary policy would follow the current trend of commercial banking, stressing the intraday management of liquidity. This is a challenge still to be explored, both in theory and in practice.[16]

Finally, we have dealt here with the implementation of monetary policy, exploring the case where the demand for central bank money were only at the intraday level, absent an end-of-day demand. It is also of interest trying to figure out how monetary policy might look like in a world without central bank money at all: this issue is taken up in the article by S. W. Schmitz in this volume. After surveying the different proposals emerging from the literature, he provides an in-depth analysis of how the tools currently available to central banks would be affected in such an extreme scenario. It turns out that monetary policy could still be effectively

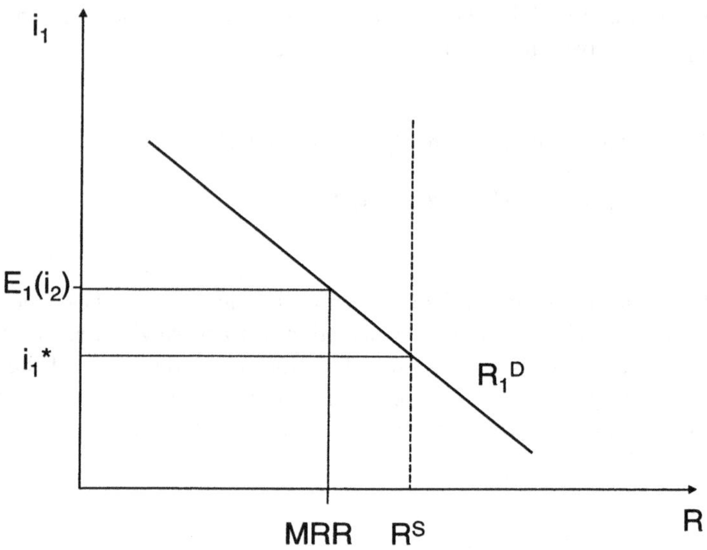

Figure 8.4 Money market equilibrium with MRR and averaging facility

managed, provided a minimum reserve requirement (in the medium of final settlement) is imposed. The legal framework is already in place, so that no new regulation is needed: central banks do have the regulatory power to set an MRR.

Conclusions

During the 1990s, substantial changes occurred in the organisation of settlement systems, leading to a convergence – in terms of risk and liquidity cost – between RTGS and MNS systems. The introduction of hybrid systems has led to an improvement of the risk-liquidity trade-off, thanks to the synchronisation of payment orders.

The management of liquidity at the intraday level has become increasingly relevant. In particular, the timing of payment orders raises a coordination problem among banks: each of them has an individual interest in deferring its own outgoing payments, in order to shift onto other banks the burden of liquidity; at the same time, there is a collective interest in anticipating payment orders, in order to improve the available information, relative to the overall position of each bank in the payment system. This 'intraday liquidity game' may lead to socially inefficient outcomes. Central banks may play a crucial role in coordinating banks, trying to implement an efficient equilibrium.

The current trend towards the hybrid systems should reduce the incentive to delay payments, and with it the uncertainty about the end-of-day liquidity position of each bank. This in turn might lower the need for an end-of-day demand for bank reserves in central bank money. Such evolution is a challenge for the implementation of monetary policy, which traditionally relies on a positive demand for central bank money. A way out is the imposition of a minimum reserve requirement, a device already in place in many countries.

References

Baglioni, A. and Hamaui, R. (2003) 'The choice among interbank settlement systems: the European experience', *Economic Notes*, 32: 67–100.

Bank of England (2004a): *Reform of the Bank of England's Operations in the Sterling Money Markets*, Consultative paper (May), London: Bank of England.

Bank of England (2004b): *Reform of the Bank of England's Operations in the Sterling Money Markets*, news release (22 July), London: Bank of England.

Bech, M. and Garratt, R. (2003) 'The intraday liquidity management game', *Journal of Economic Theory*, 109:198–219.

BIS (1990) *Minimum Standards for the Design and Operation of Cross-Border and Multi-Currency Netting and Settlement Schemes,* Basel: Bank for International Settlements.

Freixas, X. and Parigi, B. (1998) 'Contagion and efficiency in gross and net interbank payment systems', *Journal of Financial Intermediation*, 7:3–31.

Holthausen, C. and Ronde, T. (2000) 'Regulating access to international large value payment systems', European Central Bank Working Paper No.22, Frankfurt/Main.

Kahn, C. and Roberts, W. (1998): Payment system settlement and bank incentives, *Review of Financial Studies*, 11: 845–70.

McAndrews, J. and Rajan, S. (2000) 'The timing and funding of Fedwire funds transfers', *FRBNY Economic Policy Review* (July): 17–28.

Notes

1 I wish to thank all participants of the workshop at the Austrian Academy of Sciences, Vienna (June 2004), for very useful discussion.

2 TARGET is the real time gross settlement system handling large value payments in Europe; it is managed by the European System of Central Banks. BI-Rel (where BI stands for Bank of Italy) is the Italian segment of TARGET, RTGS-plus is the German one and TBF (*Transferts Banque de France*) is the French one. Euro1 is a private net settlement system, run by the EBA Clearing Company. PNS (*Paris Net Settlement*) is a hybrid system, run by CRI (*Central des Règlements Interbancaires*). Fedwire is the major (RTGS) settlement system in US, run by the Federal Reserve System. CHIPS (Clearing House Interbank Payments System) is a private system: it is the main US system dealing with cross-border and foreign exchange transactions; it was a netting system until 2001, when it became a hybrid system.

3 See Freixas and Parigi 1998, Kahn and Roberts 1998, Holthausen and Ronde 2000.

4 See Bech and Garratt 2003.

5 See BIS (1990), introducing the so-called Lamfalussy standards.

6 The use of the intraday credit facility is *de facto* limited by the available collateral. The cost of this requirement may be seen as a constraint put on the management of the securities portfolio, possibly making the bank bear an opportunity cost (should it give up better alternative uses of funds). Given that banks hold large securities portfolios in normal circumstances, such a cost is presumably quite low.

7 The interest rate applied, on an annual basis, is 36 basis points.

8 See McAndrews and Rajan 2000.

9 The fluctuation of exchange rates does not affect this process, as there is no cross-currency netting.

10 A value of α close to zero means that the first objective prevails in the loss function, while the opposite holds true for high values of α.

11 The following data can provide a rough indication of the effect of hybrids on the demand for intraday liquidity relative to daily payments. Consider that in a traditional RTGS system the ratio between the intraday liquidity used and the value of daily payments handled is about 3 per cent (such as in the 'old' BI-Rel system), while in hybrid systems such ratio may be as low as 0.2–0.4 per cent (which is the ratio between pre-funding and daily payment value in CHIPS and PNS respectively).

12 However, the Bank of England has recently announced a reform of its operational framework, leading to the introduction of voluntary remunerated reserves, to be held on average over a maintenance period. This – together with the new features of the BoE interventions in the money market – should help in reducing the volatility of the overnight interest rate, keeping its level in line with the policy target rate (i.e. the repo rate set by the Monetary Policy Committee). See Bank of England (2004a,b).

13 The detailed framework varies across countries. The maintenance period is two-weeks long in US, while it has a variable length (about one month) in the euro area.

14 You will notice that only R_1^D may actually deviate from *MRR*: R_2^D, to the contrary, is determined by the constraint, once R_1^D has been chosen. In a more realistic setting, where the length of the maintenance period is T > 2, all the daily reserve levels up to day T-1 may deviate from the required level. In the ECB operational framework, banks having a deficit (surplus) in their reserve accounts on the last day of the maintenance period may be forced to borrow (deposit) money from the central bank at penalising rates (i.e. the rates on the marginal standing facilities: minimum rate on main refinancing operations $\pm$ 1%).

15 You will notice that the elasticity of the demand for reserves increases with α: the slope of the R_1^D line in Figure 8.4 is $-1/\alpha$. In the limit, as $\alpha \to \infty$ the demand schedule is flat, leading to the 'martingale' property: $i_1 = E_1(i_2)$. To the contrary, if $\alpha = 0$ the demand is a vertical line at *MRR*.

16 Remember, however, that some central banks – like the Fed – already price their intraday credit facilities, although such a price is not intended to be a monetary policy rate.

Index

For Product Safety Concerns and Information please contact our EU representative GPSR@taylorandfrancis.com
Taylor & Francis Verlag GmbH, Kaufingerstraße 24, 80331 München, Germany

www.ingramcontent.com/pod-product-compliance
Lightning Source LLC
LaVergne TN
LVHW011133300926
849160LV00008B/627
9780415648608